KT-447-684

ANGLING
LINES

Nicholas,
I hope you enjoy these stories.
They come with my very best
wishes and kind regards,

Bruce

Tongue, May 2011

Bruce Sandison

The Press and Journal

ANGLING LINES

Fishing in Scotland

FOREWORD BY
JEREMY PAXMAN

[signature: Bruce Sandison]

BLACK & WHITE PUBLISHING

First published in this edition 2009
by Black & White Publishing Ltd
29 Ocean Drive, Edinburgh EH6 6JL

1 3 5 7 9 10 8 6 4 2   09 10 11 12

ISBN: 978 1 84502 254 9

Copyright © Bruce Sandison 2009

Previously published in the *Press and Journal* 1999–2008.

The right of Bruce Sandison to be identified as the author of this work has been asserted
by him in accordance with the Copyright, Designs and Patents Act 1988.

All rights reserved. No part of this publication may be reproduced, stored in a retrieval
system, or transmitted in any form, or by any means, electronic, mechanical, photocopying,
recording or otherwise, without permission in writing from the publisher.

A CIP catalogue record for this book is available from the British Library.

DISCLAIMER
Whilst every reasonable effort has been made to ensure the accuracy of the information
in this book, the Publisher assumes no responsibility for and gives no guarantees,
undertakings or warranties concerning the accuracy, completeness or up-to-date nature
of the information contained herein and does not accept any liability
whatsoever arising from any errors or omissions.

Typeset by Ellipsis Books Ltd, Glasgow
Printed and bound by MPG Books Ltd, Bodmin

for Ann

For salmon, trout and sea-trout,
For all fish great or small,
Let thanks be given
Before we cast
To Him who gave us all.

Contents

CONTENTS

Foreword

I have never been fishing with Bruce Sandison. But I once spent many hours cursing his name. It was four or five years ago, and a friend and I had spent the day flogging away on one of the Highland salmon rivers, with the sort of results you might expect when the sun is high in a cloudless sky and the river is low in a waterless sludge.

We had invited Bruce to dinner, during the course of which he professed himself astonished that we were wasting our time trying to winkle out salmon, when there was one of the finest trout lochs on Scotland only fifteen minutes' walk away. Well, what would you have done?

It was about 9.30 in the evening when we waved him goodbye. Perhaps we should have smelled a rat when he pointed at the hillside and said, 'It's just over the top there.' What had seemed to be a sheep track disappeared. What had appeared to be heather turned out to be gorse bushes. What had looked to be the top of the hill was just a ridge.

And when, sweating, bleeding and bitten to death by midges, we reached the loch we found that all the trout were rising approximately thirty yards beyond the limit of our casts. 'Bruce Sodding Sandison' was one of the kinder epithets when, on the tramp home sometime long after midnight, we both fell over a cliff.

I say I have never fished with Bruce. It is not entirely true, because, as the saying goes, some of the best fishing is done in print. This collection of pieces ranges widely, from his introduction to the sport in the Borders, to many accounts of his pursuit of wild trout across the Highlands.

On a gratifyingly large proportion of sorties he is outfished by his wife, Ann, or variously blown, rained, or frozen off the water. There are a number of suspicious occasions on which his wife's entirely harmless Yorkshire terrier is accused of having run off with his catch, an excuse about as plausible as having left your homework on the bus.

Many people would consider that blaming the dog for your own incompetence is the sure sign of a bounder, or at least of a man who ought to buy a cat. But Bruce is not a bounder. No-one has done more to fight against the salmon farms which have done so much damage to the rivers and lochs of the Highlands. He's a tall bloke, but on this occasion it was David against Goliath, and without the right result.

He also has a profound affection for what is, for me, the most beautiful corner of these islands, a devotion that, unlike most of us, he acted upon, moving himself lock-stock and barrel to a delightfully positioned little house at the top of a twisting track. When I am stuck in some horrible city, I often think of him, high in his eyrie above the Kyle of Tongue. In these pieces he brings that glorious part of the world to life.

Come to think of it, now I've read these pieces, I think perhaps it's time to give Bruce Sodding Sandison a call.

Jeremy Paxman

Introduction

I can't remember how I became an angler. It just seemed to happen. None of the members of my family fished. I had to teach myself the essential elements of our well-loved art: how to break rods, tie allegedly fail-safe knots, fill boots with ice-cold water, how to fall into rivers and how to hook the back of my head and everything else within range, other than fish.

But in doing so I discovered a world of endless excitement and content. A special place in which I felt enormously comfortable; unthreatened by the plague of conjugating Latin verbs, wrestling with the mysteries of geometry and the horror that was algebra, or trying to explain, yet again, to distraught parents, the reason for my constant academic disgrace.

On river and loch, other things caught my attention: piping greenshank, curlew whistling down the wind, a soaring buzzard, the fearsome smile of a wildcat. As I tramped the moors I found a host of wildflowers and I learned their names. I thrilled to the sight of autumn bedecked trees, and, in the early months of the season, to the body-chilling bite of February.

Yes, I wanted to catch fish, but it soon became clear to me that catching fish was only a very small part of the pleasure that angling brings. This firm belief has stayed with me throughout my life. It has shaped my views and opinions on the management of Scotland's fisheries, and, also, on how we should care for our precious, irreplaceable environment.

The stories in this book reflect these opinions and I am grateful to the *Press & Journal* for giving me the opportunity to recount them, firstly in my weekly angling column in that paper, and now gathered together here in book form. Some may disagree with some of the things I say and they have every right to do so. Angling is, and always has been, a broad church.

This is a personal account of one man's fishing, but it is also a book about the land I love. Our mountains and moorlands make us what we are. Every creature, human or animal, depends upon that land for survival. Therefore, whatever hurts Scotland's environment hurts us all.

In our brief stewardship of this treasure, let us strive to preserve its integrity. When we are gone, let there be no sign of our passing other than the friendly imprint of our care. This is our duty to future generations and there is no room for compromise.

Bruce Sandison
Tongue, Sutherland

1.
A Place for Everything

Wild brown trout anglers do not need to be entirely disconsolate during the close season. There is always plenty to do: sort out the rubbish in your fishing bag; clean lines; service reels; examine rods for loose rings; untangle spools of nylon; weed out unwanted flies and tidy fly boxes; check jacket pockets for left-over bits and pieces.

Doing so can lead to surprising discoveries – like where I had put my driving licence. I searched for months, never thinking I would have been stupid enough to chuck it in my fishing bag. However, the uneaten picnic remains came as a shock, as did the leaky thermos flask. And why had I carted round half a tonne of suntan lotion all season?

Some anglers are the epitome of neatness. A place for everything and everything in its place. Always in control. I am not. I'm the guy who forgets to collect the key for the boat before setting out. The man who arrives without a landing net. And, on one painful occasion, the angler who spent a day hobbling around in waders that were five sizes too small, because he had grabbed the first pair that came to hand, his wife's rather than his own.

A highlight of my season was when I persuaded a friend to walk out with me to fish one of my favourite hill lochs, Loch na Moine, to the east of Loch Craggie near Tongue in North Sutherland. My companion does not like bank fishing, or taxing hikes to get there. But Loch na Moine has some really seriously large trout and the possibility of connecting with such a specimen encouraged him to make the effort.

He tackled up and, following my expert advice, was soon lashing the water to a foam. As I put up my rod, I watched him with silent amusement. Which is when I discovered that I had forgotten to bring my reel. After an hour or so, my friend came back to where I was sitting and asked why I wasn't fishing. I lied. "James, it is pleasure enough for me to simply enjoy watching you fish. And I will be there with the landing net the instant you hook that one for the glass case."

Which reminds me that there is another very good reason for wild brown trout anglers not to be too disconsolate during the close season: rehearsing the happy memories of past fishing triumphs and disasters, of the ones that got away and the few that didn't. In the meantime, however, if you will excuse me, I really have to do something about the uneaten picnic remains and the leaky thermos flask in my fishing bag.

2.
Scotland's Other Loch Awe

Scotland's other Loch Awe is in Assynt. Unlike its vast Argyllshire namesake, this is a small, intimate water where good baskets of modest brown trout are the rule rather than the exception. Find it in OS Map 15, Loch Assynt, Scale 1:50,000 at Gd ref: 247155. Loch Awe is one of the 50 or so lochs in the care of the Assynt Angling Group; a joint venture between angling clubs and local estates intent upon preserving and prompting game fishing in the area.

The Assynt Angling Group has one of the most useful websites (www. assyntangling.org.uk) that I have come across. It gives comprehensive details of all the waters the group manages; identifying those with runs of migratory fish as well as brown trout, parking places, boat mooring locations, types of boats, area of Loch Assynt where spinning is allowed, rules and regulations, where to buy your permit and how much it will cost. Make the group website your first port of call if you are considering an Assynt angling adventure.

Little Loch Awe averages six feet in depth, is almost one mile long by up to quarter of a mile wide and lies adjacent to the A837 Ledmore Junction/ Lochinver road. Boat fishing invariably brings the best results. There are a number of tree- and scrub-covered islands at the south end of the loch and you should concentrate you efforts there. Also pay close attention to where the two feeder streams enter: midway down the west shore, and the stream that flows in from Loch na Gruagaich at the north end of the loch.

The outlet stream from Loch Awe, the River Loanan, flows through Loch Assynt to the River Inver and so there is always the possibility of encountering salmon and sea-trout. As such, treat every rise with caution and respect. It might well be yet another hard-fighting 8oz brown trout, but it could also be something much larger. This is just one of the aspects that makes Loch Awe such a wonderful place to fish. The surrounding scenery is another, with the long, grey shoulder of Canisp (846m) to the west and ragged crags of Breabag (718m) to the east.

Nearby Loch na Gruagaich (Gd ref: 242159) can also provide great sport fishing from the bank, as can Loch na Saighe Duibhe (Gd ref: 233159). But one of my most enduring memories is of a hot summer day, descending from the summit of Canisp by way of the Allt Mhic Mhurchaidh Gheir burn when we stopped to cool off in one of its crystal-clear pools Whilst it may have upset the fish in this magical stream, it most certainly comforted us.

3.
Kate McLaren

One of the most successful sea-trout and brown trout flies devised by the mind of man is the Kate McLaren. To go fishing without a few Kate McLarens in your box is to be improperly dressed. Earlier this year, on Fred Carrie's 'Wild Fishing Scotland' website forum, there was some debate about the origins of the fly and who it was named after. In consequence, I decided to establish the truth of the matter.

This was not difficult because the one person who could supply the answer was Lily McLaren, wife of the inestimable Charles Carmichael McLaren who for many years ran game fishing courses out of the Altnaharra Hotel in North Sutherland. Given that Castle Sandison is in Tongue, but a few miles distant from Altnaharra, I arranged to visit Lily and ask about the birth of the famous fly and for details of the original dressing.

Lily McLaren is a happy, smiling woman with a warm nature and ready laugh. She has a wealth of stories and knowledge about salmon and sea-trout fishing and was taught to fish by her late husband. Charles McLaren wrote extensively on the subject of salmon and sea-trout fishing, including two seminal works, *The Art of Sea-Trout Fishing*, published by Oliver & Boyd in 1963, and *Fishing for Salmon*, published by John Donald in Edinburgh in 1977.

Lily gave me an account of the naming of the fly, and of the dressing: "The Kate McLaren was first tied by William Robertson, a tackle dealer in Glasgow. The Robertsons were friends of Charles's father, John McLaren, and it was designed by John and named after his wife, Kate. The dressing is: Tail: Golden pheasant crest; Body: black-ribbed flat silver; Hackles: Black tied down the body and at the head a natural red hen, one tied over the black (must be hen so as to work properly in the water)."

Charles's parents had the Kinlochewe Hotel for many years but, during World War II, they moved to Blair Atholl when restrictions were placed upon access to certain areas of the West Highlands. After the war, the family moved back to Kinlochewe and it was there that Charles learned many of his fishing skills. Before moving to Altnaharra, Charles ran fishing courses at the Culag Hotel in Lochinver and it was there that he met Lily, when she joined one of his fishing weeks.

A few days after my meeting with Lily McLaren an envelope arrived on my desk from Altnaharra. Attached to the front of the card was a Kate McLaren, taken from Charles's own fly box, and, written on the back of the card, "With best wishes – Lily McL."

4.

A Final Fling

With the close of the sea-trout and salmon season upon us, and a distinct lack of anything fishy in the Sandison freezer, I arranged a final outing to one of my favourite waters, Loch Hope in North Sutherland. Given the sad demise of salmonid numbers along the west coast and in the Scottish islands, Loch Hope is now Scotland's premier sea-trout fishery, but because of the lack of rain this season it has been at its lowest level in living memory.

Previous attempts to persuade Hope sea-trout to respond to my well-presented flies had ended in failure, but it had rained and, this time, I was confident of success. As is almost always the case when fishing a loch for these magical trout, the best conditions are a steady south to south-west wind, light to medium in force, an air temperature higher than the temperature of the water, overcast, but warm, with the occasional burst of sunshine.

This applies to fishing a team of wet flies as it does to fishing the dap. Most of the fish taken from Hope, 500 to 600 each season, come to the dap. In my view this is simply because the majority of the anglers use that method. I prefer wet flies, however, to cover all eventualities, I took along a dapping rod as well. This was put into the safe hands of my fishing companion, my eldest grandson, Brodie. We were blessed with all of the weather conditions noted above and with an anticipatory glint in our eyes we headed smartly across the loch to fish Beat 3.

Beat 3 covers a substantial area of the south end of the loch. It extends to both banks, west and east, but in my experience the west bank is most productive; apart from the extreme north end of the east bank where a feeder stream flows in. There are always fish there, attracted by the scent of the fresh water tumbling down from Ben Hope (927m), Scotland's most northerly Munro. With the wind from the south, we set up a long drift that lasted for almost a mile before ending at the sand bar before Middle Bay.

Almost immediately fish began rising to the dap, and to the wet flies. It is some time since I have seen so many really seriously large sea-trout in the loch, and not only sea-trout, but good numbers of salmon as well, generally lying in shallow water, a few feet from the shore. We kept two sea-trout, wonderfully silver fish, and stored the memory of their capture and our splendid day in the dream-bank of our angling minds.

5.
The Curse of the Fishing Classes

I wish I could say that my fishing season has been a succession of trout-filled days. But that would be a lie and, as everybody knows, we anglers always tell the truth. Work, that curse of the fishing classes, was the problem. It seemed to get in the way of every piscatorial endeavour; although, after three decades of plying my trade people still stop my wife on the street and ask: "Oh, Mrs Sandison, has your man got a job yet or is he still writing?"

The other problem was lack of rain. Whilst the rest of Scotland had more than its fare share, North Sutherland remained almost bone dry. When the rains did come, bringing excellent runs of sea-trout and salmon into our local rivers and lochs, they arrived the week after our annual assault on the Borgie, which ended with us red-faced and salmonless. And as more fortunate anglers enjoyed great sport on Loch Hope, I was tied to my computer.

But I have a cunning plan for next year, regardless of the weather. It involves arranging an invigorating tramp out to one of my favourite waters near Scourie, Lochain Doimhain. Find it in OS Map 9, Cape Wrath, Scale 1:50,000 at Gd ref: 225429. Be warned, however, it is a lot easier to find Doimhain on the map than it is find it on the ground. You will need a compass and map and the ability to use them to arrive at this loch. And, should the weather deteriorate, similar highly developed map-reading skills are required to see you safely home.

I visited the loch in the 1980s with the late Stan Tuer, a famous Scourie angler and delightful fishing companion. When we arrived, Stan said, "Bruce, I will show you Pennell Point. The first angler to fish a Black Pennell from the point, casting a little right of centre with about 10yds of line, hooks and lands a trout of 1lb 8oz." Stan strode purposefully to the bank and, with his first cast, as if by royal command, rose and hooked a splendid trout which weighed almost exactly 1lb 8oz.

It would spoil your enjoyment if I were to tell you exactly where Pennell Point is. Suffice to say that as you arrive at the loch it should be obvious. What is less obvious is the number of nearby locations which also hold good trout, indeed, seriously large specimens of up to and over 5lb. The lochs are unnamed on the map, but their local names should help to identify some of them: Aeroplane, Boot, Pound and Otter. For permission to fish them and accommodation, contact the excellent Patrick Price, Scourie Hotel on tel: 01971 502396.

6.
Highland Streams

The majority of Scotland's rivers are more noted for their salmon than they are for their brown trout. But many of these streams can produce brown trout of exceptional size. For example, in 2005 John Sheard landed a fish weighing 10lb 2oz from a tributary of the River Deveron, the Isla, just downstream from the 'Friendly Town' of Keith. Muriel Mackay from Aviemore landed a 14lb trout from the Spey, Duncan McLaren had a 12lb 8oz fish from the Tay and a brown trout weighing 17lb has been taken from the River Ness.

With the exception of John Sheard's trout, the other glass-case specimens were taken by anglers fishing for salmon. However, the fish that I remember with most pleasure was the brown trout I caught many years ago on the River Findhorn, above Tomatin, when my father and his friend were lashing away, unsuccessfully, for salmon. I was fishing for trout and ended the day with five fish weighing 7lb 8oz, the largest being a trout weighing 3lb 8oz.

But fishing, for me, has never been about the size or numbers. Just being there, by river or loch, has always been enough. Some of the most exciting days I have had during my fishing lifetime were the ones when if I had caught two more fish, I would have had a brace. Many of these days have been spent exploring not rivers, but small streams. Perhaps this stems from when I was a youth. I learned the basics of fly-fishing on the Water of Leith above Balerno near Edinburgh, and wandered the banks of Lyne Water, a tributary of the River Tweed, filling my Wellington boots with water and hooking the back of my neck.

You can discover the same angling challenge and enjoyment by exploring the burns and little streams near you. Best results generally come after a spate, but by no means always. That is part of the challenge. You will need a light trout rod, invariably shorter than 8ft in length, 2lb to 3lb breaking strain nylon for your leader, and small flies. I fish these burns with a single fly and often use dry fly patterns. Be prepared to spend as much time watching the water as casting into it.

One of the most memorable fishing days that I ever had was spent on tiny Alt Lon a'Chuil in North Sutherland. It was September, with the surrounding moor burnished gold. There had been rain, and the water was stained peat-brown. I was accompanied by greenshank, curlew, golden plover and the smell of the rushing, foam-flecked stream. And by the happy sound of wild brown trout splashing at my fly.

7.
Geireann Mill Sea Pool

Loch nan Geireann is one of the most productive fishing lochs on the island of North Uist in the Outer Hebrides. Find it on OS Map 18, Sound of Harris, at Gd ref: 845725. The loch is known locally as Geireann Mill, because in the nineteenth century the outlet stream was used to provide power for a mill, the ruins of which can still be seen.

Park on the grassy area to the north of the A865 road at Gd ref: 843737. Follow the track past the hatchery building for a few minutes to reach the boat mooring bay at the north end of the loch. If you intend to bank fish from the west shore of Geireann Mill, then the easiest access route is from the A865 at Garry Skibinish, Gd ref: 928748.

Geireann Mill is two miles north/south by up to three quarters of a mile wide. Eighteen islands lie scattered throughout its length and on one of them, Eilean an Tighe (the island of the house), Neolithic pottery fragments have been found which suggest that much of the earthenware used in the Uists at that time was made on Eilean an Tighe.

The loch is divided by two finger-like promontories and the shoreline wanders round headlands and bays for a distance of five miles. There are excellent stocks of brown trout, as well as the chance of salmon and sea-trout. Boat fishing brings the best results and is the most convenient way of exploring this large expanse of water.

The average depth is six feet and brown trout are taken throughout the length and breadth of the loch, but most salmon are caught, from the shore, in very shallow water, particularly at the north-east end of the loch. Sea-trout tend to be found between the two largest islands, Aird Reamhar and Eilean Glas, both named on the OS Map.

But perhaps the most exciting place to catch sea-trout is in the sea pool at Gd ref: 846747, between Clett and Rubha Glas. Walk out over the sands just before low tide, a distance of three quarters of a mile, taking great care to avoid soft areas. Fish from the east shore, the rocks bordering the pool are slippery, but negotiable.

The last time I fished here the pool was alive with salmon and sea-trout, leaping and splashing in the clear waters. It was one of those rare moments when I knew that I was completely happy. The sight and sound and smell of 3,000-mile-old Atlantic, waves, curling white and green as they surged through the narrow gap in the rocks and into the pool will stay with me for as long as I live.

8.
Reach for Skyline

Skyline Loch near Altnabreac in Caithness is one of the most exciting lochs that I have ever fished. Prior to the 1970s, the loch was controlled by a syndicate and access was not generally available to members of the public. When this changed, about 30 years ago, my wife Ann and I booked the loch and tramped out to fish it one fine day in June.

Skyline is just under half a mile north/south by up to about 150 yards wide. Find the loch on OS Sheet 11, Thurso & Dunbeath at Gd ref: 010480. There are two adjacent waters, Lochan nam Breac (Gd ref: 001479), which contains large stocks of small brown trout, and an unnamed lochan at Gd ref: 015476, which to the best of my knowledge is fishless. I have to say that when we first arrived at Skyline I thought that it looked pretty fishless as well.

The loch lies at the heart of the Flow Country and a graceful red-throated diver greeted us. We walked up the west bank to get the wind behind us for ease of casting. I found, with care, that I could wade out a few steps from the bank and, as most men do, I was soon lashing out as long a line as possible in order to attract any trout that happened to be in a feeding mood.

After a fruitless hour, I glanced back to where Ann was fishing. She was kneeling in the heather, about half a dozen yards back from the edge of the loch, casting her flies on to the water close to the bank. As I watched, the rod tip suddenly dipped and the water exploded in a cascade of peat-coloured foam. I heaved myself ashore and hurried back, landing net at the ready. The trout was duly secured. It was a beautifully marked fish and weighed 2lb 12oz.

Thereafter, I never placed a foot in the loch again, even from the east shore where the water is shallower. In my experience, the trout tend to lie close to the west bank, only a few yards out, and the best chance of catching them is to keep down below the skyline (no pun intended) and cast just a few yards of line. The exception to that rule is when you see a fish rise. If you can cover it, quickly, it will invariably take your fly.

Expect blank days. We have had many on this wonderful little loch. But on its day Skyline can be an angler's paradise. The trout average 2lb in weight and they fight furiously. Seek permission to fish from the Forsinard Hotel, tel: 01641 571221.

9.
Loch Rannoch

I have never been entirely comfortable when fishing some of Scotland's vast trout lochs. This perhaps stems from breaking a sheer-pin on an old Seagull outboard motor whilst fishing Loch Awe on a nail-bitingly cold April day many years ago. We had to row back to Ford, into the wind, in the midst of a furious snow storm.

However, the exception to this generalisation is Loch Rannoch on the Road to the Isles. This is one of my favourite waters, 10 miles east/west by up to 1 mile wide and dropping to a depth of over 30 metres at the east end. Although the loch has been impounded for hydro-power generation purposes, it still manages to look natural.

And the surrounding scenery is some of the finest in Scotland. Graceful Schiehallion (1,083m) dominates the south shore, whilst the mountains of the Talla Beith and Craiganour forests crowd the northern horizon. The magnificent Black Wood of Rannoch, which still contains remnants of the Caledonian forest that used to cover much of Scotland, lies to the west of Carie.

Nearby, the Forestry Commission has laid out a number of inviting woodland walks of various lengths to suit various degrees of fitness; the ideal way to keep non-fishing members of your party happy whilst you get on with man's proper function in life, which is the removal of trout from their natural habitat.

The loch has long been famous for huge ferox trout. As far back as 1867 there are reports of a fish weighing 22lb being taken. In the early years of the last century Rannoch produced ferox of 21lb, 23lb 8oz and 18lb 8oz. In recent years, the loch still manages to produce double-figure ferox most seasons. These fish are generally caught by trolling, but some fall to flies fished from the bank, particularly in the early months of the season, close to mouths of the feeder streams that enter along the north shore.

However, boat fishing usually brings best results and it is also the most convenient method of exploring this large loch. The west end, where the water is shallow, almost always provides sport. Expect to encounter pretty brown trout that average 8oz/10oz. There are larger fish as well, including trout of up to and over 3lb in weight.

Use OS Map 42, Loch Rannoch to find your way round and concentrate your efforts in the vicinity of the bay at Finnart (Gd ref: 520574), east from Finnart Lodge (Gd ref: 525574), the shallows around Eilean nam Faoileag (Gd ref: 531576) and the bay at Eilean Mor (Gd ref: 553568). Obtain permission to do so from the Country Store in Kinloch Rannoch (tel: 01882 632306).

10.
Catch Them on the Tide

It is an acknowledged truism that into every life a little rain must fall, but bucketfuls of the stuff have been lashing huge chunks of Scotland in recent weeks. So far, however, the north has escaped and, consequently, many of our salmon streams and lochs are almost bone dry. Water levels in Loch Hope and Loch Loyal are lower now than they have been in living memory and until a sustained downpour arrives, salmon anglers on rivers such as the Helmsdale, Wick, Thurso, Forss, Halladale, Naver and Borgie despair of the chance of a fish.

However, even in these extraordinary conditions sport can still be had on the lower reaches of our rivers, when salmon and sea-trout waiting in estuaries for a spate may come in and out of their rivers of origin on high tides. This is good news for anglers fishing the Association beats of, for instance, the Naver and Helmsdale where day tickets are generally available and do not cost an arm and a leg to procure. On the little River Forss, the Sea Pool can often produce a fish when elsewhere on the stream conditions are hopeless.

In Caithness, where the River Wester enters the sea in Sinclair Bay to the north of Wick, sport may be had with sea-trout at the mouth of the river. The lower reaches of the River Halladale, near Melvich, offer similar opportunities. There are excellent current reports of sea-trout catches from the west side of the Kyle of Tongue. A friend of mine, fishing the Kyle last week, had several fish, including a sea-trout of 4lb 8oz to a size 12 Black Pennell.

Loch Hope, which I fished recently, has been dour and difficult. Nevertheless, a 12lb salmon was taken on the Dap at the end of July – the largest salmon caught on the loch for many years – and sea-trout of up to 5lb in weight have been landed. In spite of low water levels, Loch Loyal and, indeed, our other trout lochs, have all managed to send anglers home with at least something for breakfast, if not with that elusive one for the glass-case of angling dreams.

Those of us lucky enough to live in the area can often mitigate the impact of adverse weather conditions by choosing a fishing location best suited to these conditions. Sadly, this is not possible for visitors who have booked a salmon fishing holiday and arrive only to find the river of their choice so low that they might just as well have stayed at home. Happily, however, anglers are an eternally optimistic bunch and invariably manage to still enjoy their visit. After all, it might rain, and, if not, then there is always the next time.

11.
River Spey Sea-Trout

I discovered the joy of sea-trout fishing on the River Spey in the pool below the old bridge near Grantown. It was August and my wife, Ann, and I waited until dusk before launching our attack. The evening was unforgettable; the sweet smell of the river, the black shadows of bats flitting by and the sound of serious fish splashing their way upstream.

The River Spey is famous as a salmon stream, but it also used to produce some of the best sea-trout fishing in Europe. It was not unusual for upwards of 5,000 sea-trout to be taken during a season. In recent years, however, fewer sea-trout are running the river and rod and line catches in 2006 were 25% down on the 1992 to 2001 average of 4,591 fish. In 2007 they collapsed to 52% of that average.

Nor is this decline confined to the River Spey. All of the other rivers in the Moray Firth area, from the Deveron round to the Kyle of Sutherland in the north, mirror this pattern. Two of the most prolific sea-trout beats on the River Dee, Aboyne and Birse, produced only 30 sea-trout in June this year, rather than their customary 150 to 200 fish. The River Ness used to produce some 500 sea-trout each season; last year it could only manage 50.

This problem is now being addressed by The Moray Firth Sea-Trout Project; a collaborative initiative undertaken by District Salmon Fisheries Boards, Fisheries Trusts and angling associations around the Moray Firth. For more information, and to help in this important work, contact the project manager, Marcus Walters (www.mfstp.co.uk). Marcus hopes that anglers fishing the rivers in the area will let him know of any odd catches, such as unusually thin sea-trout, marked or diseased fish, or even sudden increases in numbers.

Although I have nothing other than anecdotal evidence to support my view, I believe that the decline in sea-trout numbers in Scotland's east coast rivers is not confined to the Moray Firth Basin. It seems to me that a similar situation is developing in other rivers outwith that region; in the Angus Esks, the Tay system, the Forth catchment and in the River Tweed. As such, I think that this situation should, as a matter of urgency, be examined on a much wider basis.

Sea-trout have survived in our waters since the end of the last Ice Age. They are 'miracle' creatures, as much as salmon are, and deserve the same levels of care and protection as their larger cousins enjoy. The Moray Firth Sea-Trout Project is a welcome first step in providing that protection and I am sure that anglers will support this valuable initiative.

12.
Relaxing at Rhiconich

Anglers relaxing at the Rhiconich Hotel in North-West Sutherland have more than 100 trout lochs and a spate salmon stream awaiting their pleasure. Whilst hotel guests have priority, casual visitors will generally be found fishing. The seven principal lochs have boats whilst the others lochs are fished from the bank. Fishing is by fly only and trout average 8oz/12oz in weight, with a few larger fish of up to and over 2lb.

Each season produces upwards of 500 trout, most of which are returned to fight another day. Salmon and sea-trout stocks have been decimated by sea lice from factory salmon farms but most seasons still produce sport, principally from Loch Gharbet Beag. Productive trout flies include Ke-He, Black Zulu, Blue Zulu, Black Pennell, Grouse & Claret, Greenwell's Glory, March Brown, Soldier Palmer and Sliver Butcher. For salmon use Stoat's Tail, Hairy Mary, Silver Doctor, Black Pennell, Soldier Palmer and Connemara Black.

Narrow Loch Crocach is the largest loch to the west of Rhiconich, one mile long by nearly half a mile wide, and it lies like a silver and blue butterfly on the moor. Four islands guard the approach to the western arm and the channel between the south shore and these islands is a favourite drift; although, in truth, fish may be caught virtually anywhere throughout the length and breadth of this fine water.

The loch is reached from the Ardmore road. Park at the end of the road and follow the well-made path for ten minutes. A step north brings you to the south end of the loch were the boat is moored. Crocach is best fished from the boat. This makes it a whole lot easier to visit the surrounding lochs and lochans in the vicinity, such as Loch a'Phreasan Chailitean, Loch Eileanach and little Lochan na Cloiche.

For Loch Gharbet Beag, walk down to the Rhiconich River from the hotel. There is a good, though muddy, track by the side of the stream. Gharbet Beag is just over one mile in length, pinched into an hourglass shape by narrows. The loch is generally shallow, but the narrows may be 10 feet or more deep in high water and this is where most of the salmon are encountered. Other noted lies are the Ministers Burn and Black Point on the east shore, the Tail of the Loch and Green Point on the west shore.

For further information, see www.rhiconichhotel.co.uk. Permission to fish from Rhiconich Hotel on tel: 01971 521224. Self-catering accommodation for a party of 12 guests is also available at Oldshoremore Lodge which has its own brown trout loch. Find your way around using OS Map 9, Cape Wrath, Scale 1:50,000.

13.
Take Them to Loch Brandy

Of all Angus Glens – Isla, Prosen, Clova, Lethnot and Glen Esk – Glen Clova is my favourite. I discovered it more years ago than I care to remember when, along with my wife, Ann, and our children I led the way up the steep track to fish Loch Brandy. Being an angler is an essential part of being a member of Clan Sandison. The Chinese call it 'brain-washing', but teaching the family to fish introduced them to Scotland's wild places and furnished them with a joy that will last a lifetime.

Find Loch Brandy on OS Map 44, Ballater, Scale, 1:50,000 at Gd ref: 339755. The climb to the loch, which lies in a corrie enclosed by Green Hill (870m) to the east and Boustie Ley (876m) to the west, is taxing, especially for little legs, but it follows a good track that takes you to the south shore. Brandy is 800yds long by 400yds wide, horseshoe-shaped, shallow at the south, deeper to the east and west below the crags.

The weather was less than kind when we made our journey and the corrie was cloud-filled when we eventually arrived. However, as the day progressed, the clouds lifted and the full majesty of the setting opened before us: ragged cliffs guarding the crystal-clear waters of the loch; a million years of silence broken only by the song of meadow pipits above the heather and, happily, from the loch, the splash of rising trout. By the time everyone was tackled up and ready for business the corrie was filled with sunlight and the loch ready and waiting for our well-presented flies.

Loch Brandy lies at an altitude of 609m and it only begins to produce reasonable results in late June and July. The south end is rock-strewn and uncomfortable to fish, but as you work round the shore, bank fishing is easy. Wading is not. Stay safely ashore and let the fish come to you. When conditions are right, baskets of 20/30 fish are not uncommon; nothing for the glass, but brightly marked little fish that average 6oz with the possibility of the occasional trout of up to 1lb in weight.

Our day ended with a basket of about eight trout, not one of which, unfortunately, was caught by your correspondent; a fact that I have never been allowed to forget, a small price to pay for such a memorable day. Permission to fish and accommodation, including bunkhouse and self-catering lodges, from the excellent Glen Clova Hotel (tel: 01575 550350). For after-fishing entertainment, be there on Sunday 3rd August when the Angus Beer Festival – music, song and dance – arrives in magnificent Glen Clova.

14.
The Misty Island

Travelling to the Island of Skye is always a joy, even more so since the iniquitous toll to cross the bridge was scrapped back in December 2004. More often than not I am on my way to Uig to catch the ferry to Lochmadday to fish in North Uist, Benbecula and South Uist, but from time to time I can't resist the temptation to stop and fish the lochs and little rivers that make the Misty Isle such a delight for anglers.

The adverse impact of aquaculture on Skye's salmon and sea-trout populations has been considerable, particularly on once-famous fisheries such as Loch Coruisk and Loch na Crèitheach, which flow into the sea at Loch Scavaig near Camasunary – as is evidenced in Stephen Johnson's book, *Fishing from Afar*, in which he recounts a basket of 15 sea-trout weighing 73lb, taken on a warm July night before the last war.

But for me the real pleasure of fishing in Skye is to be found amongst the many trout lochs that adorn the island. The best known of these is the Storr Lochs, a few miles north from Portree. Find it on OS Map 23, North Skye, Scale 1:50,000 at Gd ref: 501506. The loch is in fact two waters, Loch Leathan and Loch Fada, which were joined together when a dam was built to contain the lochs as part of a hydro-electric generating scheme.

The system now extends for about two and a half miles north/south by up to half a mile wide across the north bay of Loch Leathan. The setting is majestic, with the famous pinnacle The Old Man of Storr (535m) dominating the eastern horizon, backed by the ragged edges of the southern end of the Trotternish Ridge.

The fishing can also be majestic, mightily helped by the underlying limestone outcrop which give the lochs a high pH and make them the ideal home for trout of good quality. The fish average about 13oz but much larger fish are taken each season and trout of up to and over 4lb in weight are not uncommon. The largest brown trout ever taken in Skye came from the Storr Lochs and weighed an impressive 11lb 4oz.

Boat fishing brings best results, but if the wind is howling and you can't get afloat bank fish with confidence, particularly in the vicinity of the feeder streams which flow down from the Trotternish into the west shore of the loch. Fly fishing only and there is often a mayfly hatch. Offer Ke-He, Black Pennell, Greenwell's Glory, March Brown and Butchers various. Fishing is managed by the excellent Portree Angling Association and permits are available from Island Cycles (tel: 01478 613121).

15.
Loyal to Loyal

I was driving south down the Tongue/Lairg road on the west shore of Loch Loyal the other day when I was overtaken by a dipper. The little bird, best black-and-white bib-tuckered, flew past me, unconcerned and clearly engaged upon extremely urgent business. Whether angler or not, Loch Loyal in North Sutherland captivates all who visit its heather-clad banks and always delivers remarkable and unexpected pleasures.

The loch is approximately four miles long by up to half a mile wide and drops to a depth of more than 200ft below Beinn Stumanadh (627m) at the north-east end. It is a classic wild brown trout water and lies about 15 minutes' drive from my front door. Find it on OS Map 10, Strathnaver, Scale 1:50,000 at Gd ref: 620480. Find permission to fish at The Ben Loyal Hotel in Tongue (tel: 01847 521216).

Loyal hosts a resident population of 1,000 grey-lag geese and provides nesting sites for rare black-throated divers. Redshank, snipe and woodcock are abundant and the loch is often visited by osprey. The surroundings peaks are home to golden eagle, buzzard, peregrine and raven, and I have often watched otters playing with their cubs along the shoreline.

Loyal flows north through Loch Craggie (Gd ref: 615520) and Loch Slaim (Gd ref: 626535) into the Borgie River, one of Sutherland's most exciting little salmon streams, and a few salmon are taken most seasons as they head for their natal spawning grounds in the streams that feed into

Loch Loyal from the east and from Loch Coulside (Gd ref: 580435) to the south.

But the real prize here is Loyal's marvellous brown trout, which range in size from a few ounces to fish of over 10lb in weight.

Both boat and bank fishing produce worthwhile results, although using a boat makes it easier to explore the trackless east shore of the loch. There are a few shallow areas, at the north-west end and at the south end, so seek local advice before setting out and always go about your business with less speed and more caution. My preferred boat drift is down the west shore from Gd ref: 614490, past Lettermore and Loyal Lodge to Gd ref: 615454.

As ever, if you can't see the bottom of the loch then you are fishing too far out, so arrange the boat accordingly. Most patterns of traditional Scottish flies work well, but my favourite cast includes a Ke-He on the 'bob', Greenwell's Glory in the middle and a Dunkeld on the tail. Dapping also brings them up, as does dry fly on calm days. Loch Loyal rarely send anglers home without something for supper and is one of my top-ten Scottish lochs.

16.
Brown Trout and Slavonian Grebes

Most anglers that I know are as interested in what flies above the water as they are in what swims below the surface. They are as likely to be thrilled by the glimpse of an osprey catching supper as they are thrilled when catching supper themselves.

One of the most attractive places to do so is at Loch Ruthven, a few miles south from Inverness. Find it on OS Map 26, Inverness, Scale: 50,000 at Gd ref: 620276. The loch is a designated Special Area of Conservation and it is also a Royal Society for the Protection of Birds reserve, famous for its population of rare Slavonian grebes.

Ruthven covers an area of 375 acres and is two miles east/west by up to half a mile wide with an average depth of 10 feet. The brown trout are of exceptional quality and average 12oz/14oz in weight, but most seasons a few fish of up to and over 3lb are caught.

Fish rise and are taken throughout the loch, from the margins to the middle, but, generally, the most productive areas are at the east and west ends. At the east end, drift across the shallows towards the inlet stream from An Dubh-lochain (Gd ref: 629285). This tiny loch is rarely fished but it can hold good fish which run the stream from Ruthven in high water conditions.

The large bay at the south-west end of the loch can also be very productive, particularly in the vicinity of the small inlet burn and along the extreme west shoreline. Flies that work well include Ke-He, Soldier Palmer, Kate McLaren, Black Pennell, Loch Ordie, Woodcock and hare-lug, and Hedgehogs. On calm evenings, confidently offer dry flies.

Boat fishing only and outboard motors are not allowed. Ruthven can be very wild and windy at times, so take care and, if in doubt, don't launch the boat. Instead, consider a visit to Ruthven's near neighbour, Loch a'Choire (Gd ref: 626293). This delightful little loch lies to the north of Ruthven and is accessed via a short forest track from Balvoulin.

A'Choire is circular in shape and even in high winds it is possible to find a convenient bank from which to fish. The loch is sheltered by Creag Dhearg (350m) in the west and the lower slopes of Stac na Cathaig (446m) to the north. The loch contains Arctic charr as well as brown trout which give a good account of themselves.

Further details about Loch Ruthven, and boat bookings, can be obtained from Graham's Tackle Shop in Castle Street, Inverness (tel: 01463 233178). For Loch a'Choire bookings contact the Brin Estate on tel: 01808 521211 or tel: 01808 521283.

17.
Scotland's Best Ever Basket of Wild Brown Trout

The Fionn Loch near Gairloch in Wester Ross is one of Scotland's most famous trout lochs. On 12th April 1851, whilst fishing the loch, Sir Alexander Gordon Cumming of Altyre caught a record basket of trout. Osgood Mackenzie, in his book *A Hundred Years in the Highlands*, described the event: "There were four beauties lying side by side on the table of the small drinking room, and they turned the scales at 51lb. The total weight of fish caught by trolling that day was 87lb 12oz."

The loch lies at the heart of the Letterewe and Fisherfield forests, between Little Loch Broom to the north and Loch Maree to the south. The surrounding scenery is majestic and hosts 35 dramatic peaks, 18 of which are Munros – Scottish mountains over 914.4m in height. Fionn is five miles long by up to one and a half miles wide and drops to a depth of 150ft near Carnmore Bothy at the south end of the loch. Find it on OS map 19, Gairloch & Ullapool, Scale 1:50,000 at Gd ref: 950785.

Boat fishing only on Fionn, and be warned that there are sudden shallows which cover barely submerged rocks waiting to catch you unawares. Hasten slowly about your business and take great care. If you are unfamiliar with the loch it is advisable to seek advice and assistance from the Estate, or from a member of the Gairloch Angling Club. A good place to begin is down the east shoreline, about 10yds out from the bank, as is the bay on the north-east shore that is protected by Eilean Fraoch (Gd ref: 945804).

Old Boathouse Bay (Gd ref: 945782) is also productive and a noted lie for the salmon which enter the loch via the Little Gruinard River; although most anglers fishing the loch prefer to concentrate on the wild brown trout for which Fionn is most famous. Today, trolling is not allowed but even so fish of up to and over 10lb in weight are not entirely uncommon. The average is somewhat less, being in the order of 8oz/10oz, and this makes the loch a beginner's paradise. Even on a bad day, the greatest duffer in the world should catch his or her fair share, as was witnessed the last time I fished there: a dozen trout were landed. Our boat partner caught six, my wife, Ann, caught six – and I caught the rest.

All inquires about fishing the Fionn Loch should be addressed to the Letterewe Estate, Loch Maree, Achnasheen, Ross-shire IV22 2HH, tel: 01445 760207. Permission to fish is at the discretion of the Estate, which also has a number of self-catering cottages for let to visitors

18.
The Rough Bounds of Knoydart

I visited one of Scotland's most remote trout lochs last week, Loch an Dubh-Lochain. It lies at the heart of the Rough Bounds of Knoydart and can be found at Gd ref: 820005 on OS Map 33, Loch Alsh & Glen Shiel, Scale: 1, 50,000. The most convenient access route is by sea; from the south across Loch Nevis, from Malling to Inverie, or, from the north, via Barrisdale on Loch Hourn. Neither route is for the faint-hearted. After stepping ashore, both involve a hike of about five miles.

However, the rewards for doing so are beyond compare, not only from the point of view of the fishing, but also because of the majestic grandeur of the surrounding scenery: Sgurr Coire Choinnichean (796m), Aonach Sgoilte (849m) and Ladhar Bheinn (1,020m) to the north, with Beinn Bhuidhe (855m), Meall Buidhe (946m) and Luinne Bheinn (939m) to the south.

The loch is deep, dropping to a depth of almost 100ft, and is one mile long by up to 400yds wide. Look out for pretty wild brown trout that average 8oz/10oz in weight. But there are much larger specimens as well, including ferox trout, the aquatic 'wolf' that is descended from species that have inhabited the loch since the end of the last Ice Age – along with their attendant population of Arctic charr. Best results come from boat fishing and bank fishing is not allowed.

Loch an Dubh-Lochain is the headwater loch of the River Inverie, a notable salmon and sea-trout fishery that is recovering from the less than welcome impact of the fish farms in Loch Nevis. Drew Harris of Kilchoan Estate is conducting a re-stocking programme which is beginning to produce encouraging results. In spite of low water levels during my visit, several sea-trout of up to and over 4lb in weight had been caught and released, and salmon parr were abundant.

There are two other trout lochs on the hill to the south of Kilchoan, Loch Bhraomisaig at Gd ref: 785973 and its unnamed satellite lochan to the west on the slopes of Lagan Loisgte. Bhraomisaig lies at about 350m and it might test your lungs a bit getting there, but it holds some excellent trout which can exceed 4lb in weight. Neither Bhraomisaog nor its satellite surrender their residents easily, but be assured they are there, waiting for your carefully-presented fly.

Offer them Kate McLaren, Black Pennell, Ke-He, Soldier Palmer, Loch Ordie, Greenwell's Glory, March Brown, Woodcock and hare-lug, Invicta, Silver Invicta, Silver Butcher and Alexandra. For permission to do so, contact Drew Harris on tel: 01687 462724, email: drewhkilchoan@onetel.com. The estate has excellent accommodation for visitors, including a bunkhouse and self-catering cottages.

19.
The Machair Lochs of South Uist

The machair trout lochs on the island of South Uist in the Western Isles are sparkling jewels in Scotland's angling crown. And they have had an exceptional start to the season, in spite of May being the driest month in the Outer Hebrides since records began. A total of 651 fish were caught, the majority being returned to fight another day.

The principal machair lochs on the fertile western seaboard of the island are, from north to south, East Loch Bee, Grogarry, Stilligarry, Altubrug, West Loch Ollay, Bornish and Upper Kildonan. Each has a special characteristic in its own right, but they all share one thing in common: good stocks of quality wild brown trout that range from 10oz to over 5lb in weight.

I find it impossible to single out one of these lochs as being my 'favourite', they have all been good to me, more or less, over the years. But, as is ever the case in fishing, sometimes they have reduced me to tears, particularly East Loch Bee and West Loch Ollay, which on occasions can be dramatically dour; after one dour day, I renamed the latter 'Damn Ollay'.

This did not apply to two anglers on West Loch Ollay last week; they had a basket of four trout weighing 8lb 8oz. Another party had 37 fish weighing 37lb 8oz for their five-day visit to the island, including a splendid trout of 3lb 8oz. The heaviest fish taken so far this season weighed 5lb and came from that most enigmatic of all South Uist waters, Grogarry Loch.

These are the bare facts. What they do not illustrate, however, is the sheer beauty of this magical isle. June is the kindest time to be there, when the air is sweet and feels like the soft touch of a child's hand on your brow. When the machair bursts into a two-mile wide, 20-mile long carpet of wildflowers: buttercup, red and white clover, blue speedwell, eyebright, birdsfoot trefoil, harebell, wild thyme, yellow and blue pansy and silver-weed.

Drifting over the lochs, the sense of peace is an almost physical, dream-like presence. Which, of course, is exactly when a leviathan of a fish dashes at your flies and catapults you back to reality. Talking of which, flies that is, the most successful patterns so far include Green Peter, Kate McLaren, Clan Chief, Loch Ordie, Soldier Palmer and Machair Claret.

I have fished in many places, in Scotland and overseas, but few of them have ever been able to match the complete pleasure that is trout fishing on the machair lochs of South Uist. My enduring memory is of the whimsical call of curlew and oystercatcher, and the happy sound of rising trout.

20.
Blessed in Badanloch

The Badanloch waters of East Sutherland cover an area almost four miles square. They offer anglers exciting sport with wild brown trout that vary in size from a few ounces right up to specimen fish of over 9lb. Find the lochs on OS Map 17, Strath of Kildonan, and OS Map 16, Lairg and Loch Shin, Scale 1:50,000.

There are three principal lochs, from east to west, Badanloch, Loch nan Clàr, and Loch Rimsdale. They are the source of the Helmsdale River and were joined together when a dam was built to create a reservoir to feed additional water into the river when levels are low.

Boat fishing brings the best results, and allows you to more comfortably explore this vast water. An outboard motor is essential, but you will have to use your own since none are available for hire. However, in windy conditions, fishing from the bank can be just as productive.

Take care when using the outboard and hasten slowly; underwater rocks wait to catch you unawares and the water level can fluctuate during the season. The lochs are generally shallow, particularly as you move through the narrows between Badanloch and Loch nan Clàr where the water is barely four feet deep.

Badanloch has an average depth of 17ft and you should concentrate your efforts between the island of Rubha Mór and the south shore. The best fishing area on Loch nan Clàr is at the west end, where the loch begins to narrow before joining Loch Rimsdale. Trout of over 4lb in weight have been caught here and salmon are also sometimes taken.

The last of the Badanloch waters, Rimsdale is perhaps the most productive and this is where most of the largest trout are encountered. Rimsdale lies at right angles to its neighbours and is three miles north/south by up to three quarters of a mile wide.

Rimsdale is accessed from the B871 Kinbrace/Syre road at Gd ref: 740399. A track on the western edge of the forestry plantation leads to the boat mooring bay. The loch also contains Arctic charr and the most productive areas are: the bay on the east shore at Gd ref: 746356, just before the entrance to Loch nan Clàr, the south-west shore, particularly where the burn flows in from Loch Truderscaig, and the south-east shore.

The Badanloch trout are not fussy eaters and most standard patterns of Scottish loch flies will produce results, but it is generally useful to have a Kingfisher Butcher or a Dunkeld on your cast. Be aware also that the residents respond very well to the dap. More information and bookings from Brian Lyall on tel: 01431 831232.

21.
Angling in Unst

Unst in Shetland is the most northerly island of the British Isles and home to the UK's most northerly brown trout, sea-trout and salmon fishery. Since the early 1990s there had been a general decline in the numbers of fish being caught but in 2004 a group of islanders got together and decided it was time to do something about it.

Davie McMillan of the Unst Angling Club told me, "We realised that the future of our fishing was in our own hands, and that if we did not act, then nobody else would." Since then the club has been hard at work, clearing up the burns and streams through which sea-trout and salmon reach their traditional spawning grounds. The club also started a unique sea-trout restocking programme using native fish, reared in their natal streams.

The work of planting out the small fish was undertaken by school children who, in 2004, released upwards of 750 sea-trout into spawning burns. Since then, catches have improved by 25%, and continue to do so. The club operates a strict catch-and-release policy and every salmon or sea-trout caught is returned to fight again another day. More sea-trout have been seen around the island this season than for nearly two decades.

This has certainly been the case on Loch of Cliff, the largest loch in Unst, which drains into the sea at Burra Firth at the north end of the island. Salmon, perfectly shaped wild fish of up to 12lb in weight, are being caught and the largest sea-trout taken weighed 10lb. In the south, near to where the ferry arrives from Yell at the Wick of Belmont, there are additional lochs, Snarravoe, Snabrough and Stourhull, which also offer sport with sea-trout and brown trout.

Snarravoe drains into the sea at Snarra Voe through a burn which is a few hundred yards in length. The burn had become heavily silted and a digger was brought in to clear it. And the fish returned. Loch of Snarravoe is considered to be the best loch on Unst and, in times past, it was stocked with trout from Loch Leven. Today, it contains specimen brown trout, some of which local anglers reckon to be in the teens of pounds, and increasing numbers of sea-trout.

I have to declare an interest here because my ancestors came from Unst, but if you are looking for an exciting fishing holiday amidst some of the most dramatic scenery on Planet Earth, then head for Unst. You will find excellent accommodation at Saxa Vord, which offers self-catering houses, a comfortable bunkhouse, restaurant and bar (www.saxavord.com) and a warm welcome from the members of the Unst Angling Club (tel: 01957 711554).

22.
Head for Heilen

Two of the north's finest trout lochs, Heilen and Watten in Caithness, opened for business last Thursday. Heilen, near Castletown, is home to enormous trout. Over the past three years the loch has produced specimens of up to and over 6lb in weight. In June 2007, Ray Millard landed a 10lb 12oz fish and in June last year Ronald Mackenzie landed a trout weighing 11lb 10oz, the largest wild brown trout ever caught on the fly in the county.

Most fish of this size are ferox trout, a species that feeds almost exclusively on Arctic charr and which are caught trolling the depths. But Heilen is shallow, with an average depth of little more than four feet, and the trout grow to such a size because of the quantity of the food available to them. Both boat and bank fishing are available, but your correspondent has had more success fishing from the bank.

May and June are the best months on this most challenging water but don't expect it to be easy – Heilen trout do not readily give themselves up. Do expect, however, to be fishing one of the most lovely and exciting waters in all of Scotland.

Loch Watten is less demanding than Heilen and will rarely send you home without something for supper. The fish it contains are of outstanding quality and they average around 1lb in weight, although most seasons produce fish of up to and over 3lb. The loch is a substantial affair, three miles long by up to half a mile wide with an average depth of 8ft, and fishing from the boat brings better results than bank fishing.

As with Heilen, I have always found May and June to the best months, although the loch can fish very well during September. My favourite fishing areas are at the south end, near Watten Village; the north-east shore in Factor's Bay, then a drift behind the small island off the north shore down what is known as Whin Bank. Another productive drift, in a north-east wind, is from the island directly across the loch to the opposite bank by the old army shooting range.

In truth, however, fish rise and can be taken anywhere in the loch. Many local anglers simply set up a long drift, right down the middle, end to end, and do as well as those of us who prefer to fish the shallower margins. As for which flies to use to tempt the fish on Heilen and Watten, I most often fish with a Ke-He on the 'bob', a March Brown in the middle, and a Silver Butcher on the tail, all on size 12 dressings. More info from Hugo Ross in Wick on tel: 01955 604200, and at www.hugoross.co.uk .

23.
The Challenge of Loch Lanlish

Loch Lanlish, one of the famous Durness limestone lochs, produced its first trout of the season on 13th April. The fish, which weighed 3lb 8oz, was landed by Kiltarlity angler Ian MacRitchie, who was fishing a Claret Bumble on a floating line.

Most anglers have favourite lochs, generally because they have had great sport on them. But my love affair with Loch Lanlish, which began more years ago than I care to remember, was fired by the opposite reason – my inability to persuade the leviathans that inhabit this enigmatic loch to rise to my flies, no matter how carefully I present them.

Lanlish lies to the south of Balnakeil Bay (OS Map 9, Cape Wrath, Scale 1:50,000, Gd ref: 386684) and when I first fished it, seeing anybody else was the exception rather than the rule. It is a much busier place now, being surrounded by a golf course, the sixth hole of which borders the loch. However, those engaged in 'a good walk spoiled' are required not to interfere with the activities of anglers as they pass by.

Lanlish is a small loch and fishing is from the bank only. The north, west and south shores offer easy and safe wading, whilst wading down the east bank can be a bit of a difficult stumble because of the rocky bottom. There is a small island halfway down the east bank which, during the early months of the season, is home to nesting Arctic terns. Keep well clear to avoid disturbing the birds.

In bygone days, Lanlish used to produce wonderful trout of up to and over 14lb in weight. Even today, it can still give up fish of 8lb/9lb. I know, because I have seen such specimen trout and the happy smile on the faces of the anglers who caught them. My heaviest fish from the loch weighed just less than 4lb, but at times you would swear that the loch was entirely fishless.

Nothing could be further from the truth; they are there, all right, but they are incredibly hard to catch. It is almost impossible to resist the temptation to wade, which is, of course, when fish rise behind you. I don't think that I will ever 'master' Loch Lanlish, no matter how often I fish it, but I do know that I will keep on trying.

On a warm June evening, with the scent of wildflowers filling the air and the cry of curlew on the hill, there are few more wonderful places in all of Scotland to fish. Catching anything is a supreme bonus and, for me, just being there is pleasure enough. Bookings from Martin Mackay, tel: 01971 511255, email: martin@durnesslimestonelochs.co.uk.

24.
The Magic of Sionascaig

Scotland has more than its fair share of wind-swept lochs: Ericht in Perthshire, running for 15 miles from Dalwhinnie to Rannoch; Loch Shin by Lairg in Sutherland, 17 miles by one mile; Mullardoch and Monar in Inverness-shire, bleak Loch Loyne, Loch Quoich and Cluanie; Loch Lochy, Loch Arkaig, Loch Treig and the Blackwater Reservoir by Fort William.

Most of these lochs have been incorporated into hydro-electric power generating schemes and water levels fluctuate considerably. This makes their banks unstable and, often, down-right dangerous for anglers fishing from the shore. Afloat, on a fine day with trout rising and surrounded by majestic mountains, they are wonderful. However, a sudden storm could find you fighting for your life.

But there is one Scottish loch that belies its size: Loch Sionascaig, in Wester Ross. The loch is over three miles long by two miles wide and its shoreline meanders in and out of bays and fishy corners for a distance of 17 miles. There are more than a dozen islands, large and small in the loch, and, at the east end, a stream connects Sionascaig to two further substantial waters, Lochan Gainmheich and Loch an Doire Duibh.

Find Loch Sionascaig on one of my most treasured Ordnance Survey maps, Sheet 15, Loch Assynt, the 'Old Testament' of Scottish trout fishing. There is pleasure enough here to last several angling lifetimes and Sionascaig is the jewel in the crown. The loch lies at Gd ref: 120140 in the heart of the Inverpolly National Nature Reserve, guarded by little Stac Pollaidh (618m), Cul Beag (769m) and Cul Mor (849m). To the north tower the Assynt peaks, Suilven (731m) and the grey bulk of Canisp (846m).

Sionascaig holds a substantial stock of traditional Highland wild brown trout and they average in the order of 6oz/8oz in weight, but each season fish of up to and over 3lb are caught. I have reports of much larger specimens being caught as well, ferox trout in the teens of pounds taken using that old

Scots method, 'trolling'. Although the loch is 180ft deep, there are sudden, rock-strewn shallows, so hasten slowly about your business and take care.

Most of the action is around the margins, a few yards out from the shore. To tackle this most successfully it is best to fish three in the boat; bow and stern rods fishing whilst the third angler works the oars and keeps the boat in position. The third man/woman swaps places with the bow or stern rod every half an hour. In the unlikely chance of Sionascaig being 'dour', moor the boat at Gd ref: 112131 and walk south to bank fish Loch Doire na h-Airbhe, a loch that is constantly in my dreams. Bookings from: Inverpolly Estate, tel: 01854 622452.

25.
The Only Certainty is Uncertainty

The endless fascination of angling is rooted in uncertainty. Regardless of how long we have been fishing or how experienced we think we are, the unexpected invariably catches us unawares. More often than not, in my experience, these incidents happen at the start of the season, and, more often than not, when weather conditions seem to preclude angling success.

Towards the end of March, I once hosted two boys on an outing to Loch Stemster in Caithness, close to the A9 Latheron/Thurso road at Achavanich. It was cold, very cold and I didn't expect them to catch anything. However, almost as soon as their flies landed on the water, fish rose and were hooked and caught. After a couple of hours we retired, frozen, yes, but triumphant.

On another occasion, fishing Loch Stilligarry in South Uist on 1st April, more as a gesture of angling intent than with any real hope of encountering its famously large residents, a good fish rose close to the shore but just outside my casting range. Regardless of the lack of waders, I simply splashed in and covered it. To my surprise, the fish took instantly and, after a considerable struggle, I managed to beach it. The trout weighed 2lb 8oz.

My wife, Ann, once shamed the rest of the family, my son Blair and daughter Lewis-Ann and me, during an Easter holiday in Orkney. It was snowing heavily and we were unable to negotiate the minor road leading down to the west shore of Loch of Swannay where we hoped to bank fish. Instead, we parked at the north end of the loch and devised a new plan of attack, which, essentially, amounted to sitting in the car hoping that the storm would pass.

Ann, made of sterner stuff, grabbed her rod and marched off. Within a few moments she had disappeared into the blizzard. Fifteen minutes later we saw her fighting her way back, head down against the wind, covered from head to foot in snow. She also clutched in her gloved hands a wonderful trout of about 2lb in weight. A day or so later, when we managed to get down to Scruit on the west shore of Swannay, I caught two splendid trout each weighing about 1lb 8oz.

I guess that the truth of the matter resides in that old angling dictum, "you won't catch any fish unless your flies are in the water." As such, even although conditions might seem hopeless, it is as well to have a go. After all, you never know your luck, or, when I am confronted with the unexpected and welcome appearance of an eager trout, skill. But I would say that, wouldn't I?

26.
Wee Ones

As a boy, I used to start my trout fishing season on the River Tweed just upstream from Innerleithen. It was always cold and I can't remember ever catching anything. I found one of my old County of Peebles Angling Improvement Association permits the other day when rummaging through ancient document files. Can't think why I kept it, but written on the back are the words, 'WEE ONES' – must have been one of my better days.

On the front, however, was a note of the price of the day's fishing – seven shillings and sixpence, equivalent in today's currency to 37.5p but a lot from my weekly pay-packet of two pounds ten shillings (£2.50). The price of a day ticket to fish the stretch now is £8.00, and under 18s pay nothing; too late for me but good news for present day embryonic anglers. Still, it's an ill wind, OAPs get it for half price and at £4.00 that's a bargain.

In the same file, I also found a day ticket for the River Whitadder. If you are a salmon or sea-trout returning to the River Tweed, the Whitadder is first right on your way upstream. The permit cost three shillings and sixpence (17.5p) then and it costs £6.00 today. Not entirely surprisingly, I saw that I had noted on the permit: 'NO FISH'. I wonder what it was that compelled me to keep trying?

Perhaps the truth is that as anglers grow older they simply become more experienced. I wasn't aware of this alleged fact, but, in retrospect I guess that it must have happened because in due course I found myself thinking more and more about where the fish might lie, rather than about which tree or bush I was going to snag next when casting.

In those days there were few professional instructors for either salmon or trout fishing. Most youngsters were taught the rudiments by their fathers, or relatives, or by a helpful gillie. It was different for me. None of my family fished. Father was a golfer and I suspect that he thought that I was deranged to want to spend my time emptying my boots of water and extracting hooks from various parts of my anatomy.

Until, that is, one evening when he came down to collect me when I was fishing Flemington Pool on Lyne Water, another Tweed tributary. "Here, son," he said, "give me a shot at that." I handed him the rod. Dad hardly played another game of golf for the rest of his life and, one by one, I introduced my brothers and my mother to the gentle art. Thereafter, for me, family holidays took on a new and exciting meaning.

27.
The Winter of My Discontent

Now is the winter of my wild trout fishing discontent: 44 days to go until the start of the new season. One of the ways that I use to try and dull the pain of waiting is to make up lists of lochs which I intend to fish during the next year. But in spite of my best efforts, like New Year resolutions, I generally fail to honour them all.

Another tactic is to follow the format of that well-loved radio programme, *Desert Island Discs*. Instead of music, however, you decide which 10 trout lochs you would take; presuming your island is big enough to hold them, which excludes waters such as Lomond, Ericht and Shin. Here are my 10, and why I chose them.

Watten, in Caithness, because every member of my family loves the loch, and because it is where my father caught his last trout. Sletill, in the Flow Country of East Sutherland, before factory tree-farming. A wonderful, intimate loch that in those days took a hike of one and a half hours to reach, and for the black throated diver that always greeted us when we arrived.

Tangusdale, on Barra, with its castle-crested island at the south end, a magical loch on a magical isle that once gave me a 3lb trout. Stilligarry on South Uist, the call of oystercatchers and the sound of the sea and the sweet scent of a summer evening on the machair. And Oban Sponish, on North Uist, where shoals of sea-trout used to race through green and brown blankets of seaweed to take my fly.

Laidon, on Rannoch Moor, because of the day my wife, Ann, and I spent there exploring the tiny lochans to the south. Loch Leven, the first trout loch that I fished as a boy in 1953, for the kindness of my hosts, Mr & Mrs Tom Kelly and our two gillies, Big Eck and his son.

Gladhouse, to the south of Edinburgh; a hill loch in the lowlands where Ann and I once almost drowned on a windy day in 1962 when the City Fathers of Edinburgh Council controlled the fishing. I would have to take Heilen, in Caithness, a 'trout loch from hell' but containing the most beautiful fish in the world, and the most difficult to catch. And last, but not least, little Loch Hakel, a few minutes' drive from my front door.

As to my book, I would pack *The Fisherman's Vade Mecum* by G. W. Munsell, the book that got me hooked on fishing, and, for my luxury, it would have to be a fly-tying kit. With all of these, I think that I would be quite happy in my wilderness and find it paradise enow.

28.
The Family Fishing Association

Pause for thought time. I suppose the most significant event last season, for me, anyway, was the sudden realisation that the Sandison Family Fishing Association (SFFA) had grown so considerably in size. When we last held an AGM, in Wick, back in 1977, there were six of us: my wife, Ann, myself and our four children, plus one associate member (Horace Cat).

Twenty-eight years on, and our membership has grown to 32; plus a host of associates including eight cats, five dogs, two Yorkshire terriers and a goat. I won't list all the names, sufficient to say that our four children are to blame for this explosion in the Association's numbers, what with getting married and having families of their own and all that sort of thing.

Of greater concern to me is that one of the founding members of the SFFA (I won't mention names for fear of embarrassing Blair) recently came across a copy of the minutes of that meeting and is questioning their validity; to the extent of calling an Extraordinary Annual General Meeting with the sole purpose of removing the Chairman (me) from that position.

After all I have done for them: thousands of pounds in fishing tackle and clothing over the years, millions of blood knots, hundreds of miles on the oars just to put them over fish. The hours that I have spent teaching them, their children, and their children's friends and all the other hangers-on how to cast. This is the thanks I get? What an ungrateful bunch.

Maybe I did 'extend' the truth a bit when I said that the Chairman caught the heaviest trout of the season, but I completely refute the suggestion that I deliberately failed to land one of Blair's fish. Neither is there any need to make personal remarks about my eye-sight. And yes, maybe I didn't have the authority of the meeting to claim that I had caught more trout than the lot of them put together, but, after all, it was a long time ago, and it was true.

I have a feeling that I am going to be seriously discomfited by all of this digging up of the past and I know that I will just have to smile bravely and take it on the chin. After all, I really only have myself to blame for my predicament. Nevertheless, and in spite of these entirely inaccurate and false accusations, I can only repeat now what I said at the end of the minutes of the 1977 meeting: "The Chairman thanked the members of the Association for their continued support and said that he felt privileged to belong to one of the best angling clubs in the world."

29.
All I Want for Christmas

I have yet to meet the angler who has everything. Anglers always need something: another fly box, preferably filled with a couple of dozen of the best 'fail-safe' patterns tied by the world's greatest dressers; and what angler would deny that a new fly rod, just a bit longer and just a bit firmer than his present model, would be a more than welcome stocking-filler come Christmas morn? Reels, lines, landing nets, monogrammed priests, new wading jacket. Yup, I could do with a new one of those, I can hear you thinking.

In November I was in southern Chile where I watched anglers fishing for salmon on Lake Llanquihue near Puerto Varas. The lake covers an area of 330 square miles, is up to 5,000ft deep and dominated by a glorious volcano, Osorno, snow-capped and nearly 9,000ft in height. However, local anglers are hardly going to set tackle dealer cash tills ringing, because they use the simplest of fishing techniques, and the simplest of fishing equipment in their pursuit of fish.

A nine-inch section of plastic pipe acts as a reel. A couple of hundred yards of line (looked like strong backing to me) is wound round the pipe. A trace, weight and spinning lure is attached to the end of the line. The angler spins the weighted trace in an anti-clockwise direction around his head and, when enough speed has been generated, lets go. The line flies off the pipe and I have seen the lure land more than 100 yards from shore. And I have watched them catch salmon, cautiously pulling the fish in whilst winding the line back on to the pipe as they did so.

Still, not quite the same as a neatly boxed Hardy Smuggler, or a long tube marked Orvis, is it? Do we anglers take ourselves and our tackle too seriously? Do we put too much faith in the latest technological miracle offered for our piscatorial pleasure? We are certainly encouraged to do so by manufacturers and suppliers, but, then, they would say that, wouldn't they, because that's why they are in business.

When I was a boy, I did my fair share of hook-line-and-sinker work from the end of piers various from Kinghorn in Fife down to St Abb's in Berwickshire, and great fun it was too. I also served a long apprenticeship at the business end of a greenheart salmon rod, and more hours than I care to remember searching for precious, lost flies. Therefore, in the autumn of my fishing career, I am perfectly comfortable to admit that, like most of my fellow anglers, I don't have everything – a message I trust that nearest and dearest will read and will act upon accordingly.

30.
Jurassic Fishing

Jurassic Lake in Patagonia, Argentina, is being hailed as the most exciting wild rainbow trout fishery in the world. Anglers are said to catch upwards of 80 rainbow trout between them during a visit to the lake, and the fish are reported to average 10lb in weight. The heaviest fish taken during 2007 is estimated to have weighed 25lb.

A picture landed on my desk the other day of one of my friends holding a double-figure Jurassic Lake rainbow trout, and I have since logged on to the website of a company that organises fishing trips to the lake – www. wherewisemenfish.com – and viewed a number of videos showing the capture and release of some seriously large fish.

But as far as I can gather these are not really wild trout, and are only in the lake due to a failed attempt to establish a fish farm there. When the venture was abandoned, the fish were released and, because of the abundance of food in the lake, they thrived, mightily. They are now spawning in the lake and in its feeder stream and, happily, for anglers at least, there seems to be no outlet stream. The fish are trapped there for the duration of their lives.

Getting to Jurassic Lake involves a back-breaking four-hour 4x4 journey through a desolate landscape. Accommodation is in tents with wooden flooring and simple beds; sheets, duvets and blankets are provided. An additional shower tent is planned for the 2008 season. Fishing is from the shore only. Paying for the privilege of being there can also be uncomfortable, upwards of £2,000 per rod per week, excluding travel to and from UK.

I suppose that whether or not £3,000+ for a week's trout fishing is expensive depends upon individual circumstances, but the acid test, at least for me, is more basic: would I spend that amount of money and travel halfway round the world to fish in what we here in Scotland would call a 'stank' – essentially an enclosed water with no natural outlet?

My answer would be no. Neither do I want to overdose on fishing for trout that rise to whatever is put in front of their snouts. Surely the real joy of fishing lies not in the size of fish caught, but in the challenge of persuading them to rise to your flies?

I can find that challenge within a 10-minute drive from my front door, and amidst scenery that is just a spectacular and on lochs that are just as remote as Jurassic Lake. The wild trout that I catch here in Scotland might not average 10lb in weight, but they are more precious to me than anything that Patagonia has to offer.

31.
Ladies First

One woman angler is far more effective than any 10 men. The chauvinists amongst you can grouse and girn all they like, but this is a fact. From that notorious day in 1922 when Miss Georgina Ballantine landed her record-breaking 64lb salmon on the River Tay, to the present time, it has always been thus.

Those who disagree probably don't fish with female companions and consequently know little better. I do know better, all too well, and throughout my angling life I have struggled to understand the successful-female-angler syndrome. How is it that they always seem to manage to catch them whilst we poor males remain fishless?

Diana Huntingdon, fishing the River Awe in 1927, landed a 55lb salmon, and another of 51lb in 1930; Mrs Morrison took her 61lb salmon from the River Deveron in October 1924; Pauline Kirkbride's 29lb Dee fish from the Woodend Beat; Lady Burnett's 45lb Tweed salmon. There are plenty more.

This also includes the late Mrs Kelly of Edinburgh, one of the most proficient trout anglers that I ever knew. Mrs Kelly fished Loch Leven in the 1950s and I have seen her catch more trout to her own rod than the combined total for the whole of two visiting angling clubs. If there were trout about, Mrs Kelly caught them.

My daughter, Lewis-Ann, is perpetually lucky, or, as she points out, skilful. Even as a child, on her first fishing trip into the hills south of Scourie, Lewis-Ann caught fish whilst the rest of Clan Sandison thrashed fruitlessly. Regardless of the weather, Lewis-Ann always catches fish.

Ann, my long-suffering better half, is just as useful in matters piscatorial. One day, fishing a series of lochans between Glutt and Dalnawillan in Caithness, I left her to her own devices and stamped off to do business in more promising waters. I returned fishless whilst she caught three, each being over 1lb 8oz in weight.

The secret of their success is, I am convinced, two-fold. Firstly, women are persistent. Lady Burnett used to fish every minute, right up to close of play. "What's the time, Jimmy?" she would ask her gillie. "Five minutes to go, Madam," he would reply. "Right, long enough for another dozen casts." During which time she invariably hooked a fish.

Secondly, there is technique. Macho males lash out miles of line and, in doing so, often lose contact with their flies. Women dance out their cast to barely a couple of rod lengths distance from the boat or bank. On these facts I rest my case: one woman angler is far more effective and efficient than any 10 men. If this be error and upon me proved, then I will eat my landing net.

32.
Hooked on Shetland

I was once hooked by a Shetland trout. I suppose that it was just returning like-for-like. As I tried to remove the fish from my tail fly, my wife Ann's wretched Yorkshire terrier, Heathcliff, made a lunge for it. Whilst fending him off, I dropped the fish and in the process the middle fly, a size 14 March Brown, embedded itself deeply into the back of my left hand.

Ann, using the 'loop-and-pull method', was able painlessly to remove the fly, during the course of which operation I swear that I saw Heathcliff, his face twisted into a hideous, white-toothed grin, smirking at me from ear to hairy ear.

We had set out that morning to explore a number of lochs on North Mid Field: Whitelaw Loch (Gd ref: 359540), Truggles Water (Gd ref: 372547), Maa Water (Gd ref: 378552) and Lamba Water (Gd ref: 382559). Find them on OS Map 3, Shetland – North Mainland, Scale 1:50,000.

The day involved a seven-mile hike over fair to rough ground, but it was worth every step, not just for great sport with splendid little trout, but also because of the wondrous array of bird life we encountered along the way. Graceful whimbrel whistled down the wind, birds that I have only once seen on mainland Scotland, but which are common in Shetland.

Arctic Skua tumbled in amazing aerial display. Great Skua dive-bombed us as we tramped up the hill. Red-throated divers, the Shetland 'rain geese', joined us on little Whitelaw Loch. I caught a glimpse of an otter, staring curiously at me as I passed the inlet burn to Maa Water. Beyond the moor, in the midst of a silver and blue sea, towered the stacks of Papa Stour.

At the end of the day, we returned to our cottage on the shore by Scrabba Skerry at Bridge of Walls and opened a bottle of wine. "You know," I said to Ann, " I bet the trout that hooked me is telling his friends all about the huge angler he caught." "Do you think so?" she replied. "I'm certain – how he played me, the fight I put up, how heavy I was and how he carefully put me back – the works." "And do you think they will believe him?" "I don't know if fish have an equivalent for how anglers would respond to such a story, but if they have, then my guess is that the tale will be greeted with a loud chorus of, 'Aye, right!'"

33.
A Small Ramble

In a few hours it will be midnight, December 31st, 2007. When I was outside earlier this evening, the Northern Lights fingered the star-splashed sky, touching Ben Hope, Ben Loyal and the leaden waters of the Kyle of Tongue. The sound of our stream tumbling down the hill from Beinn Bhreac was like the noise of ice cubes clinking in a crystal glass. And I found myself thinking about fishing.

I remember a day when we rested at Suileag Bothy, below the towering bulk of Suilven near Lochinver in North-West Sutherland. A best bib-and-tuckered dipper bobbed and splashed in the Abhairn an Clach Airigh burn. Loch an Alltain Duibh sparkled in autumn sunlight, its surface stippled with rising trout. Purple heather and red-bedecked rowan brushed its banks.

Sorry, I'm rambling. On second thoughts, I'm not sorry. After so many years fishing, I am allowed a small ramble. Hang on whilst I pour myself a decent measure of the 'water of life'. After all, it is New Year's Eve. During my angling life I must have cast millions of times, rowed hundreds of miles up and down lochs large and small in all kinds of weather, tied thousands of casts and lost countless numbers of flies.

They have been good years and I regret nothing, not even losing that monster trout at Unthank on the South Tyne when we lived near Bardon Mill in Northumberland. Or the Tweed salmon in the Long Pool, upstream from Innerleithen, when I was 16, although I wept at the time. And the day when Ann and I almost capsized the boat in a howling gale on Gladhouse Reservoir near Edinburgh.

I taught my father to fish and used to used to make up his casts. If Dad saw a trout rise he would remain rooted to the same spot for hours, convinced that, through sheer perseverance, it would eventually rise and take his inexpertly offered fly. It never did.

Angling has been one of the greatest joys of my life. Not just catching fish, but the whole bang-shoot of the business of being at one with nature. I adore Scotland and everything it stands for: the smell, the touch and the taste of my native land; its people, lonely moors and distant mountains, its trout-filled lochs and peat-stained streams. Damn all and anyone who dares to demean this treasure.

Well, here it comes, another new year in all its pristine splendour. Another beginning. Make the most of it. Make it the best year ever. A year of happiness, a year of care, courtesy and consideration for all creatures great and small, human or otherwise. May there always be love in your life and wild trout in your loch.

34.
Haunting Memories

Some lochs haunt me. Waters where I have hooked and lost monster trout, and others where I know monsters lurk, but have never managed to tempt them to rise to my flies, no matter how carefully presented. One such loch, unnamed on OS Map 9, Cape Wrath, Second Series, Scale 1:50,000, but known locally as Calva, lies to the west of the A894 Scourie/Kylestrome road at Gd ref: 175375. More years ago than I care to remember, my wife, Ann, and I and our two children tramped out to fish it and the other unnamed lochans to the north.

The children had great sport and caught bright little trout in the lochans that gave them a good fight and lots of pleasure. I was fishing the south end of Calva, near to where a rowan tree bordered the bank. The water was incredibly clear and I had been told by Ian Hay, who owned the Scourie Hotel then, that the loch held specimen fish. I believed him. As we anglers always do. However, after two or three hours of fruitless endeavour, I was about to give up when the 'fish of a lifetime' rose and took my tail fly.

I can still see every spot on its huge body as it leapt from the water, sending crystal droplets sparkling into the afternoon sunlight. And that was the last I saw of it. Two minutes later the hook came free and I was left dejected and in utter despair. It is a feeling that, during my fishing life, I have come to know well. Very well. Another of the Scourie lochs helped to cement that feeling, the unnamed water at Gd ref: 196414. It is one of the most beautiful lochs in Scotland and whilst bank fishing halfway down the west shore, I hooked and lost another specimen trout.

Then there was that enormous trout on Loch na Moine (OS Map 10, Gd ref: 628518). After three spectacular runs, I had him to the net, a trout that I estimated to be in the order of 7lb in weight. But my landing net refused to open and the bank was unsuitable for beaching the fish. I can still see it turning on its side and heading back to the depths. Also, the enigma that is Loch a'Bhualaidh (OS Map 10, Gd ref: 537562), reached after a two-mile tramp up the hill from the west shore of the Kyle of Tongue. I have seen a basket of five trout from that loch which weighed 21lb, but I have yet to seriously disturb any of the residents.

There are others, ones that got away, not a lot, to be truthful, but I will never forget them, although they have almost certainly forgotten me. Remember to obtain proper permission if you decide to visit any of the lochs mentioned above. Speak to the Scourie Hotel (tel: 01971 502396) and Ben Loyal Hotel (tel: 01847 611216).

35.
Toftingall is Tops

Loch Toftingall in Caithness is one of the most user-friendly waters that I have ever fished. Today, a good forest track allows you to drive almost to the mooring bay, but when I first visited Toftingall, in near gale-force conditions, it involved a vigorous one and a half mile hike across boggy moorland to reach a comfortable position from which to cast at the south end.

High peat banks gave some shelter, but I was not particularly confident about any reward for my endeavours. Which doubled my pleasure when an excellent trout immediately took my carefully presented Silver Butcher and roared off like an express train towards the middle of the loch. When it came to the net, it was just under 2lb in weight, and, shortly thereafter, I landed a second fish of similar size.

Since that first visit I have spent many happy hours on Toftingall, although I never again caught fish of such size. They now more modestly average 10oz/12oz in weight, but fight with such vigour that in their initial run they seem to be very much larger than they really are. The other advantage of the loch is that it is generally rectangular/circular in shape which means that no matter from which direction the wind howls – as it often does in Caithness – it is possible to find an area of the bank from which to cast.

Locate the loch on OS Map 11, Thurso & Dunbeath, Scale 1:50,000 at Gd ref: 190525. Toftingall is approximately 160 acres in extent and has an average depth of about four feet. Personally, I prefer to bank fish, and have always had better results doing so than by fishing from a boat. I once waded across the loch, from the west to the east bank, towards the south end, without the water going much above waist level. And caught four trout in the process.

However, for those not inclined, three boats are available, along with outboard motors. The key to success and safety when using an outboard on the loch is, as it is on all lochs, to hasten about your business slowly. Be safe, not sorry. However, apart from the shallows, there is only one serious obstruction to catch you unawares: a large rock, at about Gd ref: 192519 on the OS Map, which is just below the surface in normal water levels.

Toftingall is the ideal place to introduce beginners to our gentle art, and for a splendid family day out: peaceful, serene, lots of pretty trout, a boathouse for shelter should the weather turn nasty and a lochside picnic table for sunny days and lazy evenings. Further details and bookings from Hugo Ross in Wick, tel: 01955 604200.

36.
Casting Aspersions

My youngest daughter, Jean, was fascinated by a casting clinic at a game fair we visited a few years back. Eventually, she asked me if she could have a lesson. Ignoring the implicit insult that I had been less than satisfactory as her angling mentor, I held my peace and simply agreed. I have learned from bitter experience that arguing with Jean is a fruitless undertaking that almost invariably ends in tears, mine.

The instructor soon had Jean under control, which was something I had never achieved. As I watched, I was amazed at the improvement basic instruction from a professional could effect. But, from time to time, I noticed that Jean stopped casting and fell into deep conversation with her tutor.

Eventually, she wandered over and, smugly, announced: "You know what you have been telling me about casting? Well he says it is a load of rubbish." I spluttered, searching for words with which to defend my reputation. Jean spotted my distress and moved in for the kill. "He wants a word with you, now."

Resigned, I shambled over. "What are you trying to do to me?" I pleaded. "She will never let me forget this if I live to be a hundred. You have destroyed my life." Unperturbed, he handed me a rod and a said: "Come on, Bruce, let's try to sort something out. We can't have you going about being a danger to yourself, if not to any fish that might come your way."

Most of us think that just because we thrash about with a trout or salmon rod and, occasionally, stumble into a fish, we are competent, indeed even expert, anglers. But that session at the casting clinic reminded me of the danger of misleading beginners by suggesting we can teach them to cast. Yes, we can show them how to get a fly onto the water, but, in doing so, we often infect them with our own faults and casting misdemeanours.

The wild lochs and rivers of Scotland are a priceless treasure, to be nurtured for the pleasure of present generations and for the pleasure of generations yet to come. So, in spite of my alleged failings as an instructor, I have no regrets about introducing beginners to this delight. After all, there is nothing to stop them seeking better casting advice than I can offer. Just ask Jean. Quicker than it takes you to read these words, she will confirm that it is the right thing to do.

37.
Beavering About

Scottish Natural Heritage has been working for more than a decade on proposals to reintroduce European beavers to our rivers. Now, after many set-backs, it looks likely that a group of these animals, extinct in Scotland for the past 400 years, will be released into the Argyllshire countryside.

The primary source of opposition to the reintroduction has come from landowners and the farming community. They are uncertain of the impact that beavers might have upon their properties and the potential for damage to their legitimate commercial interests.

Concern has also been expressed by some members of the angling community, who feel that beavers going about their natural business might have an adverse effect on salmon, sea-trout and brown trout stocks in the rivers that they make their home.

These anxieties are understandable, but perhaps unfounded. I, for one, would be delighted to share my day with beavers. Part of the great attraction of fishing is the opportunity it gives us, not only to attempt the removal of fish from their natural habitat, but also the chance to enjoy the wonderful and diverse wildlife that we encounter whilst doing so.

Some of my most treasured angling memories are not about the ones that got away and the ones that didn't, but about unexpected meetings with the animals and plants with which we share Scotland's treasured and irreplaceable environment: otters, red deer, wildcat, mountain hares, eagle, peregrine, wild swans, black-throated and red-throated divers, mountain aven, chickweed wintergreen, mosses and lichens, the unique Scottish primrose, and many more.

Of all of these, my favourite is probably the otter. Indeed, if, as many believe, we are reborn in an afterlife in a different form, then please could I come back as an otter? The complete outdoor life, free fishing, unrestricted swimming, fun and games and a highly developed sense of humour. Who could ask for more?

I have watched an otter take a salmon from Falls Pool on the River Forss in Caithness. My wife, Ann, and I whilst fishing Loch Ruard in the Flow Country were visited by a curious otter. It lay on its back, forepaws folded across its chest, assured and self-confident, staring at us, before diving below the waves. I have seen an otter and her four cubs, early in the morning, running along the shore of Loch Watten near the island.

For all of these reasons, I welcome the return of beavers to Scotland. They will add mightily to the pleasure and content that goes hand in hand with fishing. And bring us closer to accepting our responsibility to preserve and protect for the comfort and joy of future generations all of the things that make Scotland so special.

38.
Willie Morrison

The late Willie Morrison was one of Sutherland's best-loved fishing characters. Willie ran the Inchnadamph Hotel at Loch Assynt where he was famous for his ability as an angler, and for his laid-back, wry sense of humour. So when I heard that his grandson, 11-year-old Kenneth, had caught his first salmon last week, I knew that Willie would have been very proud of him.

Kenneth's dad, George, told me: "We were trolling home when Kenneth hooked the fish, near Skiag Bridge. He played it for about 10 minutes in fairly rough conditions whilst I held the boat off the shore. Kenneth coaxed the fish over the net and we landed it – when the red and gold toby fell from its mouth! It was a hen fish and weighed just under 5lb."

I first met Willie in the 1970s, when I wrote angling reports for a fishing magazine. Willie always underplayed his hand: "How has the fishing, been, Willie?" I would ask. "Oh, not very good," he would reply. "Have any salmon been caught?" "Let me think for a moment… well, I had a couple myself, and one of our guests had six for his day and, oh yes, there was that 4lb trout from one of the Corrie Lochans."

I remember the time I phoned Willie to ask about results for the previous month. After going through the customary routine, I was just about to end our conversation when Willie added, "And there have been some nice brown trout as well." "Tell me more," I asked. Three ferox weighing a total of nearly 28lb. I went over the following morning and photographed them.

Every evening in the hotel, after dinner, Willie would arrange the following day's fishing with his guests: which loch they were going to fish, advice on flies and tactics when needed. One evening, however, matters were not going too well because one of the assembled company had launched into a seemingly endless and detailed history of the Highland midge *Culicoides impunctatus*.

Everybody groaned inwardly as the relentless saga unfolded, until the speaker explained that it was only the female of the species that did the biting and that after biting she died within 24 hours. Willie sighed, and gently interrupted, "Yes, indeed, but there would be a lot at her funeral, I'm sure." The room erupted in laughter and sanity and good humour were restored.

Willie's great love of the broken lands of Assynt and of its fishing has continued through his son, George, and now, down to the next generation through his grandson, Kenneth. Willie Morrison's enduring legacy is the many happy memories that he left behind him, and of his kindness and unfailing courtesy.

39.
The Great Joy of Fishing

I used to work for an acerbic Yorkshireman who had an answer for all occasions. Once, whilst driving round Limekilns estate with Lord Elgin, we paused in sight of Dunfermline Abbey. Written in stone around the top of the tower are the words "King Robert the Bruce". King Robert's body is buried in the Abbey and Lord Elgin's family is descended from 'The Bruce'.

My boss chose that moment to inquire of Lord Elgin: "Have you lived here long then?" I cringed in the back of the vehicle. Lord Elgin, the soul of discretion, after a pause, replied politely: "About 700 years." "I suppose you must almost be one of the locals by now then?" quipped my boss.

He had a point. When I moved to Caithness, in spite of the fact that my grandfather was Caithness born and bred in the county, I was regarded as an outsider. At a Burns Supper one year I was asked by a local: "Are ye a liar?" I protested, "I try not to be." He insisted: "Are ye a liar?" It dawned on me that he was asking if I was a lawyer.

The way you speak doesn't really matter to anglers. Fishing is as much about shared pleasure as it is about catching fish and most piscators are as friendly and cheerful a bunch of human beings as ever trod God's good earth.

The late Angus McArthur brightened many a fisherman's day. I once sent two friends to fish the Association Water of the River Naver in North Sutherland. Angus happened by and stopped for a blether. He walked the beat with them, pointing out the lies, and gave them advice on patterns of fly to use.

I met Angus when bank fishing Loch Croispol near Durness. He was sharing a boat with a friend and they rowed over to ask if I would like to join them. Never regretted doing so, not only for the pleasure of their company, but also for their humour. Whether they had caught nothing or a creel-full, if anyone asked how they were getting on they always replied, "Just the two."

I remember fishing in South Uist with an Italian dentist. Neither of us could speak a word of the other's language but we got on just fine. I spent many months fishing in a remote region of Chile where nobody spoke English, but language was never a problem. I have even fished with non-English-speaking Japanese anglers and we communicated perfectly.

I often think that if our political masters spent more time fly-fishing and less time bickering about the Euro, health care and political sleaze, the world would be a far better place. How could anyone be anything other than agreeable when confronted with the great joy that is fishing?

40.
Less than Bored on the Borgie

A friend once complained to me about salmon fishing in Alaska. He said that after a few days he got bored catching fish. Most Scottish anglers that I know wouldn't object to the chance, just once in a lifetime, of getting 'bored' catching salmon. But it is a truism that success in salmon fishing depends as much upon being in the right place at the right time as it does upon skill, or any other of the fates in which we anglers place our trust.

For once, however, my wife, Ann, and I managed to achieve that happy state, of being in the right place at the right time, during August, on the River Borgie a few miles from our home in North Sutherland. Conditions were perfect: a falling spate, after several weeks of rain, with fresh fish running the river almost constantly. In every pool, salmon were showing, splashing and surging upstream to reach their ancestral spawning grounds.

The Borgie is my favourite salmon stream; modest in size, easily fished from the bank and set amidst some of the most splendid scenery in Scotland. The river rises from Loch Mathair Bhorgaidh, between Cnoc an Daimh Beag (295m) and Cnoc an Daimh Mor (357m), to the south of Ben Loyal (765m), Queen of Scottish Mountains. It flows north through lochs Coulside, Loyal, Craggie and Slaim to greet the sea amidst the golden sands of Torrisdale Bay, a mile or so to the west of where its neighbour, the River Naver, enters the same bay.

There are three principal beats, each fishing two rods, with an additional, moorland beat above Falls Pool. The first mile of the stream, from the sea up to near Borgie Bridge on the A836 Thurso/Durness road, is let on a daily basis. The other beats are let by the week. There are some 50 named pools, mostly man-made, and each one offers the chance of sport. The Borgie is a spate stream, but this year we have had an overabundance of the wet stuff. And the Good Lord, in his infinite wisdom, even arranged for brief, additional showers which kept the river in prime fishing condition for weeks on end.

It was against this background that we enjoyed wonderful sport with beautifully formed, silver salmon, fresh from their Greenland feeding grounds. The first purple blush of heather coloured the banks and our days on the river were accompanied by golden eagle, buzzard, heron, dipper and piping greenshank. By the end of our visit we had encountered more than a dozen fish, with Ann landing her first-ever salmon, and, do you know, we were not bored at all, not even for a single minute!

41.
Life's Unkindest Cuts

Even up here in laid-back North Sutherland, life's unkindest cuts sometimes come from the least expected directions. For instance, from nearest and dearest. I was in the kitchen and all I did was mention cooking fish. "Don't ask me anything about that," responded my wife, Ann. "Why ever not?" I replied. "You are a master of the art."

This was greeted with silence. "Honest," I continued, "I mean it, and I speak from years of experience. You are an expert when it comes to preparing and cooking the trout I catch." "I have forgotten what a wild brown trout looks like," she said. I blundered on. "That's impossible. How can anyone forget something like that?"

"Easy," she replied, "because you don't catch any, that's how. When did you last come home with something for supper?" "That's unfair . . ." "And it's unfair of you to complain that I don't serve trout." "All I said . . ." I started. "I know what you said, Bruce, but how do you expect me to cook trout if you don't catch any?"

I retired, hurt, to ponder this truth. I never seem to find enough time to go fishing. So far this season I have managed only a handful of outings: freezing on Loch Loyal in March, blown off Loch Hope in June, a day grandson-sitting duty on Loch Craggie, a few sessions on the oars for visiting friends. If I had managed to catch just a couple more trout I might even have had a brace.

It seems to me that years get shorter as they pass by. I remember when years were proper and each month as long as a lifetime, each day endless. What changed that? What happened to time? It never used to be like that: always in a hurry, unforgiving, brash and unfeeling. There was always time to go fishing when I was a boy.

My introduction to trout fishing in Sutherland came during a school holiday. We stayed in Strathnaver with a lady much given to religious fervour but not above removing the odd salmon from the river at the first stroke of Sabbath's ending. I fell in love with the area then and dreamed about living and working in the far north and being surrounded by some of the finest wild trout fishing in the world.

I do so, now, and, to be truthful, I suppose time is only what we make of it. So I have started. It is my birthday in a few weeks and I have devised a cunning plan for a whole week of trout fishing. Perhaps I might even come home with something to keep Ann happy – maybe I should warn her to clear a large space in the freezer? After all, you never know your luck, do you?

42.
About the Length of a Small Battleship

Lochan Bealach Cornaidh lies cupped between two arms of Quinag (808m), one of Scotland's most dramatic mountains. Spidean Coinich's sheer cliffs guard the south shore whilst the vast buttress of Sail Gharbh towers to the north. Reaching Bealach Cornaidh will involve you in a vigorous, soggy, forty-minute moorland tramp over gently rising ground.

Use OS Map 15, Loch Assynt to find your way round. The loch lies at Gd ref: 209281. Park in the old quarry on the east side of the A894 Skiag Bridge/Unapool road. Directly across from the quarry, follow a well-defined stalker's path heading north-west over Druim na h-Uamha Moire. This track ends after about a mile, after which you are on your own, so always carry a compass and map in case of bad weather.

Cornaidh is approximately 440yds long by 220yds wide and it is fished from the shore. Wading is possible along the north bank, but take care, because the bottom here is boulder-strewn and uneven. The east end, where the Allt na Bradhan burn tumbles out, is easily accessible and as you near the burn, there is a promontory on the north-east corner that makes an ideal casting platform.

The shallow western bay offers the most comfortable wading. The bottom is sandy and you will be able to cover a wide area of water. This bay is also useful for cooling off body and soul during hot summer days when the fish are not rising. Happily, however, lack of trout is not generally a problem at Bealach Cornaidh. The lochan has good numbers of fish, the majority of which are pink-fleshed.

Trout vary in size from a few ounces right up to splendid fish of over 2lb in weight. Therefore, treat each rise with caution and respect. Neither are the trout too fussy about which pattern of fly they take. Start with trad-itional patterns, such as Black Pennell, Ke-He and Silver Butcher. If that doesn't work, tempt them with something more 'exotic'. Keep a brace for breakfast; carefully return the rest to fight another day.

Whilst in the vicinity, sort of, consider a further expedition to the group of lochs that lie between Sail Garbh and the main road. These lochs, nan Eun and its unnamed satellite waters are very rarely fished and yet I have reliable reports from fellow anglers (who would never, ever, embellish any of the stories they tell me) that there are some particularly large trout here; the length of one such resident being described as about the same length as a small battleship. Worth a look?

43.
Sheildaig Diamonds and Fairies

In the hills to the south of Shieldaig Lodge Hotel near Gairloch, lie Diamonds, Spectacles, Aeroplanes and Fairies, the names of a group of excel-lent trout lochs fished from the hotel.

The hotel is situated on the shores of Loch Shieldaig where, after dinner, you may watch eider duck rooting amongst the reed-fringed shallows or wander through the old woodlands followed by the sound of cuckoo and finch.

The Fairy Lochs – Fairy and Top Fairy – are a short walk from the hotel and they hold trout that average just under 1lb in weight. Good baskets are the rule rather than the exception and the lochs contains larger fish as well. Trout of over 6lb in weight have been taken here.

The other, smaller, lochans are close to Top Fairy, so if sport is slow on the Fairies it is a simple matter to restore self-confidence with a few casts on Aeroplane where baskets of 15/20 8oz trout are unexceptional. Bank fishing, and flies to offer include Soldier Palmer, Grouse & Claret, Whickham's Fancy, Kingfisher Butcher, and Alexandria.

Loch Bad na h-Achlaise, another of the hotel waters, lies close to the B80567 road to Red Point. This loch fishes well throughout the season and the most productive area is in the west section of the north bay. In calm conditions, dry fly works particularly well on Bad na h-Achlaise. A boat is available, although bank fishing can be just as rewarding.

If you enjoy a decent walk with your fishing, then head for the lochs that lie to the west of Baosbheinn (875m), the 'Wizard's Mountain'. There are seven, all of which drain into the sea at Eilean Horrisdale. These waters are accessed by a good track and furthest out is Loch a'Bhealaich, reached in about three hours. A boat is moored at the north end, but bank fishing, particularly in the sandy, shallow waters, can be just as good.

Loch a'Ghobhainn (Gowan) is the best of the Sheildaig Forest waters where boat fishing brings good results. Trout here average three to the pound, but heavier fish of up to and over 2lb in weight are often taken. Next north is Loch Gaineamhach, full of hard fighting little trout, safe wading and excellent back fishing.

Loch Braigh Horrisdale is the ideal place for beginners, and for a family picnic; not too far for little legs to walk, a good boat, sandy beaches and trout that fight with great dash and spirit.

The final loch is Bad a'Chroatha, close to the road. There are two boats here and, in high water conditions, the chance of sport with the occasional sea-trout or salmon.

For further information, contact Shieldaig Lodge Hotel, tel: 01445 741250, website: www.shieldaiglodge.com (hotel residents have fishing priority).

44.
The Trout Lochs of the Auchentoul Forest

Elegant Ben Griam Beg (580m) and her graceful neighbour Ben Griam Mor (590m) stand like blue-grey sentinels above the wind-burnished moors of East Sutherland. Man has watched over these lands for thousands of years, as is evidenced by the remains of a hill fort on the summit of Griam Beg, built and occupied more than 2,500 years ago and the highest such Iron Age hill fort in Scotland.

These people were farmers and hunters and their larders must have been laden with red deer and with salmon, trout and sea-trout taken from the Helmsdale River and from lochs of the Auchentoul Forest. During excavations at the site round stones with holes in the middle were found and these could have been used as weights on fishing nets.

This is not a technique that I would recommend you try today, unless you are anxious to spend some time as a guest in one of Her Majesty's prisons, but good fishing is readily available for a modest charge, even on two feeder streams of the famous Helmsdale River – Scotland's 'other' Bannock Burn – and on the Abhainn Frithe.

The trout lochs of the Auchentoul Forest include Loch an Ruthair, next to the A897 Helmsdale/Melvich road; Loch Culaidh, adjacent to the track out of Greamachary; Lucy Loch, near to the railway line; Lochan Dubh, to the north of Auchentoul Lodge, and Loch Arichlinie, a 40-minute tramp south-west from an Ruthair.

Loch an Ruthair is the principal water, one and a half miles north/south by up to half a mile wide. Three boats are available, and boat fishing brings best results. However, in windy conditions, bank fishing can be productive; at the north end and the north-east corner where three burns flow in, but, for better quality trout, all down the west shore.

The loch holds a plentiful stock of traditional, frying-pan sized fish, but, in recent years, under the stewardship of Angus Ross, the head keeper of the estate, careful management techniques have greatly improved the size of the residents. A few years ago a fish of 6lb 8oz was taken and today good numbers of trout between 2lb and 3lb are not uncommon. Also, whereas the flesh of the trout used to be white, now the flesh of the larger fish is salmon-red.

For me, however, Loch Arichlinie is the real 'gem' here, especially for those new to fly fishing. The trout may not be very large, but catching upwards of 50 small trout in a day is a great way to introduce the beginner to our well-loved art. Arichlinie is also very beautiful, remote and peaceful, all that is best is about trout fishing in Scotland.

For further information and bookings, contact Angus on tel: 01431 831227.

45.
Take the Strain

Single strands of horsehair are almost invisible in water, particularly running water. It is the perfect material for making the perfect cast. Guaranteed to fool even the most circumspect trout. All you need is an accommodating cuddie. Proffer a carrot at the front end whilst carefully snipping off a few strands of tail hair from the rear.

You will discover that the strands are a lot thicker than you might think, and that they are naturally tapered. Wet the hairs, then join them together with dexterous blood knots. Be gentle. With patience, you should end up with a cast of about 8ft to 9ft in length, constructed from three or four strands, depending upon the size of the horse's tail.

If at first you don't succeed, like Robert the Bruce and his spider, try, try and try again. It is worth persevering because horsehair makes the most lethal cast that I have ever used. The trouble involved in preparing it is well worth the effort of doing so.

I first used horsehair when I was a boy and I have caught trout of up to 1lb 8oz with it on the River Tweed near Innerleithen. Provided that you maintain a constant strain, avoid slack line and keep in touch with the fish, horsehair is amazingly strong. But an ill-considered snatch, jerk, or a moment's inattention, and it breaks like worn thread.

Prior to action, test the cast. To do so, I attached a fly and hooked it up to a wire fence. I then pretended that I had risen a fish, and 'struck', and the cast snapped. I tried again, but this time only raised the point of the rod, rather than striking, and the cast held.

Even when I simulated a trout stripping line from the reel, provided that I kept an even strain, the cast remained intact.

My proudest moment came one evening when my father and I arrived at Innerleithen to find the Tweed in spate; a brown, turbulent flood, sweeping seawards loaded with chunks of trees and broken branches.

Dad moaned about the weather, and a wasted journey, and got into conversation with another similarly dismayed angler. But, being young, I set off, much to their amusement, for my favourite part of the river with my horsehair cast and a small dry fly.

I fished the fly downstream, close to the bank, carefully searching back eddies and quiet places beneath overhanging branches. Wading was quite impossible, so I knelt, and on occasions lay full length on the ground in order to get my fly into inviting, fishy corners. Within an hour, I returned triumphant to show off the four brown trout that I had caught.

46.
Lies, Damned Lies and Anglers

There are lies, damned lies, and anglers. I am one of the latter, signed, sealed and delivered into the piscatorial art for nearly six decades. Beyond all hope. Which is why living and working in North Sutherland is the only place for the likes of me. Plenty of room to go fishing.

And if I were to live several lifetimes, there would still be insufficient time to explore all that this amazing land has to offer in regard to fishing for salmon, sea-trout and brown trout. Best of all, for me, are the brown trout, wild creatures that have survived in our lochs since the end of the last Ice Age, a precious, irreplaceable treasure.

My permit costs me £5.00 per season from the local angling club. Visitors pay more, but, whatever, it is value-for-money fishing the likes of which is rarely available anywhere else in UK. For instance, a day on the chalk streams of England, the Test and Itchen, will set you back upwards of £100.00. For that you are allowed to fish for stocked, hatchery-reared brown trout and foreign rainbow trout: bag-limit, four fish and then you stop fishing.

Salmon fishing is also more expensive down south. A day on a prime beat of the Spey, Dee, Tay or Tweed can cost an arm and a leg, in the region of up to £300.00 per rod. However, a rod on the association waters of world-famous rivers such as the Naver and Helmsdale in Sutherland costs less than £30.00 per rod per day.

Access to many other salmon and sea-trout fishing beyond the Great Glen rarely costs more than £40.00 a day. Granted, most of these streams are spate rivers, where good water levels are all-important for good sport, but they still represents an angling bargain where there is always an excellent chance of a fish.

Most of this sport, and particularly the wild brown trout fishing, is readily available to local and visiting anglers alike. The Scourie Angling Club issues visitor permits on 30 waters. Several hundreds of the Westminster Estate lochs are also open to the public on payment of a small fee. At Lochinver, there are years of exciting fishing available from local estates, again at a very reasonable cost.

You will be made more than welcome by the Lairg Angling Club who have fishing on Loch Shin and a number of other classic wild trout lochs. The same applies to the angling clubs in Dornoch and Golspie and on the Kyle of Sutherland and elsewhere in the far north. Show up, pay up, fish in a proper manner, with rod and line and fly, and you will always be welcome.

47.
Spring into Summer

It must be summer – white smoke and sparks are billowing skywards from a chimney in the village and the local fire engine is racing towards the scene. It happens every year, the consequence of burning peat all winter, but it is a sure sign that summer has arrived, as certain as the arrival of the first swallows.

When we lived in Caithness, we also had a peat burning stove and, one day, when I was busy on my mid-morning jog, I looked back to see smoke pouring from the chimney of our house. I made it home in record time and dialled 999.

The fire brigade and a police car arrived within five minutes of my call and I was impressed when a young constable leapt from his vehicle and ran towards me. Barely pausing for breath, he announced, "I was out on Loch Watten last night and caught a cracker on a Ke-He, it was just over 3lb in weight!"

Life is like that in the far north, a question of priorities: the house may be in flames, but talking about fishing is far more urgent business. I would not have it any other way for all the supermarkets, cinemas, nightclubs and theatres in the world.

So far this season, trout have been almost entirely absent from our diet. A preliminary expedition was a hypothermia-inducing disaster; a steely surface, untroubled all day by sight of a single fin. At last, however, now that the weather has decided to behave, it is time for a visit to Loch Haluim, one of the most attractive and productive trout lochs in all of Scotland.

The loch lies in shadow of Ben Loyal (765m), the Queen of Scottish Mountains, and is reached after an invigorating hike of some three miles from the A836 Lairg/Tongue road. Park at Inchkinloch at the south end of Loch Loyal and contour westwards round the hill to find the loch (see OS Map 10, Scale 1:50,000, Gd ref: 555455).

Loch Haluim adorns the moor like a silver and blue butterfly. It is three quarters of a mile long by up to half a mile wide, resplendent with a multitude of inviting bays and fishy promontories. This is bank fishing for wild brown trout at its very finest. Good baskets of fish are the rule, rather than the exception, and Haluim is the perfect place to introduce beginners to the gentle art of fly fishing.

Start at the north end of the east wing of the butterfly, where a small feeder stream, the Allt Fhionnaich, flows in, and work south. One of my favourite areas, however, is in the vicinity of the promontory at Gd ref: 560455, where the loch narrows. Even on a bad day, you will still catch breakfast here.

Don't expect to hook one for the glass case on Haluim – a 1lb fish is 'big' here – but the residents rise readily to most patterns of artificial fly and they fight hard. Having said which, Haluim is surrounded by a series of rarely fished named and unnamed lochans where you might encounter the fish of your angling dreams, so be prepared!

For permission to fish Loch Haluim contact Loyal Estate on tel: 01847 611291.

48.
Mushrooms and Trout

Loch Dun Mhurchaidh on the Island of Benbecula is an excellent place for finding mushrooms, and for catching wild brown trout. Both are of outstanding quality and will provide a meal fit for king and commoner alike.

However, the mushrooms are a lot easier to locate than the trout, but persist, because Dun Mhurchaidh has some splendid fish. The loch may be found on OS Map 22, Benbeclua, Scale 1:50,000 at Gd ref: 795545 between the B892 Balavanich road and the minor road from Knock Rolum in the west to Market Stance in the east.

Dun Mhurchaidh is a large, shallow water, three quarters of a mile north/south by up to a quarter mile wide. It is fished from the bank and the most frequent mistake visiting anglers make is to wade.

Approach with caution, particularly in the early morning and at dusk when large trout glide into the margins to feed. Wading only scares them out into the middle. Trout average in the order of 10oz in weight, but there are good numbers of fish of over 1lb in weight and I have seen much larger fish, certainly up to 4lb, when I have disturbed them with an ill-judged cast.

Mount your attack along the north-east arm of the loch, then down the east shore to the small island at the south end. The trout do not give themselves up easily, but Dun Mhurchaidh is one of the most exciting lochs to fish on the island. Should the going get tough on Dun Mhurchaidh, repair to the more angler-friendly Olavats to restore your self-confidence. These two waters are considered to be amongst the most productive of the Benbecula lochs and are managed by the South Uist Angling Association.

West Olavat is at Gd ref: 795513 whilst East Olavat may be found at Gd ref: 804504. Fish either from boat or bank, but boat fishing is perhaps the most profitable means of exploring all the fishy nooks and corners. My favourite is East Olavat which is scattered with a number of small islands alive with a wide variety of wildlife. The water is peat-stained and Olavat trout reflect this colour, beautifully golden and brightly red-spotted. They average 10oz/12oz in weight, but there are also good fish of over 1lb.

If the angling fates are still being unkind, take yourself to another of my favourite Benbecula lochs, Ba Alasdair at Gd ref: 857494 where catching breakfast, lunch and supper is guaranteed. Approach via the B981 and at Hacklet (Gd ref: 813483) follow the minor road north signposted to Kilerivagh and Craigastrome. Park at Gd ref: 861490.

Ba Alasdair can't be seen from the road, but a five-minute walk westwards will bring you to the south end of the loch. This is one of the most beautiful lochs in the Hebrides and it is scattered, at different levels, over a wide area. The southern section, Loch an Fheidh (Gd ref: 859485) and its outlet stream may be easily crossed to gain the hill and the higher part of the system, known as Bluebell Loch (Gd ref: 850493).

On the way up the hill, have a cast or three in two unnamed lochans: Gd ref: 855488, and 852484. Both lochans have the reputation of holding very large, dour trout. A round trip of all the waters here will involve you in a walk of about three miles amidst wildlife, flora and fauna that is every bit as exciting as is the fishing.

49.
The Limestone Lochs of Durness

High on most anglers' list of 'must fish' places are the famous Durness Limestone Lochs in North-West Sutherland: Caladail, Borralie, Croispol and little Lanlish. I have known and loved these wonderful waters for more than 30 years and they have an irresistible appeal that draws me back to them again and again, regardless of whether or not I catch anything.

The Keoldale Sheep Stock Club has the sole fishing rights to Borralie and Lanlish, and also rights on lochs Calladail and Croispol. There are two boats on Caladail, two on Borralie and one on Croispol, whilst Lanlish is fished from the bank. For bookings and information contact Martin Mackay, the secretary of the stock club, on tel: 01971 511255.

Be warned, however: the limestone lochs are not for faint-hearted anglers. If you are accustomed to catching 'limit bags' on commercial, put-and-take fisheries, you will find that the Durness waters will test all of your angling skills to their uttermost limits. Be prepared for blank days, but, when conditions are right, you could have the angling experience of your wildest dreams.

These lochs are crystal clear and every mistake is severely punished. When a trout eventually decides to rise to a well-presented fly, it does so furiously, and at tremendous speed. If you are not paying attention, all that you will feel is a vicious tug, and all that you will see is uproar in the water as the fish disappears back into the depths.

As is always the case, a decent wind helps mightily to disguise evil intent, but, quite often, and particularly in the evenings, the lochs are dead-flat calm and there is no place to hide. This is the time to change to dry fly and to fish fine and far off. Indeed, I know a number of anglers who exclusively fish dry fly on the limestone lochs and they invariably produce as good results, if not better, than those of us who stick to traditional wet fly patterns.

My preferred cast, when fishing Caladail, Borralie and Croispol, generally includes a selection from the following, depending upon the weather and all the other gods in which we anglers put our trust: Ke-He, Black Pennel, Loch Ordie for the 'bob', Greenwell's Glory, March Brown, Grouse & Claret for the middle, and, for the tail, Silver Butcher, Silver Invicta and Dunkeld. More often than not, I fish them on size 14 hooks.

The exception to the above is when I tackle little Loch Lanlish, the trout loch from hell. There are times when I would swear that there was not a single fish in the loch. Then, suddenly, after a few hours of fruitless casting, a rising trout will almost pull the rod out of my hand. In days past, Loch Lanlish has produced amazing trout in the teens of pounds, and even today fish of up to and over 8lb in weight can still be caught. Sadly, however, not by me.

My heaviest Lanlish fish weighed just under 4lb and the fingers of both of my hands would be sufficient to total up the rest of the trout that I have taken there. But, in spite of my apparent lack of success, I can think of few other lochs that I would rather fish. If you seek some of the most challenging fishing in Scotland, amongst some of Scotland's most majestic scenery, then head for Durness and its famous limestone lochs. I promise that you will not be disappointed when you do.

50.
The River Inver

Let's visit the River Inver this morning. The river flows into the sea at Lochinver in North-West Sutherland and is fished from the Inver Lodge Hotel (tel: 01571 844496, website: www.inverlodgehotel.co.uk). The hotel has fishing on the Upper Inver and the Lower Middle Inver. There are three principal pools on the Upper Inver, Loch na Garbhe Uidhe, where the flow from Loch Assynt tumbles in, Lochan an-Iasgaich which is a wide extension of the main river, and Turn Pool, just downstream from Lochan an-Iasgaich.

Lower Middle Inver is separated from the Upper Inver by a long, private stretch, and it has three principal pools, Mackenzie's Stream, Brachloch Pool and the Ministers Pool. Having said which, the runs between all these pools, given the right water conditions, are all capable of producing fish and deserve a close look and a few casts as you pass by.

Lochan an-Iasgaich is a wonderful pool; wide, with a substantial flow rushing in even in low water conditions. It is easily accessible and wading is safe and comfortable. It is possible to ford the river at the neck, but received wisdom advises you not to do so, because of the possibility of disturbing any salmon lying in, or moving up through the well-oxygenated water.

However, I have to confess that I have often waded the neck because reaching the south bank would otherwise involve a considerable hike upstream to access a footbridge in order to do so; which may account for the fact that, in spite of my best efforts, I have rarely prevented the residents of the pool from going about their lawful business.

But there can be few more scenic places in which not to catch salmon. The pool is overlooked by one of my favourite Scottish mountains, Quinag (808m), and the whole graceful ridge, from Spedean Conich in the south to Sail Gorm overlooking Unpool and Kyle Strome in the north, dominates the horizon.

Turn Pool, where Allt an Tiaghaich Burn bustles in, has been kinder to me. I remember one September evening, as I was weighing up the relative merits of a few more casts or a retreat to a refreshing pint in the hotel, when my fly stopped in midstream. I tightened into a fish, a salmon of about 6lb in weight and spawning-red, so I carefully unhooked the fish and returned it to the stream.

A few moments later a much larger fish took, and after a considerable struggle I managed to bring him to the bank. I did not weigh him because he too was returned, but I estimated the salmon to weigh in the order of about 14lb/15lb. I wish I could say that I returned him without a moment's hesitation, but that would be telling less than the whole truth.

Still, good behaviour brings its deserved rewards. A few weeks later a side of beautifully smoked River Inver salmon arrived unexpectedly at Castle Sandison, courtesy of a friend with whom I had been sharing the Beat. "That's nice," said The Manager, my wife, Ann. "Why don't we send it to Blair? He won't often get the chance of River Inver salmon in China, will he?" Dutifully, I did the deed and posted off my prize to my son. I didn't actually tell him that I hadn't caught the fish, but rather hoped that he might just assume that I had.

51.
Savage Entertainment

I do not need a calculator to total up the number of salmon that I have caught during my lifetime. The fingers of two hands will do nicely, thank you. Nobody could ever accuse me of being anything other than a deeply committed conservationist when it comes to the removal of the King of Fish from its natural habitat.

This is as much due to lack of patience as it has to do with lack of skill. I get bored. Perhaps if there were more salmon about, I might be encouraged to fish for them more often, but spending a small fortune to fish a stream that seems to be devoid of fish – at least that is what invariably happens to me – seems to be the height of lunacy.

I remember once hearing a disgruntled salmon angler complain about how much his single fish of the week had cost him: "That damned fish has cost me the best part of £2,000," he moaned. One of the locals quipped, ungraciously I thought, "Then just be grateful that you did not catch two."

For me, salmon fishing has always been a bit like waiting for a bus: nothing for ages and then two come along at once; or, on one memorable occasion when I was fishing the Thurso River, five, during the space of a couple of hours. However, even five salmon do not make a 'summer', and this is why I prefer fishing for wild brown trout.

With wild brown trout, there is always the chance of sport, even when water levels are less than kind, and tramping the hills and moorlands of this wonderful land of ours in search of sport keeps me fit. I have never been captivated by the well-ordered calm of lunch in a comfortable fishing hut by the banks of the stream.

But I confess that the thrill of hooking and playing a spring salmon is one of the supreme experiences of our art and there are few more challenging rivers upon which to try to do so than the River Kirkaig near Lochinver in Sutherland. The river is fished from Inver Lodge Hotel (tel: 01571 844496, website: www.inverlodgehotel.co.uk). Inver Lodge is, in my opinion, the finest fishing hotel in Scotland.

I must warn you, however, that the Kirkaig is not a river for wimps. Much of it is mountain goat country and you will have to work hard just to reach some of the pools, particularly on the Upper River, before you even begin to cast a fly. Nevertheless, the Kirkaig is a joy to fish, a turbulent, busy, rocky stream that will fully test every aspect of your angling skills.

Fishing ends at Falls Pool, where a 60ft high waterfall, pouring down from the Fionn Loch, is insurmountable by salmon. Falls Pool is reached after an invigorating 40-minute hike from Inverkirkaig, with the towering mass of Suilven (731m) crowding the horizon. After clambering down the side of a cliff to reach the fishing stance at Falls Pool, anglers then have to climb back up to find a faint track that leads downstream to the lower pools.

One of my favourites is Otter Pool, reached after a scary scramble down a tree- and bracken-covered, steep slope. The neck of the pool is narrow and casting in the traditional fashion is virtually impossible. I position myself at the neck and simply extend line from the reel, sweeping my fly over inviting lies. And, whilst doing so, I know that there is no place in the world that I would rather be.

52.
How Big Did You Say It Was?

Honest although we anglers undoubtedly are, there are times when even the best of us exaggerate when it comes to describing the length of fish that escape from our clutches. "How big did you say it was?" In time-honoured fashion we stretch out our arms, palms perpendicular to the ground, to indicate the length of the fish. But nobody ever believes us.

One of my acquaintances has a fail-safe method of dealing with these situations, primarily because he has only one arm – although he can tackle up and tie on a cast at twice the speed it takes me to do so. When he is called upon to demonstrate the length of his 'one that got away', he smiles, sticks out his arm and says, "That size." Hard to argue with such logic.

A few years ago, however, a one-armed angler fishing Loch Shin in Sutherland had no need to resort to subterfuge. He returned to the boat-house bearing irrefutable evidence: a magnificent 6lb brown trout. This vast loch regularly produces specimen trout of similar and even greater size.

Loch Shin is one of the largest freshwater lochs in Scotland, 17 miles long by up to three quarters of a mile in width. Find it on OS Map 16, Lairg and Loch Shin, Scale 1:50,000. During the 1950s, the water level of the loch was raised by 30ft when a dam was constructed at Lairg as part of a hydro-electric power generation scheme, and because of its size Loch Shin can be an intimidating place to fish.

Fluctuations in water levels, due to the operation of the power station, can make the margins unstable and, in some areas, downright dangerous for bank fishing. Boat fishing is safest and brings the best results and is the best means of exploring the loch. A reliable outboard engine is essential, as is a good knowledge of boat handling. In stormy weather the loch can be as wild as the sea, so, if in doubt, don't go out.

The loch contains excellent stocks of traditional Highland wild brown trout that average 8oz in weight, as well as a strain of trout introduced from Loch Leven. Most seasons produce trout of over 4lb in weight and the loch also contains Arctic charr, although they are rarely caught. There are also huge ferox trout in Shin, fish of enormous proportions, and, in the opinion of your correspondent, it is only a matter of time before the loch produces a British Record fish.

As always, on large, deep waters, a general rule is that if you can't see the bottom then you are fishing too far out. It is important to hold the boat in the most suitable fishing depth and in order to do so it is advisable to fish with three in the boat: two rods, bow and stern, fishing whilst the third member of the party minds the oars. Operate a rotational system – half an hour on the oars, then change over for an hour's fishing.

Shin trout are not fussy eaters and rise readily to most patterns of artificial flies. My list would always include Ke-He, Black Pennell, Loch Ordie, Black Zulu, Soldier Palmer, Greenwell's Glory, March Brown and

Silver Butcher. However, if you have ferox in mind, then you will have to adopt the old Scottish method of trolling: a live or dead bait on a strong trace, fished at a depth of 20ft/40ft. Savage entertainment, but the chance of the fish of your angling dreams.

53.
The Ones That Get Away

The best trout always rise at lunchtime, when you are balancing a cup of scalding coffee and wrestling with a leaky tomato sandwich. You never catch them, but me, I always try. One of the largest trout that I have ever missed rose whilst I was having lunch on the shores of Loch of Girlsta on mainland Shetland.

I rushed to the water's edge and whistled my fly out over where its nose had been. The trout grabbed and three seconds later broke my cast in a flurry of frenzied thrashing. I staggered back, blistered by hot coffee, cursing furiously. My companions never flinched. "More coffee, Bruce?" was all the sympathy I got.

I was telling this story to my wife, Ann, and my son, Blair, one lunchtime as we lazed on the banks of Loch Borralie in North-West Sutherland. "Yes, Dad," said Blair, "you have told us that story before – about how you lost the 6lb trout in Shetland – but if I remember correctly last time round it was 4lb. Grown a bit since then, has it?"

Loch Borralie is one of the famous Durness limestone lochs. The water is crystal-clear and drops to a depth of 100ft towards the north end. It contains wild brown trout of exceptional quality; silvery fish, beautifully marked, deep-bodied with bright, salmon-pink flesh. But they are circumspect trout and do not give themselves up easily.

The loch also contains specimen Arctic charr, descendents of the species trapped in the loch by receding glaciers more than 8,000 years ago. Divers, studying the biology of the loch, have reported seeing enormous trout during their work, huge, dark shapes swimming serenely by and estimated to be in the teens of pounds in weight.

All of which makes Borralie one of the most exciting lochs in Scotland to fish. A place where there is always the chance of catching that elusive 'one for the glass case'. Boats are moored at the south-west corner of the loch where the water is shallow and so clear that you can make out individual markings on the stones on the bottom. This area is a nursery for small fish, and the most productive part of the loch, in my opinion, is along the south-east shore.

Draw an imaginary line at an angle of 45° from the point of the island, south-east to the far shore, and concentrate your efforts within this triangle. The water is golden-coloured, reflecting the stones on the bottom, shading to emerald green and then dark blue as the bottom shelves into the depths. Position the boat just where the water deepens and look out for action.

As you drift north, high crags crowd the shoreline and I have seen trout rise here just inches from the bank. In normal water levels it is possible to drift through these narrows between the island and the shore and this area can also produce good sport. But perhaps the best of all times to fish Borralie in the evening, from the west bank. The water is deep close to the shore and large fish sometimes cruise up from the depths to feed in the shallows.

As I pondered these matters a large trout rose before us. I leapt to my feet and cast over the spreading rings. The trout took my fly, and, yet again, a few seconds later, broke my cast. I slumped to the ground, dejected. "How big was that one, Bruce?" asked Ann. "At least 4lb," I replied. "Aye, right Dad," said Blair unkindly, "and no doubt by next week at least 6lb!"

54.
Shades of the Shah

Highland factors in nineteenth-century Scotland held absolute power over their laird's tenants. One such man was Donald Munro, agent to Sir James Matheson, owner of the islands of Lewis and Harris which he purchased with money made trading in opium in the Far East. Munro was known locally as 'the Shah' and he was universally feared and despised. In the later years of the century he held nearly every important official position on the islands and few were able to resist his demands. But because of Munro's cold brutality, the people of Great Bernera, a small island off the west coast of Lewis, were forced to do so.

The islanders brought their stock to the mainland for summer grazing, but, a year after year, Munro reduced the area of land they could use, insisting each time he did so that the islanders built, at their own expense, stone walls to keep their cattle from impinging on his ever-expanding sheep farm. Eventually, in 1874, he denied all access and when the Bernera islanders complained he served eviction orders on them. In the ensuing fracas, Munro had one of the Bernera men arrested and thrown into jail.

Three hundred people marched on Stornoway to demand the release of their neighbour and the charges were dropped. However, not content, Munro then pursued three other Bernera men through the courts. When they were found 'not guilty', Sir James Matheson intervened and shortly thereafter sacked his odious factor.

Great Bernera is more peaceful today, but shades of the Shah linger, memorialised in the broken stone dykes that scatter the gold and heather moors. It is also a lot easier to reach the island than it was in times past: a causeway now joins Great Bernera to mainland Lewis. The island, which is well-known for the quality of its wild brown trout, divides East Loch Roag from West Loch Roag and can be found on OS Map 13, West Lewis and North Harris, Scale: 1:50,000.

There are more than 20 lochs and lochans on the island, all of which contain brown trout varying in size from a few ounces in weight up to fish of over 2lb; wild trout that have survived virtually genetically intact since the end of the last Ice Age. The principal water is Loch Baravat (Gd ref: 155355), a long, narrow loch extending for a mile north/south by up to 300yds wide. A convenient road gives easy access to the west bank where, unlike many Lewis lochs, there is comfortable and safe bank fishing. The north-west bay in particular can be very productive, as can be the south-west bay by Hacklete.

When fishing the east bank, concentrate your efforts in the vicinity of the Dun at Gd ref: 156356 and in the south-east arm of the loch at Gd ref: 158353. There are four adjacent waters, all of which are well worth a cast or three: Ionail (Gd ref: 156355), na Ceannamhoir (Gd ref: 159355), School Loch – unnamed on the OS map but at Gd ref: 159365 – and Lochan Sgeireach (Gd ref: 151353). School Loch is reputed to hold the largest fish and you should pay particular attention to the west shore where School Loch flows out into Loch Ionail.

As with all the Great Bernera waters, fish them early in the season because in the later months weed growth can become a problem. Whatever, there is enough fishing on Great Bernera to keep you busy for a month, let alone a day, and plenty of adjacent attractions to keep any non-fishing members in your party happy whilst you do so.

55.
That Sinking Feeling

The River Don is probably the finest brown trout stream in Europe and April is the finest month in which to launch your attack. In the early part of the season, the upper river produces excellent sport with hard-fighting trout that range in size from a few ounces right up to specimen fish fit for the glass case of your angling dreams.

In its beginnings, the river has the character of a classic highland stream as it flows swiftly past some of Scotland's most dramatic castles: Corgarff, Glenbucket, Craigivar and Kildrummy, the home of 'Bobbing Johnnie', the Earl of Mar, who raised the clans in support of the Old Pretender at the start of the 1715 Jacobite Rebellion.

I had my own, personal, rebellion on the Don a few years ago when I was dragged into Dam Pool on the Castle Forbes water by an enormous trout. Well, to be truthful, not exactly dragged in, but very nearly so and I very nearly drowned in the process.

It was a hot day, one of those days when you just know that you are not going to catch fish but keep on trying anyway. A swathe of tall rushes that bordered the bank of the pool had been cut and the lay on the surface, awaiting removal. The water was crystal clear and I saw the trout coming to my fly, a Greenwell's Glory.

It was one of the most enormous fish that I had ever seen and everything seemed to happen in slow motion, although in reality it was all over in a few seconds. The trout grabbed with such force that I took an involuntary step forward and tumbled head-first into the pool. The last thing that I remember hearing was the sound of the reel screaming in anger.

Lying on the bottom of the pool, I opened my eyes and noticed fronds of weeds, like green gossamer threads waving in the current. It is entirely true that in those situations your whole life flashes before you. Happily, the water level was low and, being 6ft 4ins in height, I managed to struggle upright, head just above the water, and stumble safely ashore. But I will never forget that trout. It was yellow in colour and must have been at least 7lb in weight.

The largest trout that I have had from the Don was a fish weighing 2lb 8oz. Again, it was a hot day, and, again, it also almost had me into the pool with it. I was fishing downstream from Pitfiche on the Monymusk Water, where the river was divided by a small island that had been formed due to the low water level.

The far bank bordered an inviting pool, shaded by trees, and I guessed, had I been a trout, that I would be sheltering out of the midday sun beneath their cooling branches. A shingle promontory provided a casting platform, but is was suspiciously unstable. I inched down it, wading ever deeper, trying to get my flies to sweep the water beneath the trees.

I decided to risk one more cast, and, as I did so, the shingle began to give way and I felt myself slipping. I turned, and fell on my hands and knees, fighting my way back up the promontory. Which is when the trout took. Safely back on terra firma, with the trout still on and leaping furiously around the pool, I gathered what remained of my dignity and landed it.

56.
Keeping the Cats Happy

I made three cats very happy last week. Well, to be entirely honest, two out of the three: Nelson, our senior, one-eyed moggy, doesn't seem to enjoy eating trout as much as he used to. He just toyed with my offering. The other pair scoffed the lot and meowed for more.

Would that it were always so easy to make them happy, but they probably don't realise just how difficult it is to persuade trout to rise so early in the season. It was my first outing, 27th March, and I approached the occasion more as a matter of honour than as a serious attempt to remove a few fish from their natural habitat.

The weather was cold, with a biting wind, and I was less than confident of success. Loch Hakel is my local water, a few minutes' drive from Tongue in North Sutherland, and the only other anglers fishing that afternoon were a pair of goldeneye ducks; winter visitors, easily recognisable from the white patch between eye and bill.

After an hour of savage entertainment I was considering abandoning the task and heading home when, as is often the case, the first trout grabbed my middle fly, a particularly attractive March Brown. Thus encouraged I fished on and ended up with three trout weighing 1lb 10oz. Nothing for the glass case, but more than enough for me and for our felines.

The last fish took with a mighty rush, stripping line from the reel. Given that a large fish in Hakel is rarely over 1lb, I was convinced for a moment that I had hooked a sea-trout; the loch drains into the Kyle of Tongue and although rarely caught, sea-trout are not unknown. When I beached the fish, however, I saw that it was a brown trout of about 10oz in weight.

This is one of the most significant characteristics of the fish in Loch Hakel, and, indeed, in many of our Highland lochs. Although they may be modest in size, they fight splendidly and always give an excellent account of themselves. They are very pretty fish too, beautifully marked, perfectly shaped and almost golden in colour.

The majority are also pink-fleshed and wonderful to eat. I took my fish home, cleaned them and cooked them in a frying pan with a little oil; which is when the cats, alerted by the smell, arrived to help me in my labours. I ate half of one fish before I succumbed to their wailing and it was, quite simply, superb.

I have never been able to understand why some anglers don't eat the fish they catch. For me, the point of going fishing is to be able to eat that which I catch. Otherwise, I could argue, what is the point of fishing – is it just for the adrenalin rush you experience when you actually manage to hook a fish?

In my view, and this is a view that I know is shared by my wife, Ann, who is also an angler, eating the catch is as important as catching the fish. Nevertheless, angling is a broad church with a catholic congregation so each to his own, and I guess that at least two of our cats would be happy to subscribe to that opinion as well.

57.
Singing in the Rain

Music is an angler's best friend. Not many people know that, but, honestly, it is true. I discovered this fact as a youth when fishing the Tweed downstream from Manor Bridge. The river here tumbles into a deep pool, pounding a rocky outcrop on the far bank before sweeping on to the gentle glides near Neidpath Castle.

Trout were rising constantly but persuading them to take my flies was beyond my skill; which was probably because at that stage in my angling life I was as skilful with rod and line as I was with a golf club. Green-keepers used to shudder in horror when they saw me coming, which was one of the reasons why I took up fishing.

It was raining, hard, and I fished on automatically and without much hope. I began to hum an aria from George Frederic Handel's *Messiah* – a work I had recently discovered and enjoyed. Nobody was about, so I burst into song: "He shall feed his flock, like a shepherd…" It suddenly occurred to me that given the number of fish I was catching I wouldn't be able to feed anybody, let alone a whole flock of them.

This is when the trout 'took'. Delighted, I began to concentrate, seriously. The trout stopped rising. I thought that I had just been lucky. I began singing again. Another trout rose and took the middle fly, a March Brown. This seemed to be too much of a coincidence, so I sang again, loudly. As long as I did, fish rose to my flies. With six in the basket I retired happy.

Years later, I gained a degree of notoriety when I used this method whilst filming a TV show with Paul Young. We were running out of time and the fish were refusing to cooperate. In desperation I decided to give them a bit of Handel's *Messiah*.

I strode over to the producer. "Set the camera up on me and I will catch a trout," I said. "Are you sure, Bruce?" "Yup," I replied, "when I start singing, you start rolling." He gave me a strange look. With the camera in action, I cast and sang, "He shall feed his flock…" The moment flies landed, a trout rose, was hooked, played, and released. In truth, I was surprised, but not half as much as the producer.

That is exactly how it happened, neither more nor less. Nothing was 'fixed'. To this day I still meet anglers who don't believe it, but it is surprising how many times I hear the dulcet tones of companions having a bit of a tune to themselves when fishing.

I regularly sing to trout. It doesn't always work, but it is surprising just how often that it does. Perhaps it is simply coincidence, that the trout would have risen to my flies anyway, regardless of whether or not I was warbling. Or maybe it's a physical thing, that singing relaxes mind and body, and, as such, your actions are more natural and less forced.

How many times have you hooked a fish when you were not looking, or thinking about something entirely different from the job in hand? I know that some of the best trout that I have ever caught have come to me at these moments. I have developed this into a technique which I use when all else, including singing, fails. I call it 'The Art of Thoughtless Fishing'. Try it some-time: after all, you have nothing to lose and it could mean the difference between a blank day and one for the glass case!

58.
Book Worms

Angling books generally divide into two categories: how to do it, and how I did it. One of the most useful 'how to do it' volumes, which I discovered when I was a boy, is G.W. Maunsell's *The Fisherman's Vade Mecum*, published in 1933. This was the first angling book that I read and, in spite of its somewhat dusty title, one of the finest.

In the same category, Peter Lapsley's *Fly Fishing for Trout*, published in 1992, is perhaps the best modern equivalent, at least when it comes to trout fishing. Of course, the works of that great all-rounder, Hugh Falkus, remain unsurpassed in the field of salmon and sea-trout fishing.

In the 'how I did it' category, *Fishing From Afar* by Stephen Johnson, published in 1947, is a classic. Johnson wrote the book as a POW in Stalag Luft III during the last war. He describes fishing Loch Coruisk and the Kilmarie River on the Island of Skye. I also admire John Inglis Hall's account of the River Truim, *Fishing a Highland Stream*, published 1960.

Another great 'how I did it' volume is Roderick Haig-Brown's *A River Never Sleeps*. Haig-Brown spent most of his adult life on Vancouver Island, fishing the Campbell River. The last volume in this category, *Early Scottish Angling Literature* by Professor Norman Simmonds, was published in 1997. His book is a complete delight.

There is, however, another genre in angling literature: the fishing novel or memoir and in my opinion these are the hardest of all to bring off. Many have tried and failed, few succeed. John Buchan, writer, poet, statesman and angler, is one who did. His novel *John MacNab*, published in 1925, gave its name to the bagging of a stag, salmon and a grouse in a single day; although in the book the wager was to "kill a stag or a salmon." Grouse were not involved.

Another writer who produced a book involving fishing is the American Norman MacLean. His work *A River Runs Through It* was published in 1976 after he retired as Professor of English at the University of Chicago. The book has been described as "one of these rare memoirs that can be called a masterpiece." MacLean's father was a minister and a fly-fisherman, and the opening words of book are compelling: "In our family, there was no clear line between religion and fly fishing."

I am pleased to say that the inspirational flame that brought us *John MacNab* and *A River Runs Through It* still burns brightly today. This is more than apparent in a novel that I have just finished reading, *Salmon Fishing in The Yemen* by Paul Torday, published by Weidenfeld & Nicolson at £12.99.

The constant thread of the story is salmon, and the author clearly knows what he is talking about. The hero of the tale is Dr Alfred Jones, a middle-aged fisheries scientist in an obscure government department who, against his better judgment, agrees to help a Yemeni multimillionaire introduce Atlantic salmon to that desert country. The unfolding story is a roller-coaster ride embracing politics, marital stagnation, unrequited love, murder and mystery.

In the 1950s, I spent two years in what was then Southern Arabia and is now Yemen. The author's evocative descriptions of the landscape transported me back to those days; the dry river beds, hill-top towns with 'high rise' buildings, ornate palaces, a proud, independent people and, above all, the searing heat of the desert. This is an angling novel for all seasons and I heartily recommend it.

59.
Fishing a Border Stream

The snow has all but gone. It is warm and the sun is shining. A good-to-be-alive moment. Like most anglers, these comforting conditions evoked in me memories of past expeditions and this morning I found myself thinking about the River Whiteadder in the Scottish Borders. I first fished the river for brown trout as a boy, near Abbey St Bathan's, along with my father and one of his friends. River fishing for brown trout is not abundant up here in North Sutherland and I often miss the sweet smell of a river and the excitement of casting a trout fly into a fast-flowing stream.

I began my angling life in that fashion: guddling for trout in the Meldon Burn near Eddlestone, falling into the Water of Leith whilst attempting to retrieve a snagged fly; filling my Wellington boots in Manor Water, struggling in the dark to mend a broken cast on Lyne Water, and the unforgettable agony of losing a huge trout upstream from Innerleithen; the shared apprenticeship of everyone blessed with the incurable pain of angling.

Some years later, when I married the girl in my life, we chose to spend our first days together at Abbey St Bathan's, in the Gardeners' Cottage in the grounds of Abbey St Bathan's House. It was spring-time and the river bank was bright with daffodils. The water was crystal clear and busy with best-bib-and-tuckered dippers. We enjoyed wild brown trout for breakfast most mornings and the happy memory of that time has stayed with us ever since.

The Whiteadder rises from Clints Dod (398m) in the Lammermuir Hills and after flowing through a substantial reservoir, hurries by Cranshaws, Ellmford, Abbey St Bathan's, Preston and Churnside to join the Tweed a mile upstream from Berwick. Along the way it gathers in a number of substantial tributaries, including Crook Burn, Whare Burn, Eller Burn, Bells Burn, and Blackadder Water. All the feeder streams hold good stocks of native wild brown trout, although the river is stocked from time to time with 10-inch trout to supplement the natural population.

The Whiteadder Angling Club manages the river, from Clint Dod to near Churnside, and has being doing so since the 1930s. Permits are available from a number of sources, including The Riverside Restaurant in Abbey St Bathan's (tel: 01361 840321) and from R. Welsh, Fishing Tackle Shop, Castle Street, Duns (tel: 01361 883466). In 2006, a Men's season ticket was £15.00; Ladies, Children and Senior Citizens, £7.00. Day tickets for Men were £6.00 and for Ladies, Children and Senior Citizens, £3.00.

Downstream from Chirnside, to its meeting with the Tweed, the Berwick & District Angling Association manage the river and the principal quarry here is, of course, salmon and sea-trout. I have been unable to establish exact catch statistics, but I think it is fair to say that runs of fish into the Whiteadder are steadily improving. This is primarily due to the closure of the North-East Drift Net Fishery and the hard work of the Tweed

Foundation. For more information about the Association water contact Dave Cowan on tel: 01289 306985. Costs vary depending upon the time of year, but expect to pay in the order of £15/£25 per rod per day.

Above all, for me, the real joy of fishing this lovely little stream is for its brown trout. They might not fill that glass case of your angling dreams, but they will fill you with supreme delight. On a warm spring day there are few more wonderful places to fish. Tempt them with these good friends of mine: Messrs Greenwell's Glory, Partridge & Orange and March Brown.

60.
Dear Santa

Dear Santa

I want to thank you for all the lovely presents you gave me last year, particularly for the handkerchiefs, socks and underpants and for the matching pen and pencil set. They were very nice. I am sorry that it has taken so long to send my 'thank-you' letter, but after last Christmas I had a bad cold in my nose and it took me some time to get better.

I was wondering if you might be able to let me have different presents this year. You see, I'm an angler and I like fishing for wild brown trout and sea-trout and, occasionally, for salmon. The equipment I use at present, like its owner, is getting on a bit and not quite as active as or efficient as it should be. For instance, if I had had a landing net that actually clicked open when I tried to use it then I wouldn't have lost that 6lb trout last September.

Do you fish, Santa? I guess that it must be pretty cold most of the time up there in Lapland, but I have read that in the summer months there is great fishing for grayling. I once tried to come and see you, many years ago, but only managed to get halfway up Finland; the roads then were just oil-sand-covered and driving was difficult. We stopped at a place called Viitasaari and went fishing on Lake Keitele, but didn't catch much.

We will be spending Christmas this year in Finland with our son, Charles, and his family. What a pity that you will be away on business, otherwise I could have jumped on a plane and flown north to visit you. We love being in Finland at Christmas time. Charles and his wife, Nanna, take us to a lakeside sauna where we roast in 80°C temperatures before jumping through a hole in the ice into the lake. It is quite bracing, but I'm sure that you know all about that and will have a sauna of your own in the grotto.

Here is the list of some of the presents that I would like to have this year and I hope that you might be able to help. Can I have some wild brown trout, please? They don't need to be very large, anything over 2lb in weight will do. If you could put them into a loch near were we live at Tongue in North Sutherland that would be very good. Loch Hakel, a few minutes from our home, would be perfect.

Maybe you can arrange for some sea-trout as well? If you could write my name down their lateral line and put them into Loch Hope, which I often fish, then other anglers would know that they were for me and not for them? Oh, and would it be possible for you to turn the wind down a bit when I fish Loch Hope – a gentle south-west breeze, slightly overcast and not too warm would be just about right, Santa.

Some really bushy dapping flies and a decent fishing line would be welcome stocking-fillers, but if you really want to make my Christmas memorable, then a week's fishing up your way next season would be most acceptable. Although we will be in Finland when you come to Tongue I have arranged for a friend to put out hay and carrots for the reindeers and I have left a large dram on the front stoop to warm your work.

Best wishes

Bruce

61.
Fishing Round the
Kyle of Tongue (East)

Few areas in Scotland offer anglers more, or more varied, trout fishing opportunities than those which can be found around the Kyle of Tongue in North Sutherland. Today, let's look at what is on offer to the east of the Kyle. You will need OS Map 10, Strathnaver, Scale 1:50:000 to find your way round.

Loch Craisg (Gd ref: 599578) is a small water near Braetongue a few minutes' walk from a convenient track. Like most of the lochs in the area it has a good population of small trout and is fished from the bank. Further east, and accessed from Dallcharn, is Loch Cormaic (Gd ref: 627581), one of the local angling club waters (Ben Loyal Hotel tel: 01847 611216 for permission) where boat fishing brings the best results.

The prime loch here, however, is Loch nam Breac Buidhe (Gd ref: 650570) and it lies a mile south from the A836. Park at Gd ref: 657586 and follow a peat road. This reaches Breac Buidhe after about 30 minutes. The loch is 600yds long by 300yds wide. Bank fishing only, and begin your assault in the vicinity of the island at the north-west corner.

Work anti-clockwise round to the outlet stream that flows through the forest to the Borgie River. The south end is the most productive area where there are attractive bays and promontories where good fish lie. The trout are of excellent quality and average 10oz in weight with the possibility of encountering larger specimens of up to and over 21lb.

Breac Buidhe and the lochs noted below are leased to the Borgie Lodge Hotel (tel: 01641 521332). Contact them for permission to fish. The other lochs available to visitors lie to the north of the A836, enclosed by the Skerray ring road. Loch Modsarie (Gd ref: 649618) is close to the west arm of the road and a boat is moored at the north end. Modsarie fish rise well to the fly and bank fishing is as productive as boat fishing.

A spot of leg-work is required to reach the remainder of the Skerray lochs, the most notable of which are Loch Skerray (Gd ref: 665600) itself and its near neighbour, Loch a'Chaoruinn (Gd ref: 668601). There are a number of other small lochans here, all of which offer the chance of good sport with trout that average 6oz/8oz, and the occasional larger fish of up to 1lb in weight.

But the most enigmatic of the little lochs here is immediately adjacent to the A836 and has the longest name, Loch Dubh Beul na Faire (Gd ref: 647593). It also has some of the largest fish. On a calm summer evening I have seen huge trout cruising amongst the reeds. And that is the problem: the whole loch is virtually covered with reeds. This makes it very difficult to cast without becoming seriously caught up.

Wait for a decent wind before launching your attack and then do so using a traditional, 17ft/18ft long dapping road. Attach a large, busy dapping fly – something tempting, like a Loch Ordie or Black Zulu, preferably tied on a barbless hook – and insinuate the fly into the clear water spaces amidst the reeds. You should also take great care to avoid the live electricity cables that run along the south shore. Although I have never managed to connect with one of the monsters here, I have reports of a fish of over 6lb being hooked a couple of years back. Go thou and do likewise.

62.
Fishing Round the Kyle of Tongue (North)

This morning, using OS Map 10, Strathnaver, Scale 1:50.000, turn right to Melness and park near Melness House at Gd ref: 580608. A signpost on the left points the way out to Loch a'Mhuilinn at Gd ref: 570609; another of the waters leased by the Kyle of Tongue & District Angling Club.

The walk is an easy 20 minutes and fishing is from the bank only. Loch a'Mhuilinn is approximately half a mile long by 300 yards wide and exits to the sea at Talmine Beach (Gd ref: 586626); an excellent place to park non-fishing members of your tribe whilst you get on with the proper business of the removal of wild brown trout from their natural habitat.

On arrival at the loch, the best tactic is to work anti-clockwise round the shore because crossing the extreme south end can be a muddy business. The trout are not large, although from time to time there are reports of serious specimens being lost, but they are very pretty little fish which fight with dash and spirit.

My favoured fishing area on a'Mhuilinn is on the west bank, where the main feeder stream enters the loch. Indeed, and particularly after heavy rain, the stream itself can produce splendid sport. Stay well back from the bank and cast into the stream. Let your flies swing round and into the loch. Years of silt, washed down by the rain, have built up a considerable bank here. Fish lie waiting for the current to bring them food.

For a proper adventure, follow the minor road out to Achininver and park at Gd ref: 566646. This is the start of an all-day expedition to the Ben Hutig (408m) hill lochs, most of which don't see an artificial fly from one season to the next. This is a six-mile round trip and the going can be rough to rougher. Travel light: rod, reel, nylon and few flies, wet weather gear and compass and map.

A mile up a good track will bring you to Loch na h-Uamhachd (Gd ref: 556658). Now climb due west, past Loch nan Clach Geala (Gd ref: 551656) to reach Lochain na Seilg (Gd ref: 539656) below the crest of Ben Hutig. Descend south-west over the moor to find Loch Fada and Lochan na Breac Buidhe (the loch of the yellow trout) at Gd ref: 530643.

Careful map reading should take you south now to the unnamed lochan at Gd ref: 530635 and, from there, to the head of a track (Gd ref: 548632) leading back down the hill to the road at the township of West Strathan. Walk north for half a mile to reach your car.

The trout in these waters vary in size from a few ounces up to fish of over 2lb in weight. The joy of fishing here is in discovering where the big fish lie and finding the answer to this question will test all your angling skills. But there are few finer places to do so; the western horizon is graced by Ben Loyal, Ben Hope and Foinaven. Northwards, over the waves, the next stop is Iceland. To the east, Rabbit Islands and deserted Eilean nan Ron guard the entrance to the shallow waters of the Kyle of Tongue.

And for the perfect end to a perfect day, stop off at the famous Craggan Inn (tel: 01847 601278) at Talmine for welcome rest and recuperation.

63.
Fishing Round the Kyle of Tongue (West)

I can't pretend that I have had much success on Loch a'Bhualaidh, but I know someone who has, indeed, several people. This little loch lies west of the Kyle of Tongue and is overlooked by the graceful bulk of Ben Hope (927m), Scotland's most northerly Munro – Scottish mountains over 914.4m in height.

My wife, Ann, and I have fished Loch a'Bhualaidh on several occasions and the best that we have managed is a few fish of around 1lb in weight. However, a few years ago a local angler came up to Castle Sandison to show me the basket of trout he had taken from the loch that morning. There were five fish, two of them over 5lb in weight, the smallest being 2lb 8oz. In September, two Welsh anglers tramped out to a'Bhualaidh and were rewarded with half a dozen trout weighing a total 9lb 5oz.

In spite of our lack of success we keep going back, not only because of the chance of a specimen trout, but also because it is such a wonderful place to fish, remote, peaceful, very beautiful and surrounded by outstanding flora and fauna. It is certain that during the course of the day you will see buzzards and, almost certain, catch a glimpse of a golden eagle soaring above the moor in search of lunch.

To find Loch a'Bhualaidh, hang a left after crossing the Kyle use OS Map 10, Strathnaver, Scale 1:50,000. Follow the minor road south past the council depot for about a mile and a half. Just before a bridge over a small stream at Gd ref: 565568 you can park safely in a disused quarry. Walk back, north, up the road for 100 yds to find the start of the track out to the loch at Gd ref: 538563.

Do not be tempted to climb from the quarry to find the track. It is rough going and not advisable. I know, having done it to my severe discomfort. As you walk back up the road, keep a sharp lookout on your left for the track. In its beginnings it is very faint, hardly more than a rabbit track, but once safely on it the way ahead is easy; past the north end of Loch Fhionnaich, known locally as the Goose Loch and full of small trout, then climbing gently to reach a'Bhualaidh after a hike of about 30 minutes.

The loch is approximately 550yds long by some 100yds wide and moderately sheltered from the prevailing wind. Bank fishing only and my advice would be to approach cautiously keeping well back from the bank to avoid disturbing any fish that may be feeding in the shallow water. I haven't really found a significant feeder stream and I guess that the loch gathers its water by run-off from the surrounding landscape.

The outlet stream is at the south-east end of the loch and drains east down the hill to Goose Loch. On such an intimate water you may expect to encounter fish almost anywhere, but my favourite part of a'Bhualaidh is the south end, in and around the vicinity of the outlet stream. Exactly what patterns of fly to use is very much a matter of personal preference. I tend to stick to my old friends Messrs Black Pennell, Ke-He, Soldier Palmer, Woodcock & Hare-lug, Greenwell's Glory and Butchers various.

The loch is leased by the Kyle of Tongue & District Angling Club and visitor permits won't break the bank. Contact the Ben Loyal Hotel (tel: 01847 611216) for details.

64.
Hugh Matheson

I was sad to hear about the passing away in September of Hugh Matheson of Baleshare, one of the Hebrides' best loved and most respected gillies. Hugh spent his entire working life on the Uists, firstly as a gamekeeper with

South Uist Estate and, after 1960, as Head Gamekeeper with the North Uist Estate. He had a passionate regard for his native land and for its Gaelic culture and traditions. As well as being a fine singer, he had encyclopaedic knowledge of game fishing in the islands.

My first glimpse of Hugh was in the Lochmaddy Hotel. As I entered the lounge, I noticed a group of four young men who seemed to be bombarding an elderly gentleman with questions about where the best place/places were to fish for salmon, sea-trout and brown trout, as well as with requests for details about flies and tactics. At the time, I thought that they were being a bit robust in their pursuit of knowledge, but, then, from their accents, they were clearly not from North of Mr Hadrian's Wall.

I listened as Hugh responded to these inquiries with grace, courtesy, patience and kindness. When I was introduced to him later, I suggested that his inquisitors had been fortunate indeed to benefit from his knowledge and experience. "Well," he said, "they are visitors to the island, here on holiday and it is good to be able to try and make sure that they enjoy their stay and catch a few fish."

At dinner that evening I was sitting at a table near to the one occupied by the visitors. Therefore, I was horrified, and angered when, in loud voices, they began to complain that Hugh had not told them more or given them even greater detail about fishing on North Uist. I went over to their table and asked them what they did for a living. One was a stockbroker; another was a lawyer, whilst the other two did not respond to my question.

I said to the stockbroker, "If I was to ask you what where the best shares to buy you would just tell me?" This was greeted by silence. I asked the lawyer, "And I could just walk in to your office with a legal problem and expect you to give me your advice completely free of charge?" The silence deepened. "If you have any respect for probity, gentlemen, don't you think that it might have been polite to ask Mr Matheson to spend a day or so with you in his professional capacity?" With which I excused myself.

In retrospect, I suppose that I should have just held my tongue, but their attitude and their rudeness was insupportable; criticising in public a man who had just given them a vast amount of information, information that had come from a lifetime's experience of fishing in North Uist and given it without let or hindrance. I was damned if I was going to let them get away with it.

I have met many gillies during my angling life, and, without exception, they have been some of the finest friends that I have ever had. But times change, and I think that the 'old school' has passed on. I suppose that is the nature of the beast. But it seem to me that fishing and field sports are becoming ever more commercial and that much of the simple pleasure of being out on hill, river or loch, like a lightly hooked salmon, has gone forever. I am glad that I have had the privilege of meeting Hugh Matheson, one of the 'old school', and I will always remember him with great fondness.

65.
Fishing with Flora

Benbecula, 'the mountains of the fords', lies between North and South Uist in the Outer Hebrides and is joined to them by causeways. In 1746, Flora MacDonald crossed the South Ford onto Benbecula and tramped five miles north to Market Stance. From there, she and her party followed a rough track west round the south shoulder or Rueval (124m) to Rossinish to meet Bonnie Prince Charlie, where he was disguised as her maid, Betty Burke, and carried to safety, 'Over the sea to Skye.'

For her part in the adventure, Flora MacDonald was imprisoned in the Tower of London where she remained until 1747 and her release under the Act of Indemnity; supported by the sum of £1,500 which had been raised for her by public subscription. Some years later, she was visited by Dr Samuel Johnson, who said of Flora, "Her name will be mentioned in history and if courage and fidelity be virtues mentioned with honour."

I guess that the escape committee had neither the time nor the inclination to stop along the way for a few casts in the lochs they passed. This is a pity, because they all contain wonderful trout ranging in size from three to the pound up to specimen fish fit for the glass case of your angling dreams. Find them on OS Map 22, Benbecula, Second Series, Scale 1:50,000.

The track starts on the A865 at Gd ref: 805536 and it is possible to drive from here to the first loch, Ba Una (Gd ref: 818519). This is the perfect place to park non-fishing companions, or little ones new to the gentle art of the removal of trout from their natural habitat. Ba Una has a sandy beach for the bucket and spade brigade and a large stock of small, accommodating wild brown trout that rise readily to most patterns of fly.

For those intent on more serious adventure, follow in Flora MacDonald's footsteps past Loch Hermidale (Gd ref: 826525) and Loch na Deigh fo Dheas (Gd ref: 833530), both of which are also blessed with good stocks of modest trout, to find Loch na Deigh fo Thuath at Gd ref: 834535. Leave the track here and head north, fishing the east bank of the loch along the way. Deigh fo Thuath is linked by a small stream to island-scattered Dubh Loch (Gd ref: 828544) which invariably provides good sport with excellent quality trout.

Turn west now, and cross the hill to the ruined shielings on the shores of Loch na Beire at Gd ref: 833542 by the Sound of Flodday. You may not find vast trout in this loch, but it is surrounded by a vast sense of complete peace and serenity and is a magical place to stop for lunch and recuperation. Hike west from na Beire to reach Loch na Deigh fo Thuath again and return to the Market Stance/Rossinish track fishing down the east bank.

Back on the track, an arm heads south-east. Within a mile, this leads to one of my favourite Benbecula lochs, Scarilode, at Gd ref: 846523. There are ruined shielings here overlooking the sea at Oban Haka. Within living memory they were occupied. A surveyor in the late 1940s commented: "The family at Scarilode has two children going to school at Rossinish. There are no roads, the holding being from six to eight miles from Gramsdale." Save Scarilode for a special day out. Get there if you can. You will not be disappointed.

66.
Laid Back on Laidon

This morning, after weeks of seemingly endless wind and rain, the sun shone. Our lochs and rivers are full, and in many cases overflowing. Looking south from my workroom window there are lochs where no lochs should be; acres of flooded land spiked with the tops of sunken trees and even the track up to our cottage as been awash for several days.

Exactly what havoc these storms have caused to salmon spawning reds is unclear, but one thing is certain, when the 2007 season arrives there should be no shortage of water. Scotland's most watery area, however, is Rannoch Moor, 305m above sea level and a wilderness of angling delight, silver-ribboned by the six-mile length of Loch Laidon.

Loch Laidon is inconveniently laid out on two OS Maps, the east section on Map 51, Loch Tay, the west end on Map 41, Ben Nevis. This morning, let's visit the east end, accessed along the tortuous B846 road from Killiecrankie, past Loch Tummel, Dunalistair Reservoir and Loch Rannoch to its end at Rannoch Station.

Some years ago I wrote about Loch Laidon and mentioned that it was the ideal beginner's loch, where baskets of 20 fish were the rule rather than the exception. Shortly thereafter, I was accosted by two anglers who told me that I was talking nonsense: they had fished the loch and caught twice that number of trout.

Laidon fish are not large and average in the order of three to the pound, but, believe me, there are much larger specimens as well. The heaviest fish taken weighed 11lb and is cased on the wall of the Moor of Rannoch hotel (tel: 01882 633238) and a trout of 9lb 8oz was caught in 1999. My wife, Ann, and I saw one of the largest trout that we have ever seen whilst fishing at the west end in the vicinity of Eilean Iubhair.

Boat fishing helps mightily to explore this long loch, and one might be available from the gillie who looks after the loch (tel: 01882 633246), otherwise it is bank fishing all the way. The north bank is the best place to start, following a track that margins the shore for several miles. After a mile or so, a series of feeder streams tumble into the loch from Stob na Cruaiche (739m) and where they do you will invariably find sport.

To the south of Laidon lie a series of small lochs and lochans that are rarely visited or fished as they lie in an area of Special Scientific Interest, and because they require a fair degree of leg work over the soggy moor to reach. We fished them once, having obtained prior permission to do so, and enjoyed a memorable day; mooring the boat on the shores of Laidon and tramping south, disturbing an outraged wildcat in the process.

We visited Lochan Ruighe nan Sligean, Lochan a'Mhaidseir, Lochan Ghiubhais and, the furthest out, Lochan na Breac. All of these lochs produced splendid little fish, brightly red-speckled and great fun to catch. Neither were they too fussy about what flies they took; all the standard patters worked well, as they do on Laidon: Ke-He, Black Pennell, Soldier Palmer, March Brown, Greenwell's Glory and Butchers various.

Our day was sunny and very hot, but you should never fish here without keeping an eye on the weather. Be well-prepared: a storm can come rushing in from Glencoe quicker that you can mutter Macdonald. Talking of which, storms that is, it has suddenly started raining again up here. No, wait a moment, it is sleet! Winter has arrived.

67.
Down to the Sea

It is many years since I fished for anything other than salmon, trout or sea-trout. But as a boy, like most of my peers, I regularly fished in the sea. My brother and I used to haunt Newhaven Harbour in Edinburgh, fishing for anything and everything that came our way, which was mostly small cod. There were two pier heads at the exit of the harbour and at weekends they were invariably crowded with boys fishing with hook, line and sinker.

Thinking back, it is a miracle that there were not more frequent accidents as we swung the line round our heads to launch our hooks out into the deepest water that we could reach. It is also remarkable, given that boys on the opposite pier were doing the same thing in our direction, that tangled lines were the exception rather than the rule. When that happened, the boy who shouted 'cutty!' first had the right to wind in and free his hooks, cutting and dumping, if necessary, any line that got in the way.

Today, when we visit Auld Reekie and stay in a convenient hotel over-looking Newhaven Harbour, the pier heads are devoid of boys fishing and the harbour waters seem to be devoid of the shoals of sprat that we easily caught with a treble hook to use for bait; the former probably something to do with health and safety regulations, the later more likely because of pollution and the decline in sea fish stocks.

Nevertheless, up here on the north coast of Sutherland, more and more people seem to be taking up fly fishing from the shore, particularly for sea bass. This is still a relatively unknown venue for catching *Dicentrarchus labrax* and it is only in recent years that bass have been encountered in any substantial numbers; the species is more commonly caught in warmer waters, and mostly in the Solway Firth in the vicinity of Luce Bay between Newton Stewart and Stranraer.

Exactly why we now have bass in the far north is not clear. It probably has something to do with global warming, a rise in sea temperature, but as it is with so much else of what goes on in our seas, this is only conjecture. A dozen years ago I had reports of sea bass being caught from the beach at Dunnet Bay in Caithness, and there is no doubt that the species is now relatively common in the shallow waters of the Kyle of Tongue.

The Kyle is well-known as a sea-trout fishing venue where some 150/200 sea-trout are caught most seasons, but my friend Tony Possnett, a regular visitor, told me a couple of months ago that he had been having great sport with sea bass from the shore near the bridge across the Kyle narrows. One evening, he delivered a brace to us, each weighing about 14oz. They looked splendid, streamlined and silver. They were wonderful to eat and had been caught on a Black Pennell.

Like sea-trout, the best time to fish for bass is two hours before and two hours after low tide. As the tide ebbs and flows a swift 'river' is formed and a fly cast out into the flow brings results, well, it does for Tony; I still have to see if it does the same for me. Tony tells me that they fight extremely well and give great sport. I will investigate this matter later this week and you will be the first to know the result.

68.
The Loneliness of a Long Distance Salmon Fisher

I have never found catching salmon to be boring, probably because it happens to me so infrequently. If I had one more finger I could count the number of salmon I have caught during my angling life on the digits of both hands. Or, to put it another way, 11 in total, five of them being taken during an unforgettable morning on the Thurso River.

As a youth, I fished relentlessly for salmon on the Tweed. From opening day in February until close of play in November I haunted the river, regardless of weather conditions. The closest I came to realizing my dream was losing a huge fish in a pool upstream from Innerleithen. But it was on a trout rod and it soon broke me, and my heart.

So I resigned from the fray and concentrated my efforts on fishing for wild brown trout. But, from time to time, I still go salmon fishing. One of the principal pleasures of doing so, at least it is for me, is using a salmon rod. Mastering the art of wielding a double-handed salmon rod efficiently is as engrossing as is the excitement of actually hooking anything, let alone landing it. Which is just as well, given my success rate.

My father was made of sterner stuff. I taught him to fish. He was a golfer really, but one evening when a game had been cancelled he drove down to where I was fishing a tributary of the Tweed at Flemington on the River Lyne. He sat in the car, watching, as I caught a few small trout. Eventually, he came over to where I was fishing. "Here, give me a shot at that," he said, and from that moment on he hardly touched a golf club again.

Father rarely caught anything, but he thought about little else other than fishing and his dream was to catch a salmon. He also thrashed the Tweed to no avail, and various other Scottish salmon streams, including the Spey and the Findhorn, with similar results. But towards the end of his life he treated himself to a day at Stanley on the River Tay.

I still have a grainy old black and white photograph of him standing in the pouring rain on the bank of the river at the end of the day. He is proudly holding up a salmon of about 12lb in weight, the first and last fish that he ever caught. During the fight, the reel fell off Dad's rod and he ended landing the fish in by winding the line round his arm, then, at the last moment, falling on the salmon in the shallow water and wrestling it ashore.

Apart from the Thurso fish, my salmon have come from the Beauly, Loch Hope, Inver, Kirkaig, Halladale and East Loch Ollay on South Uist in the Outer Hebrides. The Ollay fish gave me most pleasure, caught on a trout rod, from the bank and 'expertly' manoeuvred ashore through treacherous rocks. I would say that, wouldn't I? But John Kennedy was with me and he said, "Well done," which was high praise indeed.

I was almost on the point of giving up the pursuit of salmon when my son announced that his next posting was to be in Russia. Quizzically, I inquired, "Anywhere adjacent to the Kola Peninsula by any chance?" "I don't see why not," he said. I instantly felt the old salmon fishing urge flood back and smiled. "Well, in that case I think that I had better drag out the Bruce & Walker and start practising again." "Whatever you say, Dad, you certainly need it," he replied.

69.
Reincarnation, Anyone?

Those who believe in reincarnation – returning after death to live their lives again in another form – should, if at all possible, try to avoid coming back as a salmon. Well, not if they want to live a fulfilling life in peace and harmony with their natural surroundings. *Salmo salar*, the King of Fish, is perhaps the most pursued of all creatures on Planet Earth, apart, that is, from *Homo sapiens* itself.

Throughout history salmon have been hunted with relentless, almost maniacal intensity. Even our Pictish ancestors, who regarded salmon as a symbol of wisdom, targeted the species for food. Because the fish are so predictable, I suppose that salmon have only themselves to blame; returning with unfailing regularity to the river that gave them birth, and to exactly the same part of the river where they themselves were spawned.

During the Late Middle Ages, and well into the twentieth century salmon was a major export earner for Scotland's economy. Recent estimates suggest that the value of rod and line salmon angling to the Scottish economy today is in the region of £100 million per annum; and upwards of 275,000 of Jock Tamson's Bairns regularly engage in some form of angling, be it for salmon, sea-trout, trout, coarse fish species or in sea fishing.

The earliest piece of salmon legislation that I have found is dated 1278 and it relates to the Border Esk. In that year at Carlisle Assizes it was determined because of "the great destruction of salmon coming up to spawn and likewise of the young fry going down to sea", that "no net shall be placed at weirs save by conservators appointed, and that the meshes shall be wide enough to let salmon fry through, viz., of four thumbs length."

The most bitter dispute concerning salmon also featured the Border Esk, when the English built a fish trap at Netherby on their side of the river, to capture returning salmon. From about 1474 until 1837, as soon as the Scots destroyed the trap, the English rebuilt it. Finally, with both sides arming themselves for full-scale battle, Sir James Graham, the English proprietor, agreed to breech the trap to allow fish upstream.

Ultimately, however, the English won the day. In 2005, in spite of the fact that two thirds of the river's length is in Scotland, the Border Esk was officially declared to be an English River. Scottish anglers fishing the Esk now have to pay an additional fee of £63.50 to the English Environment Agency for the privilege of doing so; an outrage, in my view, and sanctioned by, of all people, the Scottish Parliament.

70.
Broken Dreams

If anybody knows what happened to the year 2006 trout fishing season please let me know. I turned my back on it for a moment in March and when I looked round again it was the end of September. Fishing seasons were proper when I was a boy. Now, they fly by with the speed of a lightly hooked 6lb brown trout heading for the middle of the loch.

My wife, Ann, and I had a serious May outing to a group of lochs on the east side of Ben Hope reputed to hold excellent trout and rarely visited. After the 10-mile hike there and back, I can understand why they are rarely visited and if they do contain said excellent trout, then said excellent trout remained singularly undisturbed by our presence.

I also had an early-season fling in Orkney and I use the word 'fling' advisedly. The wind was Orcadian-wild and unremitting. I had a look at Boardhouse and decided to stay alive, rather than launch a boat. Eventually, we parked at the south end of Loch of Skaill and whilst Ann cowered in the car I had a cast, literally a cast, before retiring hurt.

Loch Caladail, one of the Durness limestone lochs, was also unforgiving. I spent a day there with Caladail-expert Malcolm Muir from Kilbarchan near Glasgow. In spite of the fact that conditions were near perfect, we failed miserably. Not a single, solitary fish showed the slightest interest in our flies. Malcolm was fishing dry fly, with a small, black hopper, whilst I offered more traditional, wet fly fare, but to no avail.

Loch Hope has, I suppose, been kindest to me this year, apart from breaking my trout rod whilst wrestling with the oars in a life-threatening force 6 gale. The following day, when fishing Beat 1, the perfidy of sea-trout became all too apparent. I had grabbed the bottom and top sections of a spare rod from the garage and arrived at the loch only to find that they came from different rods and didn't actually 'fit'. Half a mile of black tape affected a reasonable repair and, full of hope, we launched the boat.

Towards the end of the day, still fishless, I was drowning my sorrows in a cup of coffee and had forgotten that my flies were lying on the water a foot or so from the boat. I glanced at a fly on the water and said to my companion, "Hey, look at that amazing fly, it looks perfect!" "Yes," he replied, somewhat condescendingly, I thought. "It's yours." At that precise moment a considerable sea-trout rocketed from out of the depths and head-and-tailed on the fly, thus saving us from a blank day.

71.
Saving the Day on Loch Watten

I have never been so wet and cold since the last time I had been so wet and cold. Only one other boat was on the loch, and its occupants sensibly threw in the towel at about lunch time. We fished on, not because we are masochists, but because it was our last chance to fish Loch Watten that week. Our host, Neil from Hugo Ross's tackle shop in Wick, seemed to be impervious to the weather. His enthusiasm never flagged and he was clearly determined that we should have the best chance of a fish or three, regardless of the miserable conditions.

Loch Watten is one of my favourite waters and I have fished it for near three decades. When we lived in Caithness, on a hill over looking the loch, I could be afloat within minutes of arriving home and frequently was. Now, since flitting from Caithness to the wilds of Sutherland, 50 miles away, the opportunity to do so is limited. I can think of few other lochs that contain such wonderful wild brown trout and I had been looking forward to visiting them again. As such, I was quite prepared to put up with being soaked to the skin in the process.

The loch lies midway between Wick and Thurso and is three miles long by up to half a mile wide. Watten is shallow, with an average depth of around eight to nine feet and fish may be caught from the margins to the middle. The pH level is in the order of 8.0 and trout thrive mightily in the lime-rich waters. I have never had much success bank fishing and invariably fish from a boat. In the early days when I fished the loch, the boats were typical of the far north: heavy, leaky old tubs that were a nightmare to get afloat and generally uncomfortable once they were. I have lost more fish than I care to remember when my line snagged on protruding nails and other obstructions, but, well, a boat is a boat is a boat and they were the only game in town.

Matters have improved today. The mooring bay at the Watten Village end of the loch has been upgraded, complete with car park, and getting afloat is no longer a heart-attack inducing experience. Hugo Ross has invested in a fleet of excellent boats; stable, spacious and easy to handle, they even have rod clips to hold the rod upright when moving about the loch. Reliable outboard motors are also supplied and the whole operation of getting afloat is a hassle-free experience, and, in my view, pretty well unique in the far north.

The one thing that Hugo can't arrange, however, is a gentle, south-west breeze and rising trout. Hunching our shoulders against the downpour, we slipped behind the island and began a drift down the Whin Bank towards Railway Bay. Almost immediately, fish began rising to my flies, all of which I missed. My companion, Mark Bowler from the magazine *Fly Fishing & Fly Tying*, fared little better and he is one of the most successful anglers that I know, or, as his so-called friends sometimes aver, 'lucky'.

Just before the onset of hypothermia, a splendid trout rose to Mark's black hopper dry fly. It was played, landed, photographed and released. The fish looked to be nearer 3lb in weight than 2lb, and it was utterly beautiful. A few minutes later we were motoring back to the mooring bay, freezing, yes, but amazingly content.

72.
Spotal

Arriving for the first time to fish North Uist, Benbecula and South Uist is like an angling dream come true. Driving west from Lochmadday, you are confronted by a seemingly unending vista of lochs, some of which, like Loch Scadavay, are scattered with islands and tangled promontories, each of which is festooned with its own small lochs. Scadavay extends to the south of the

A867 Lochmaddy to Clachan road and even this smaller southern section can provide several days' sport.

The famous, lime-rich machair lochs that line the west coast are generally easily accessible from the main roads, but reaching many of the more remote east-coast lochs requires a fair degree of fitness, as well as determination and the ability to use a compass and map. Also, be prepared for sudden, less than pleasant changes in the weather. In these airts a sunny day can turn into a nightmare quicker than you can mutter Grouse & Claret.

My wife, Ann, and I have fished in this wonderland for many years and never tire of going back for more. Each time we do, we discover new delights and new waters to explore. Many visitors make straight for the well-known lochs, such as East Loch Bee, Grogarry, Stilligarry, Bornish and West Loch Ollay on South Uist, justly famed for the quality of their wild brown trout. But, over the years, we have tramped ever further into the wilderness in search of the utter peace – and some really outstanding fishing – that only these places can provide.

South Uist is graced by three fine mountains, north to south, Hecla (606m), Ben Corodale (527m) and, the highest, graceful Beinn Mhor (620m). They dominate the eastern horizon and guard the approaches to three of the most remote lochs on the island, Spotal, Corodale and little Loch Hellisdale. Find them on OS Map 22, Benbecula, Scale 1:50,000 at, respectively, grid references 834367, 831331, and 828310.

Hellisdale is best approached from the end of the minor road at Arinambane (Gd ref: 792285) via Bealach Crosgard and Glen Liadale and it is reputed to hold some good trout. Head off for Corodale from the A865 at Gd ref: 768341. Aim for the bealach between Hecla and Ben Corodale then descend down Glen Usinish to reach the loch. As you do so, think of the fugitive Bonnie Prince Charlie; he tramped this way in 1746 when he hid from his pursuers and held 'court' in a cliff-top cave nearby.

My favourite, however, is Spotal, one of the loveliest lochs that I have ever fished. The last time I visited, I did so as part of an adventure hike from Lochskipport (Gd ref: 829385) at the end of the B890. I tramped out past Loch Bein (Gd ref: 843373) to gain the north edge of the Ben Hecla horseshoe, then followed the ridge round over Beinn na h-Aire and Ben Scalavat to reach the summit of Hecla. I descend via Coir Rudale by tiny Loch a'Choire to fish Spotal.

Not so many years ago, sea-trout used to run to the loch from Loch Skipport and Caolas Mór, however, the advent of fish farming has brought an end to that. But Spotal still retains its magical grace and the brown trout, although not large, are big enough for me. As I turned to leave the loch, I noticed an otter watching me curiously from the far shore, and, overhead, the Hecla golden eagles marked my progress home across the moor.

73.
The Flow Country

The Flow Country of Caithness and East Sutherland became a battle-ground during the 1980s when factory-tree farmers clashed with conservationists. These peatlands were amongst the last remaining examples of untouched blanket bog on Planet Earth. Exploiting them simply to grow exotic, tax-avoidance conifers was considered to be one of the great acts of environmental vandalism of the late twentieth century.

For many years, when we lived in Caithness, we visited the Flow Country regularly to fish its myriad lochs and lochans and to enjoy its splendid isolation and wonderful wildlife. Our four children all fished (I think the Chinese call it brain-washing) and I have treasured memories of the many happy days we spent there as a family, sometimes catching a few trout, and sometimes not.

Our favourite waters were around Altnabreac Station. You will find them on OS Map 11, Thurso & Dunbeath, Scale 1:50,000; Garbh Loch (Gd ref: 037467), Caol Loch (Gd ref: 027485), and Skyline Loch (Gd ref: 011479). To the west of Altnabreac, we fished a series of five small waters, Lochan Airigh Leathaid (Gd ref: 991390) and, across the railway line and approached from Forsinain in Strath Halladale, Loch Sletill (Gd ref: 959471) and little Loch Leir (Gd ref: 955458).

Invariably, when arriving at most of these lochs, we would be greeted by a curious black-throated or red-throated diver. One afternoon, an otter called to say hello as we fished from a boat. He swam round us and then, lying on his back with his forelegs crossed on his chest, watched us for a few minutes before diving again below the waves.

Buzzard, hen harrier, golden eagle, golden plover, greenshank and dunlin were constant companions. Red deer marked our progress over the moor, and once, memorably, we caught a glimpse of a wildcat, yellow eyes ablaze, peering at us from behind a clump of rushes.

Lochan Airigh Leathaid was one of the most challenging of these lochs. Getting to it involves a long, bumpy drive south-west from Loch More, past Dalnawillan Lodge and Dalnaganachan. Park at Gd ref: 005390 and walk west up the hill to reach the loch within 20 minutes. They remain hidden until you are on them, so take a compass to make sure you don't walk by. We did, the first time, and only discovered our mistake on looking back.

There are three main lochs, all small, and two further waters that are even smaller. They have been stocked in the past with brown trout taken from the Thurso River, although at times you would swear that they were entirely fishless. Nothing could be further from the truth because they hold excellent quality trout that average 1lb in weight, and others that are much heavier.

Bank fishing is the rule, and it is best not to wade. Stay ashore. Wading will only scare the fish out of reach. A bushy fly on the 'bob', Ke-He, Soldier Palmer or the like, March Brown or Greenwell's Glory in the middle, and an attractor on the tail should do the business, maybe, but crossing the fingers also helps.

I encountered one of the largest brown trout of my angling life when fishing the most northerly loch, a fish I estimated to have been well over 5lb in weight. I still feel the sense of utter loss as it charged off to the centre of the loch, breaking my cast in the process. Even nicer was returning to my wife, Ann, with my tale of woe only to be greeted by a handsome brace of trout weighing 4lb.

74.
Give Me a Tune

I am not really a salmon angler, as anyone who has ever seen my Spey-casting will avow. Indeed, given that the family refer to my trout casting technique as 'father's affliction', it is remarkable that I ever manage to hook anything other than bushes, trees, fence-posts and myself.

But before you reach for the violin, I must attest that I have enjoyed every moment of my angling life. I have no regrets, not even about loosing that huge salmon in the pool below Coo Ford on Tweed upstream from Innerleithen when I was a boy.

Good things happen to those who fish, even to your correspondent. I have had a trout fly named after me: The Bruce, designed by Adrian Latimer, a friend and author of some fine angling books, including *Wild Fishing in Wild Places*. To celebrate the birth of the fly, Adrian devised the Loch Lanlish Challenge; Lanlish, one of the famous Durness limestone lochs, holds trout of prodigious size.

Adrian contributed a half bottle of year-2000 champagne, to be awarded to the first of a group of our friends who took a trout of over 3lb from Lanlish when fishing with The Bruce. I am looking at the bottle as I write. It is dust-covered and will probably remain safe from any form of human interference for at least the next decade.

Another good thing arrived last week: a pipe tune called 'The Bruce', written for me by one of Scotland's most noted pipers and composers, Pipe Major Sandy Forbes. Sandy served during the war with the Seaforth Highlanders and studied with the legendary Pipe Major Willie Ross. At the age of 19, he had the distinction of being the youngest holder of the Pipe Major's Certificate in the British Army.

Sandy is an angler and his father, who was head keeper on the Kerrow Estate in Inverness-shire, taught him to fish. Two years ago, he asked me to arrange a day's fishing for himself and his friend from Inverness, Pipe Major Duncan Macdonald. I happily agreed and spent a day with them trout fishing on Loch Craggie in the shadow of Ben Loyal, 'Queen of Scottish Mountains'.

It was an unforgettable day, not only because we caught a few trout, but also, for me, for the pleasure of hearing the banter the pair exchanged. At one stage, when things had gone a bit quiet, Duncan said to Sandy, "You know if you had just brought your chanter with you and played a tune, we would have been catching a lot more trout."

When we decided to finish, I started the outboard and motored back up the loch to the mooring bay. The argument began as I was securing the boat. "Now," said Sandy, "we must pay you for arranging the day and for the hire of the boat." The more I said that it wasn't necessary, the more determined they were to do so. I held my ground, until, in a flash of inspired genius, I said to Sandy, "OK, then, Sandy, why don't you just write me a tune instead?"

Two years later it arrived and it is splendid. I can't play the chanter, let alone the pipes, but I know someone who does: my granddaughter Jessica. She has promised to learn the tune, a jig, and to play it for me on my birthday next month. I have great confidence in the result. After all, she was taught to play by Pipe Major Sandy Forbes.

75.
When All Else Fails

When all else fails give them the 'turning flee', a technique best practised from the stern (blunt end) of a loch boat. As the boat is being rowed forward at normal pace, the angler casts at right angles to the moving vessel.

Cast as long a line as you can comfortably manage. When the flies land, feather-light, of course, bring the tip of your rod down until it is parallel to the water, about two feet above the surface. Keep the rod at right angles to the boat. Do not retrieve the flies. Let them be.

Fish will rise to the flies almost as soon as they land, or, and more often, at the precise moment when the flies begin to "turn", compelled to do so by the forward motion of the boat. There is no need to strike. The fish hook themselves.

I was introduced to the technique many years ago by a wonderful Ayrshire gillie who also introduced me to a splendid variation of one of Scotland's most popular trout flies, the Black Pennell. His version was tied with a yellow tail, rather than with the traditional golden pheasant tippets, and it has been a good friend to me ever since.

The turning flee works well in all weather conditions, including that angler's curse, a dead-flat-calm. I had splendid sport one hot summer day on Sweethope Lough in Northumberland. Within an hour I took half a dozen trout whilst most of the other boats returned 'blank'. The Manager, my wife, Ann, was rowing at the time.

When Clan Sandison lived in Caithness I often caught my first trout of the season whilst fishing the turning flee on Loch Watten in early May, about 7.30pm, as my son, Blair, rowed me past the broken fence at the north east end of Factor's Bay.

Blair reminds me to this day about what he calls, "my luck"; claiming that it was only his prowess on the oars, rather than my casting skill that brought about the desired result. The lies some anglers tell.

But like everything in angling, nothing is certain. I remember fishing Loch Caladail in North-West Sutherland, when, because my companion was not allowed to row due to a congenitally 'bad back', I was on the oars all day.

Fishing conditions were difficult, but by the close of play my partner had caught four splendid trout, each weighing about 2lb, and all caught on the turning flee. As fish after fish was hooked, played and landed, I found it hard to keep a fixed grin of supportive pleasure in place.

Consequently, when I had my annual outing with a young fishing friend, I hobbled about a bit on the way down to the boat. "What's up, Bruce?" he inquired. "Oh, nothing, just a bit of a bad back this morning." "No problem," he replied courteously, "I'll row." At last I would be able to show off my skill fishing the turning flee.

When the boat was drifting, and we fished traditionally, casting in front of the boat, he rose and caught trout whilst I remained fishless. When he rowed back up to the start of another drift, I lashed away at the turning flee but to minimal avail.

By the end of the day I had little need to invent a sore back. Mine was on fire, my neck was blazing, my bum was sore and my heart ached. If I had caught just two more trout I would have had a brace.

76.
Loch Leven

I remember Loch Leven in its glory days when the whole 3,500 acres could erupt with the splash of rising trout; wonderful fish, head-and-tailing, surface-feeding on myriad insects, beautiful trout, small heads, perfectly proportioned, brightly spotted with a yellowish underbody. Blank days were rare then.

I fished Loch Leven during the 1960s, but even then it was obvious that the loch was in trouble; water quality was deteriorating and algal blooms becoming an ever-increasing problem. In the mid-60s one of my friends persuaded his father, an occasional angler, to fund a couple of days on the loch. The water was thick with suspended globules of slime and few trout rose.

It was a hot day and our benefactor, who liked to do things properly, laid aside his rod and produced his hip-flask. Unscrewing the top, he scooped up water from the loch, and, drinking with relish, said, "Ah, that good old Loch Leven water!" We drank our whisky neat. That evening, he excused himself during dinner and the following morning, before breakfast, he left for home.

As the loch water continued to deteriorate and trout resorted to bottom feeding, anglers began to desert the loch. A few months after the notorious toxic algal bloom of 'Scum Saturday', in June 1992, when Loch Leven was declared to be a public health hazard, the owner applied for and received permission from Scottish Natural Heritage to introduce rainbow trout.

Although I understood the commercial sense behind the decision, it seemed to me to destroy everything that I loved about the loch; its premier position in the history of Scottish trout fishing and, indeed, in trout fishing around the world. Loch Leven progeny has been used to stock rivers in the Argentine, Chile, Falkland Islands, India, South Africa, Kenya, Australia and

New Zealand. Introducing rainbow trout turned Loch Leven into simply just another put-and-take commercial fishery.

A few years back I booked a boat to find out for myself how the loch was fishing. My companion was Mark Bowler, editor of the magazine *Fly Fishing and Fly Tying* and we were determined to explore as much of the loch as we could in search of sport. Few other anglers were out and the harbour was packed with empty boats.

We fished Castle Island and Alice's Bower, Sunken Rock, St Serf's South-East Point, Sandy Point, West Point and Carden Spot. The only natural rises we saw were in the late afternoon, for about 10 minutes, off Sandy Point, where Mark hooked a rainbow trout on a size 18, black, dry fly. When landed it weighed 3lb 10oz and had an ugly, open, blood-red wound on a gill cover.

Since then, faced with mounting financial losses, the owner has decided that Loch Leven should revert to being brown trout only and the hatchery closed. There are still 30 boats available for anglers, but at the end of the season this will be reduced to six.

Although the glory days have gone, water quality is improving and I believe that in time the loch will flourish again. In my view, less fishing pressure will certainly not harm the recovery process. The recovery probably won't happen in my lifetime, but it will come, I think, sooner rather than later. Whatever, before I hurtle off to that great trout loch in the sky I intend to make one further pilgrimage to this shrine of all things excellent in angling – if not for the fish, then at least for old times' sake.

77.
Three of the Best Round Lairg

There are three excellent wild brown trout lochs to the north-east of the village of Lairg in Sutherland: Loch Craggie, Loch Dola and Loch Tigh na Creige. They are easily accessible along forest tracks and offer a range of sport that will suit both beginner and expert alike. There are boats on all of the lochs and fishing is strictly by fly only.

The prime water is Loch Craggie, probably one of the finest trout lochs in Scotland; three quarters of a mile long by up to 400yds wide. The average weight of Craggie trout is in the order of 1lb but most seasons produce fish of up to and over 3lb. They are beautiful trout, wonderfully marked, perfectly shaped, pink-fleshed and fighting fit. The harbour is at the south-west corner and this area is perhaps the most productive part of the loch.

From the harbour, carefully fish round the little island and then drift north down the west shoreline, a few yards out from the bank. The water is crystal clear and the boulder-strewn bottom of the loch here provides great cover for fish. The water is shallower off the east bank, but the north bay has a sandy bottom and this can also produce good sport. There is also Mayfly hatch on Craggie, generally towards the end of June.

Loch Dola is much smaller than its neighbour, but it has two little islands of its own where trout rise readily to the well-presented fly. However, in truth, trout rise and may be caught all over the loch. The water is more coloured in Dola, but the trout are very pretty and average 10oz/12oz in weight.

Loch Tigh na Creige is the most distant loch, slightly smaller than Loch Craggie and much more a Highland loch in character. The water is peat-stained. But it is a beginner's paradise and the perfect place to introduce new-comers to the joys of fly fishing. The north shore is where to begin. Drift past the promontory and islet where the principal feeder burn enters and on into the north-east bay. Creige trout average in the order of 8oz/12oz and there are lots of them, including the occasional fish of over 1lb in weight.

Traditional patters of Scottish loch flies will do fine. Use a bushy fly on the 'bob', such as Ke-He, Soldier Palmer, Black Zulu, Blue Zulu; in the middle, March Brown, Woodcock & hare-lug, Greenwell's Glory or Grouse & Claret; and an 'attractor' on the tail such as Silver Butcher, Silver Invicta or Kingfisher Butcher. They all produce fish.

Apart from the lochs noted above, fishing can also be arranged on Lairg Angling Association waters; including mighty Loch Shin, one of the longest lochs in Scotland, 17 miles north/south by up to one mile wide, and also on Loch Beannach, which the angling club stocks with native brown trout. Beannach is approached via a forest track and the boats are moored at the north-east corner.

David Walker of Park House in Lairg factors the three Lairg lochs and knows more than most about fishing in and around Lairg. Contact David on tel: 01549 402208.

78.
Swanning over Swannay

Of all Scotland's islands I love Orkney best, perhaps because it was the first Scottish island I visited. I was too young to fish then, but the memory of the kindness of the people we stayed with remains with me today. When I took my own family to Orkney, we were intent upon trout fishing. We booked a caravan and my wife, Ann, asked the owner if the caravan would be close to a trout loch. She replied, "Which loch would you like me to put it at?"

Of all Orkney's trout lochs, I love Loch of Swannay best. We first fished it from the bank near Dale during a family holiday. I managed to take a trout of 2lb, but soon discovered that Swannay was fickle; one day brightly accommodating, the next unrelentingly dour. Maybe this is why it attracted me, knowing the quality of the fish it contained, but never knowing if I was going to catch any.

The loch lies in the north of Mainland and covers an area of 670 acres. It is two miles north/south by up to half a mile wide and has an average depth of approximately 12ft/15ft. Swannay is peaty and generally exposed to the wind. When it howls, the loch can become discoloured and it often takes a few days before it becomes fishable again.

Most anglers boat fish which makes it easier to explore the water. As in the majority of Orkney lochs, there are shallow skerries and deeper 'pots', so when motoring around it is wise to hasten slowly and to have a spare sheer pin for the outboard in case of accidents. And, as always, it is best to stay seated when fishing, not only for reasons of safety, but also because standing up only alerts and alarms the fish.

Local anglers generally concentrate their efforts at the south end; carefully fishing round the small island of Muckle Holm and drifting north down the east shore towards Scruit. The south bay, where Burn of Etherlegeo flows in, near the Orkney Trout Fishing Association hut, and west to Southend can also be very productive, given the right conditions.

Exactly what the right conditions are is not so easy to describe. We have caught trout on Swannay during the middle of an April snowstorm, and on flat calm, hot summer days. The best advice that I can give is to just go fishing, hopefully, whatever the prevailing conditions might be.

As to what flies to offer, that is almost as enigmatic as the loch itself. Once, after a blank day, I was chatting to an angler who had been fishing round Muckle Holm. I had watched him from the shore, and he seemed to be casting at lightning speed, quickly bringing his flies across the surface to cast again. He had a splendid basket of six trout weighing in the order of 10lb and he gave me a piece of advice: "Never fish Swannay without a Black Pennell on your cast," he said.

I have followed his advice ever since, and sometimes it works, and sometimes it doesn't. I guess it's the way you fish the flies, rather than the precise patterns used. Other Swannay regulars insist that the most successful fishing method is using dry fly. Some days, I try everything, and some days they all work. There again, sometimes I try everything and they don't. But whatever happens, I keep going back.

79.
Sea-Trout Delight

July is the witching month for sea-trout and, for many anglers, fishing for them represents the pinnacle of the piscatorial art. Sea-trout take the fly with fierce savagery, almost pulling the rod from your hand and they fight spectacularly, leaping and tail-dancing across the water like bars of pure silver.

My first encounter with sea-trout occurred many years ago one mild July night below the old bridge across the Spey at Grantown. There is something magical about fishing at night; the sound and smell of the river, the heart-stopping splash of rising fish. The Spey produces some 4,000 sea-trout each season and is Scotland's premier sea-trout fishery.

Since then, however, most of my sea-trout fishing has been done in the bays and inlets around North Uist and on Loch Hope in North Sutherland. In the 70s and 80s some of the best sea-trout fishing in Europe could be found in the Outer Hebrides. My favourite North Uist location is at Oban Sponish, reached after a vigorous two and a half mile tramp south from the Lochmaddy/Clachan road (see OS Map 18, Sound of Harris).

Oban Sponish (Gd ref: 880645) is a long inlet from Loch Eport, narrowing as it enters the sea. There is a rock bar at this point and when the tide recedes it acts a barrier, keeping sea-trout trapped until the next high tide. Another beautiful sea pool where sea-trout roam is in the north of the island, a few miles east of Sollas where the road touches the sea at Loch nan Geireann (Gd ref: 846748).

Walk out over the sands at low tide to where the Rubha Glas headland reaches over to touch Clett in the west. A gap here has produced a sizable pool through which the tide pours, bringing with it both sea-trout and salmon. Fish the pool from the west shore. Close to the gap at the seaward end the bottom is sandy and this is where to concentrate your efforts. Since the arrival of aquaculture in the Hebrides, sea-trout numbers there have fallen dramatically, but it is still worth having a cast at these locations, because there are few more wonderful places in the world to do so.

My regular sea-trout venue now is Loch Hope, half an hour's drive from my front door. The loch produces approximately 500 fish each season, as well as reasonable numbers of salmon. The loch is four and a half miles long and divided naturally into three sections: North End, Middle Bay and South End. South End (tel: 01847 611216 for bookings) is the most productive area and it is divided into the three beats. I had my first outing on Beat 3 (see OS Map 9, Cape Wrath, Gd ref: 452518) towards the end of June.

The wind was perfect, from the south, drifting the boat gently down the Beat's one-mile-long west shore. The only oar-work required was a few strokes now and again to keep the boat about 25/30yds out from the bank. Of the three 'offers' I had, one, a sea-trout of 2lb 8oz, was successfully played and landed. The other two were from seriously large fish, both of which I managed to hook but then lost. The last was a veritable monster of incredible power. I still see the turmoil in the water as it dashed at my fly (a size 12 Woodcock and Hare-lug), and feel the sense of desolation when, a few moments later, it was gone.

80.
Admiral Lord Nelson

Not many people know that Admiral Lord Nelson (1758–1805) was a fly-fisherman. I didn't until a friend, Roy Christie, sent me two amazingly beautiful trout flies, a Carshalton Cocktail and a Carshalton Dun. They are similar in style to the flies the victor of the Battle of Trafalgar would have used when he fished his local stream, the River Wandle. It flows through South London and joins Old Father Thames at Wandsworth.

However, by the end of the nineteenth century there were 90 mills along its 11-mile length and pollution from them soon killed the stream as a trout fishery. The mills continued to empty untreated waste into the river until by the end of the 1960s the Wandle was officially declared to be an 'open sewer'. Now, thanks to the work of the Wild Trout Trust, the river is being rescued and restored.

Nelson's love of fishing was noted by another angler, Sir Humphrey Davy, the inventor of the Miner's Safety Lamp. He commented, "Nelson was a good fisher; as proof of his passion for it, he continued the pursuit even with his left hand." I find it hard enough to tackle up with both hands, never mind one, but there are some advantages to being single-handed: when asked how big the fish was that got away all the angler need do is to extend his forearm, palm of the hand vertical, and say, "That big."

I guess it is really only anglers who marvel at the sheer beauty and artistry of the perfectly tied artificial fly and Roy Christie's work seemed to me to be finer than anything thing else that I had seen in more than... well, many years angling. Roy can be contacted on reversedparachutes@yahoo. co.uk Find out more about the work of the Wild Trout Trust on www. wildtrout.org.

The only problem I now face is the thought of having to fish with the flies. They will get wet, or I might snag them on an underwater obstruction. I would lose them. And I don't tie flies. So I propose to mount the pair in a display case and hang the result close to my desk so that I can enjoy the sight of them whenever I sit down at my computer. Call me a wimp, but that is how it works for me.

However, there is no doubt whatsoever in my mind where I would use them: at Paradise Wood on the River Don, a few miles north of Monymusk. I am more certain than I have ever been in my whole life that Don trout would be unable to resist them. And I am sure that Admiral Nelson would approve, mightily.

81.
The Trout Loch from Hell

Being a Scot means that at an early age you are invariably introduced to the joys of rugby, golf and trout fishing. Well, to be precise, boys are, rather than girls, although my wife, Ann, has played golf and is also an angler. But as a boy, I was never particularly joyful with the rugby bit; lying under a muddy heap of vandals on a freezing Saturday morning did not seem to me to be the best way to spend precious school-free weekends.

Golf appealed for a while until my father, pushed beyond endurance, roared: "Get out of my sight until you can watch where your damn ball goes!" This was understandable. Not only did it cost him a half a dozen balls to get me round, but it also took five hours and endless embarrassments with other players. I used to 'tack' up the course like a yacht in distress and only rarely on the fairway that I was meant to be playing.

That left trout fishing and none of my family fished. This seemed to be reason enough for becoming involved. At least I would be left to my own devices. No more twisted ankles and demonic sports masters. Goodbye to dissident fairways and scrabbling under gorse bushes searching for seriously slashed grey orbs of gutta-percha.

Fishing promised freedom, and even the worst duffer in the world has a chance of catching fish. In spite of what angling gurus might preach, believe me, if a fish is there, spots your fly and wants it, you will catch it. I have seen, all too often, so-called 'experts' ending the day red-faced and fishless whilst the duffer comes home with at least something for breakfast if not one for the glass case.

I persisted in this belief for years until the day I came eyeball to eyeball with the trout loch from hell: East Loch Bee on the Island of South Uist. I have thrashed bloody Bee to foam more times than I care to remember but have yet to take a decent fish from its shallow, brackish waters. Yes, I have caught trout, but fish so small that I hardly noticed them even although I was looking all the time.

A causeway divides the two sections of Loch Bee, east and west, and the whole system almost cuts the north end of South Uist in half, stopped from doing so only by floodgates at the east, Loch Skiport, end. Some South Uist anglers claim that West Loch Bee is the more exciting fishery. It may well be but I can't really comment: the last time I fished West Bee if I had caught two more trout I would have had a brace.

What is beyond doubt, however, is that East Loch Bee is a first-class trout loch. My son, Blair, was Secretary of the South Uist Angling Association for a number of years and never missed an opportunity to send regular details of fish that he and his friends took there, including gripping action shots of said fish being caught.

I have seen fish of over 4lb taken from East Loch Bee and in spite of repeated failure, I keep going back; in the sure and certain knowledge that the longer I remain fishless, then the sooner it is that I will break my duck – or, in this case swan, because the loch is home to more than 100 of these graceful creatures. But tempus fugit and if I'm not careful I could find myself under these wretched gorse bushes again, hunting for lost golf balls.

82.
What Does Angling Mean to You?

What does angling mean to you? Is it relaxation, sport, escapism, or is it an overwhelming compulsion to compete and show that you are top dog? Does it mean more and bigger fish, a bite every cast, getting value for money, an excuse to tie exotic never-fail-patterns of artificial flies? Or is it just a way to avoid cutting the grass, painting the spare room or doing the weekly shopping on a Saturday afternoon?

The short answer is that few of us really know what compels us to go fishing. Perhaps components of all these feelings and contradictions lie embodied in the heart of every angler; not permanently, but as recurring bits and pieces of the nonsense that follows us throughout much of our fishing lives.

Attitudes change, even angling attitudes. The callow, aggressive youth bristling with club badges today is often the happy old codger of tomorrow. Pleased enough to be out on river or loch and not too much concerned about catching trout.

I once met two such happy old codgers on the shores of a Sutherland loch. I had watched them, earlier, in pouring rain and a strengthening breeze, fishing behind a small island at the south end of the Loch Hakel near Tongue.

Later, I came across them after lunch, relaxing by the dying embers of their lochside fire. I stopped to talk as anglers do. They politely apologised for not being able to offer me a cup of tea, but generously proffered something stronger.

The sum total of their ages, one announced, was 150 years. They told me that they had been fishing companions since before I was born. Looking at them, I guessed that they were busy fishing before most present-day anglers had been born and I felt privileged to make their acquaintance.

During our blether it became clear that they had fished throughout most of Scotland and that they had enjoyed every moment doing so. They were traditionalists, their only nod to modernity being carbon fibre rods: "I was sad to put my cane rod away", said the elder of the duo, "but the wrists were going and I needed something lighter."

He added, "But it is nice to see a young fellow like you still using one." I have fished with a cane rod all my life and it is unlikely that I will change. My rod was made for me by a Mr Stott who lived in a cottage near the Roman Wall in Northumberland and was a former employee of Hardy Bros in Alnwick.

I left them re-launching their boat and, from the hill, watched them row back up the loch in record time and turn into a drift. A few moments later I saw the tip of the bow rod bend into a fish, whilst the stern rod reeled in and reached for the landing net. They seemed to epitomise everything that is dear to me about my favourite pastime: companionship, shared pleasure and the chance of the odd trout.

I don't pretend that I have all the answers, or even some of the answers as to what makes an angler, but I am certain that the characteristics and courtesy described above are an essential part of that process, and that they only come with the passage of time.

These truths can't be forced upon people, but perhaps we should try, for the benefit of our dearly loved art, to try to emulate these traits. If fishing means anything or has any lasting importance, then that is what it means to me.

83.
Flying High

For some anglers, fly-tying becomes an all-enduring passion, at least as important as catching fish and almost an end in itself; bits of fur and feather cobbled together round a hook with the single purpose of fooling fish into thinking that the imitation is the real thing; an irresistible, delicate and dainty morsel.

Except, that is, for my own efforts. These generally start life as an attempt to tie a standard pattern, such as a size 16 Silver Butcher, and end up looking

The Loch of the Night, Flowerdale Forest

The Duck Loch,
Kyle of Tongue

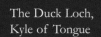

The Kyle of Durness

Stormy day on Loch Hope

Loch Pityoulish, Aviemore

Macgregor's Leap, River Lyon, Perthshire

River Spey at Craigellac

Loch Ailsh, Assynt

Loch Dubh an
Lochain, Knoydart

Loch na h-Oidhche, Wester Ross

Loch Arkaig, Lochaber

Kyle of Tongue and Castle Varrich

Foinaven and Loch an Tigh Shelg

Humpy Bridge Pool, River Forss

Fishing the Thurso River at Westerdale

Jake Smart on Plantation Loch, Altnaharra

Falls Pool, River Forss, Caithness

Buchan Burn, Glen Trool

East Loch Bee, South Uist

Gorm loch na Beinne,
Wester Ross

Ann Sandison,
River Borgie

like a prehistoric monster; more likely to tempt pterodactyls than they are ever likely to tempt trout. I have little aptitude and fifteen thumbs.

One of the most innovative fly-tyers I know is Peter Fluck, of *Spitting Image* fame, the satirical political puppet show that was a popular TV programme of the 1970s and 80s. Peter and I fish together from time to time and he never travels anywhere without his fly-tying material, neatly collected together in an impressive, multi-drawered, mahogany box that rides importantly on the back seat of his car.

Which is how it came to grief one morning when my wife, Ann, borrowed Peter's car to go deliver the children to school. Taking a corner too fast, she applied the brakes fiercely and the drawers slipped out depositing half a ton of hooks and feathers in a jumbled heap on the floor. Ever philosophical, all Peter said was, "Needed a good clean out anyway."

Two of Peter's most memorable dressings had political connotations: the Geoffrey Howe, a scarlet hackle with a bright yellow streak down the body, and the Edwina Currie, slim-shanked, but a well-bodied piece of work with great big staring eyes. He eventually abandoned them, confessing that both were useless; the flies that is, not the people that gave them their name.

Choosing the flies to tie on to your cast is one of the most important moments of the fishing day. It all depends upon weather, water height, wind conditions, surface fly-life, insects under shore-side stones, how you are feeling that morning and, in my case, whether or not I have remembered to take any flies with me.

Flies, of course, get stuck in places other than a trout's mouth: such as thumb, finger, back of neck and bum; and, on one memorable, painful instance, the nose. I am happy to say that it was not my nose, but the nose of an illustrious angler who once edited one of Scotland's national newspapers.

He had been fishing Loch Leven using a small, double-hooked Dunkeld, a bright yellow and black concoction. After 'the accident' he had to suffer the ignominy of driving back to Edinburgh so attired; much to the amusement of the toll attendant at the Forth Road Bridge and to his long-suffering wife who tried to brush it off, and to the staff of Edinburgh Royal Infirmary who had the task of removing it.

But, deeply embedded single hooks can be safely removed by the loch-side. The technique is simple, effective and painless. Loop a length of fishing line, or string, round the shank of the fly, just above where the point has entered the flesh. Press down hard on the eye of the fly, and, whilst doing so, jerk the loop, firmly, back and slightly up and away from the angle of the hook's entry. The fly pops out without leaving a mark. Honest.

84.
Hopping Mad on the Kirkaig

Anglers who look good, feel good. Also, because of their natty attire, they are erroneously judged to be more expert in the gentle art than their less well-dressed neighbours; not that I have noticed any real truth in this supposition. However, clothing manufacturers capitalise on this presumption and target their advertising to take advantage of piscatorial vanity.

This vanity is most obvious in the rarefied stratosphere of superior salmon fishing and most in evidence by those who hail from south of Mr Hadrian's Wall. They dress in the same fashion, men and women alike: checked shirt, cravat or tie, woolly jumper, Tweed, moleskin or loden breeks, long stockings rounded off with garter-tabs in green, red or mustard. Open-toed sandals are *de rigueur* at breakfast.

Every season brings a flood of them to the north of Scotland. Their vehicles clutter up our single-track roads. The raucous din of their conversation dominates hotel dining rooms and lounges. They command our habitat as though it were their God-given right to do so; unaware of the complex issues we face in connection with preserving and protecting it.

They know little of our history or traditions and seem to care about them even less. For them, it is only a holiday, a welcome break from a bleak urban existence. The redeeming grace of their presence is that they spend a lot of cash in pursuit of their pleasure – in salmon angling terms upwards of £80 million each year.

This helps to sustain thousands of jobs in rural Scotland. Therefore,

I suppose, it is as well to "hack it". The Lord in His infinite wisdom made us different in speech, manners and in dress. Who am I to criticise? I myself sometimes wear similar clothes when salmon fishing, although I would not part with my decrepit deerstalker for all the designer-headwear in Christendom.

Sad experience, however, determined me to ditch one vital item of "designer-gear": the breeks. They give the lower legs no protection whatsoever from midge-attack. The damned brutes burrow into the folds of the wool stockings and feed ravenously. You thus become a mobile dining room, a sort of meals-on-legs for our voracious little friends. Everywhere you go, the midges go as well.

Over the years I have tried all the propriety brands of repellent. None seemed to work. Perhaps the wretched beasties have developed immunity to them, or perhaps the change in our climate has given them a new lease of life. This certainly appeared to be the case when a friend and I fished the River Kirkaig in North Sutherland a few years ago. The river was in perfect condition, salmon were showing and, for once, we appeared to be in the right place at the right time.

So were the midges. Whole armies of the beasts. I really wanted to catch a salmon but found that it was entirely impossible to last for more than a few moments in a battlefield where the midges held all the advantages. My legs were on fire and my stockings were like tenement buildings for midges. Ignominious retreat was the only option and I fled the scene scratching furiously.

Ever since, I have been the one at breakfast wearing ankle-length trousers, and, by the river, the head-enveloping anti-midge net. It might not look beautiful, but at least it allows me to get on with the job in hand in relative peace and comfort – if only it was as simple to tone down the mighty buzz made by some of our friends from the south.

85.
Skill or Luck?

There are anglers cleverer and more skilful than I am. So-called friends remind me of this constantly. Even nearest and dearest refer to my casting technique as "father's affliction". Few admit that I occasionally catch fish. With the evidence before them on the kitchen scales they talk scathingly of luck and the stupidity of trout.

But I think that fish are cleverer and more skilful, than anglers, that is. Biologists argue that if fish possess a brain and are capable of sensitivities, in the way that we understand the meaning of that word, then they must be rudimentary. Before being engulfed by a flood of evidence to the contrary, tell me, what do you make of the following events?

I was fishing the Tweed midway between Peebles and Innerleithen on a stretch called 'The Girlie'; downstream from the railway crossing by the cottage – you know the place. The evening epitomised the best that Tweed can offer; perfect water and air temperature, river height, wind force and direction, hatching flies and gentle sunlight.

I was inching down a run that I knew held good trout. There was a deep 'hole' towards the far bank and I was convinced that I would tempt one of the residents to take my fly: a Greenwell's Glory tied on a cast made of single strands of horsehair acquired at great personal risk from an unsuspecting Clydesdale. But in spite of my determined efforts not a fin did I see.

I waded quietly to the bank to walk back and begin again at the head of the pool when I noticed a local angler standing watching me. He gave a cheery wave and marched into the river, casting as he went. Water flew from his progress like waves cascading off the deck of a deep-sea trawler.

As though by royal command a large trout rose and five minutes later he landed it. I am vague about its exact size. I did not want to rush up and examine it because I would have drowned the man on the spot. But it looked to me be about 2lb in weight.

The line whistled out again, and, yet again, another trout rose, was hooked, landed and despatched. With casual disdain the angler reeled in, stowed his landing net and marched off. "Good night!" he called. "Hope you manage to have some sport."

Tell me, were the fish I failed to catch the clever ones? Were the two that the local angler caught just educationally subnormal? Was my fine tackle and delicate casting simply a waste of time? Does artistry really matter?

Consider the number of fish that we catch in relation to the number available to be caught. Is it only the dumb ones that end up gasping in our grubby grasp? Or is there, in the dark green of the river, an Aztec-like fishy society that requires regular sacrifices to be made to an Air God?

Was it by accident or by design that you caught that beauty last season? You recount the breathtaking events by heart – difficult wind conditions, casting under the trees, the high bank, the superb, inch-perfect cast, the lightning strike, avoiding the weeds and so on. But be honest: did you take the fish or did the fish take you?

The largest wild brown trout that I have ever caught weighed 4lb 8oz and it took my tail fly when I wasn't looking. I was pouring myself a cup of coffee. I have never caught another wild trout of that size although I have been looking all the time. Who do we really think that we are fooling, the fish or ourselves?

86.
Safety Afloat

I have a love/hate relationship with outboard engines. In truth, mostly hate. The majority of them are noisy, smelly, unreliable things, much given to letting you down when you most need them.

I have to say, however, that my own engine is very user-friendly; a 3.5hp Yamaha that I bought nearly 20 years ago. Because my wife, Ann, and I mostly bank fish hill lochs, a whole season can pass without the engine being used. Nevertheless, when I do take it out, it always starts virtually 'first pull'.

A couple of oars and two strong arms used to be sufficient when I started fishing. On Loch Leven, in the old days, however, four arms were required because the Leven boats were huge, comfortably accommodating three anglers and two boatmen; or, when I first fished it as a youth, two adults and an over-excited small boy. Big Eck and his son where on the oars that day and they were the best in the business.

I enjoy rowing, but many anglers seem to have forgotten how to do so; the simple joy of working with wind and waves, conserving energy, inching through a storm, hugging the shore to reach your destination safely. Modern anglers are ill-used to handling small boats and hardly a season passes without some dreadful accident.

Yet there are few regulations governing the use of loch boats. Saint and sinner, non-swimmer or otherwise, anglers step straight in and push off regardless of experience. When they do so, they put their lives and the lives of others at risk.

Perhaps the time has come for some kind of examination, which anglers must pass before taking charge of a boat and awarded only when they can demonstrate they are competent to do so.

I envisage a practical test, covering physical fitness, rowing techniques, boat handling, weather lore, outboard motor maintenance, life saving and survival tactics in the event of an accident. It could be organised and managed by organisations such as the Scottish Anglers' National Association and funded by the Sports Council.

Whether or not the tests should be compulsory is a matter for debate. I think that they should be. One life lost is one too many. Yes, accidents would still happen, but at least the people involved in them would be better able to cope with their situation.

In the meantime, here are a few simple rules to keep you safe when afloat. If there is any chance of a storm, stay ashore and fish from the bank. Inspect the boat thoroughly before setting out. Tie in each oar with a length of twine attached to a thwart. Tie in the outboard engine to the transom. If you don't know the difference between the thwart and a transom, take up golf.

Fill the petrol tank before setting off. Take spare fuel. Refill the tank at lunch time, when you are ashore; never try to do so when afloat. Regularly check the tightness of outboard motor locking pins during the course of the day. Carry a basic tool kit and spare sheer-pins and know how to use them.

Wear a life jacket. Never stand up in a boat. Stay seated. When changing places make sure that only one person moves at time. Remain in your place until your companion is seated. Only one person should be in charge and nobody argues with him. Don't get into or out of the boat until told to do so. If the boat is not fitted with boat-seats, don't use an all-purpose, portable one. Invariably, they alter the point of balance of the boat and make it unsafe. Don't drink and drive. Be safe, not sorry.

87.
Look Before You Leap

The most valuable lesson I learned when in the army in Southern Arabia was that time spent in reconnaissance is seldom wasted. This applies as much to fishing as it does to dealing with military matters. It has served me well over the years and freed me "frae monie a blunder and foolish notion".

There was not a lot of trout fishing in the vicinity of the Barren Rocks of Aden, but I knew somewhere that there was, in Kenya, so I decided to spend my leave there. I planned in advance, sending for and reading whatever I could find about fishing opportunities and suitable accommodation.

It took me a micro-second to settle on a hotel. Looking down the list, my eye was drawn to one entry: The Izzak Walton Inn at Embu, a few hours drive north-east from Nairobi. Seemed about right to me and it was. I spent two weeks fishing the small, deep streams that flowed down from the snow-capped heights of Mount Kenya (5,195m), and lazy evenings lounging in the garden amidst the scent of jacaranda trees.

For old times' sake, this afternoon, I typed the name of the hotel into my web-browser and up it came, large as life and still flourishing. I had found the hotel after a search that lasted a couple of months. My computer found it in about three seconds. Do the same today if you are searching for accommodation and good fishing. There never has been so much information so readily available at the touch of a button.

Nevertheless, finding a good trout fishing hotel in Scotland is not as simple as it might at first seem. In truth, in my experience, they are few and far between. What most anglers want from a fishing hotel is comfortable accommodation, decent food, knowledgeable advice, sound boats and reliable outboard engines, and a friendly place in which to swap stories at the end of the day with fellow guests.

These matters are personal and what is right for me may not be right for you. However, I unhesitatingly recommend the Scourie Hotel in North-West Sutherland (tel: 01971 502396), Inver Lodge Hotel at Lochinver (tel: 01571 844496), The Merkister Hotel, Orkney (tel: 01856 771366) and the Ben Loyal Hotel in Tongue (tel: 01847 611216).

I am happy to add another name to that list, the Overscaig Hotel on the shores of Loch Shin on the road between Lairg and Scourie. There has been a coaching inn here for many years and it is now under the ownership of Martin and Jan Fraser. (They have a first-class website and you can access it through http://www.overscaighotel.co.uk.) The hotel has been substantially modernised, boats refurbished and new Yamaha 4hp engines provided.

For the brown trout anglers, there is exciting fishing on Loch Shin, one of Scotland longest lochs, adjoining Loch a'Ghriama, the River Merkland and Loch Merkland. The average weight of trout is in the order of 8oz, but all these lochs are capable of producing much larger specimens. Best of all, perhaps, for those who like their fishing really wild, there is the possibility of exploring some of the remote lochs that lie in the hills to the north of Overscaig between Ben Hee (873m) and Carn Dearg (796m).

The Lairg Angling Club (http://www.fishing-highland.co.uk) also have boats on Loch Shin and fishing on Loch Craggie, considered by many to be one of the finest trout lochs in the north. Martin and Jan Fraser at the Overscaig Hotel (tel: 01549 431203) will be happy to help and advise.

88.
Head for the Hills

Some like their fishing rough. None of your namby-pamby, park-by-the-bank, step from the car straight into the boat for them. Unless the loch lies at the end of a four-mile long gut-busting hike it's not proper fishing. The more remote and wild the location, then the better they like it, regardless of the size or number of trout caught.

The Manager, my wife Ann, and I fall into this category, as well as into various nauseous peat bogs along the way. Once, hiking out to Loch Sletill in the Sutherland Flow Country, Ann sank up to her waist in a bog. I was ahead and didn't see the incident, but, fortunately our son, Charles, who, even as a youth was built like a tank, was on hand to rescue his mother.

Experience is the only certain antidote for such disasters. The more you walk the moors, the more you come to spot danger areas in advance. Caution is the watchword. Be safe, not sorry. But provided you take proper care you will come to little harm. The golden rule is to travel with a friend, rather than alone, and preferably with someone tank-built like Charles.

Scottish hill loch fishing is a multi-faceted joy. Not only does it take you into some of the most glorious places on Planet Earth, but it also keeps body and soul fit and trim. We rarely, if ever, see another soul during our expeditions: Our companions are the plants, birds and beasts of the moors and mountains: blaeberry, wild thyme, greenshank, eagle, raven, wildcat, red deer and otter, and, occasionally, brown trout.

Travel light and prepare carefully. All you really need is your rod and reel, nylon for making up casts and a few flies. A telescopic rod is ideal for the job. Daiwa and Shakespeare both make inexpensive, excellent telescopic rods. I have used one for years. They are first-class, light, easily transportable and able to cope with most of the wild trout to be found in our hill lochs.

Carry everything in a waterproof back-pack; fishing gear, spare clothing, whistle, torch, compass and map, food and drink and be comfortably shod. For more serious expeditions take along a lightweight tent. Obtain permission from the owner of the fishing before setting out and always let someone know where you are going and when you expect to be back.

Two of our favourite hill lochs lie to the south of Melvich in Sutherland, Loch na h-Eaglaise Mor and Loch na h-Eaglaise Beag (OS Map 10, Gd refs: 855590 and 862600); a six-mile round trip over a seriously boggy moor. There used to be boats on both lochs but they have gone now. I would be surprised if these lochs were visited more than a couple of times a year, but they hold marvellous fish; particularly Eaglaise Beag which, if you happen to be there at the right time, can produce specimen trout of up to and over 2lb in weight.

There are thousands of lochs to choose from, most of which rarely see an artificial fly from one season to the next. If you are not too comfortable about going 'solo' on such expeditions, think about visiting the Sheiling Guest House in Ullapool (tel: 01854 612947). Duncan MacKenzie, the owner, is an experienced hill walker and expert angler. He will guide you to some fine hill loch fishing on the craggy paradise peninsula that lies between Loch Broom and Little Loch Broom in Wester-Ross.

89.
Tibbie Shiels

Anglers like some lochs better than others for a variety of reasons, not all of them to do with whatever success or failure they experience when fishing them; I have had more blank days on East Loch Bee in South Uist than I care to remember and yet I still love being there. Loch Lanlish at Durness and Loch Heilen in Caithness will break your heart trying to catch the trout that they contain, but for me they are irresistible.

St Mary's Loch near Selkirk in the Borders is high up on my list of best places to be; more for its literary associations than for the quality of its fishing, although it can often offer great sport. The brown trout average in the order of 8oz, with a few much larger specimens, and there is a population of voracious pike and perch. Most of all, however, I value St Mary's for Tibbie Shiels Inn.

Isabella (Tibbie) Shiels, with her husband, Robert Richardson, and their family settled there in 1823. Robert was a mole catcher on Lord Napier's estate and when he died suddenly the following year Tibbie determined to support herself and her children by taking in guests. Thus a legend was born. Throughout her long life (Tibbie died in 1878 in her 96th year), the great and the good of literary society took Tibbie and her inn to their hearts and made it and her famous.

The 'giants' amongst her guests, all of whom enjoyed trout fishing, were Sir Walter Scott and his inner-circle of friends: John Wilson, professor of moral philosophy at Edinburgh University, Scott's son-in-law, John Gibson Lochart, James Hogg, the 'Ettrick Shepherd' and Thomas Todd Stoddart, author of the first book describing Scottish fishing: *The Art of Angling as Practised in Scotland* and published in 1835.

Wilson contributed to *Blackwood's Magazine* under the pseudonym of Christopher North and he wrote about their fishing exploits on St Mary's featuring James Hogg as 'The Shepherd'. One of the best ever angling put-downs that I have read is given by 'The Shepherd' in response to an over-boastful fisherman:

"Poo, that was nae day's fishin' ava, man, compared to ane o' mine on St Mary's Loch. To say naething about the countless sma' anes, twa hunder about half a pun', ae hundred about a haill pun', fifty about twa pun', five-and-twenty about fowre pun' and the lave rennin' frae half a stone up to a stane and a half, except about half a dozen, aboon a' weicht that put Geordie Gudefallow and Huntly Gordon to their metel to carry them pechin to Mount Benger [where Hogg lived] on a haun-barrow."

It was rumoured that Tibbie had a soft spot for James Hogg for towards the end of her life she is reported as saying, "Yon Hogg, the Shepherd, ye ken, was an awfu fine man. He should hae tae'n me, for he cam courting for years, but he just gaed away and took another." Hogg died in 1835 and during his last illness he was nursed by his wife and by Tibbie Shiels.

Tibbie was admired by all her famous guests: Sir Walter Scott, Robert Louis Stevenson, who was also a trout fisherman, the historian Thomas Carlyle, the poet William Wordsworth, Prime Minister William Ewart Gladstone and many more, and the inn that she established is as welcoming today as it was in the days when Scott and his friends fished St Mary's. A statue of Hogg sits on the hillside overlooking Tibbie's inn and the loch where he found so much companionship, pleasure and happiness.

For information about fishing and Tibbie Shiels Inn, contact tel: 07515 944361; email: info@tibbieshiels.com; website: www.tibbieshiels.com.

90.
Ultima Thule

Brown trout fishing in Shetland is spectacular; not only because of the number of lochs available – about 400 – and the quality of the fish that they contain, but also because of the sheer beauty of the surroundings. My wife, Ann, and I discovered this angling treasure many years ago and we have been returning ever since.

Shetland trout fishing offers something for everyone, from beginner to expert alike. There are easily accessible, excellent roadside lochs and other more distant waters where having a compass and map and knowing how to use them is as essential as having a fishing rod. A short sea journey from Mainland Shetland opens up even more angling opportunities on the adjacent islands of Unst, Yell, Fetlar and Whalsay.

The one thing that there is never enough of for the angler visiting Shetland is time, in spite of the long, glorious summer days when it rarely gets really dark. So to make the most of an angling expedition to the northern isles, plan your visit for the 'simmer dim' months of June and July.

Most of the fishing in Shetland is in the care of the Shetland Anglers Association and it is available to visitors for a £15.00 season ticket. This probably makes it the best value-for-money trout fishing to be found anywhere in Europe. Boats are also available on some of the lochs and the use of them costs £20.00 per week. Shetland anglers are very welcoming and always ready to help visitors with local knowledge on tactics and tackle.

For permits and further details, contact the Rod and Line Tackle Shop in Harbour Street, Lerwick (tel: 01595 695055) or speak to the association secretary, Alex Miller on tel: 01595 695903 during the day or tel: 01595 696025 in the evening. Essential reading is the book that the association publishes which gives details of more than 200 of the main lochs, as well as providing information about the patterns of flies used to tempt their fish.

Deciding where to start will be your only problem and to help you along the way here are a few of my favourite Shetland waters. Whilst nothing is certain in fishing other than uncertainty, they should provide you with a few good memories to store away in the dream-bank of your angling mind.

For a week's fishing, you should consider: Loch of Tingwall, step from the car into the boat; similarly, Loch of Benston, considered by many to the best Mainland loch; wonderful, shallow Loch of Spiggie at the south end of Mainland, from boat or bank; Loch of Huxter on the island of Whalsay with the chance of a specimen fish; the gem that is Loch of Vollister on the Island of Yell, a 30-minute walk across the moor from the road; and a wild day out exploring the lochs to the north of Ronas Hill (450m).

To make things easy for yourself, plan to stay with Marjorie and Gordon Williamson at Herrislea House Hotel near Lerwick. Gordon is one of Shetland's best known and most knowledgeable anglers and he will make all the arrangements required to ensure that you have an unforgettable holiday. Contact Gordon on tel: 01595 840208, email: herrislea.house@zetnet.co.uk. Make this the year that you begin an angling love affair with Shetland.

91.
The Road to the Isles

Take the 'Road to the Isles' this morning and enjoy a day fishing for wild brown trout amidst the hills of North Morar. There are eight lochs to explore and you will need OS Map 40, Loch Shiel, Scale 1:50,000, Second series to find your way round. These lochs are in the care of the Loch Morar Angling Angling club and at present no permission is required to fish them. However, as a safety precaution, you should contact the Loch Morar

Superintendent, Viv de Fresnes (tel: 01687 462388), before setting out to let him know where you are going and when you intend to return.

A good track starts south of Mallaig at Glasnacardoch (Gd ref: 675960) on the A830. This leads east and brings you to the north shore of the largest water, Loch an Nostarie after a hike of 15/20 minutes. Nostarie is about half a mile wide by half a mile long, but it leads through narrows to two further interconnecting waters, Lochan a'Mheadhoin (Gd ref: 693948) and Loch a'Bhada Dharaich (Gd ref: 696945).

Bank fishing all the way and excellent sport with a wide range of fish that weigh in the order of 8oz/10oz, as well as trout of up to and over 2lb in weight. A year or so ago a ferox trout of over 10lb in weight was taken, so treat every rise with respect. The wind will dictate from which part of the loch you launch your attack, but given the shape of Nostarie you should always find a comfortable place from which to fish.

A series of little streams enter the north-east corner of Nostarie and this is a good start point. Work round the finger-like promontory and into the bay with the small island. The south end of the loch, where it narrows prior to flowing into Lochan a'Mheadhoin, should also be carefully examined. However, in truth, as is generally the case when hill loch fishing, trout may be taken from all round the shoreline. Try to avoid wading as it only scares the trout out into the depths.

You will need at least a full day to do justice to Loch an Nostarie and its adjacent waters. This means, happily, that you must return to explore the lochs further to the east: Eireagoraidh (Gd ref: 720955) – do not attempt to wade here, it is dangerous to do so – and its satellite lochans to the south, Loch Mhic Leannain (Gd ref: 713949) and Loch na Ba Glaise (Gd ref: 715940). Eireagoraidh is accessed from Glasnacardoch track. Reaching the last of the two waters named above will tax lungs and limbs and you will definitely need a compass in case of adverse weather conditions.

There is one other water here, which can also provide good sport: Loch a'Ghille Ghobaich (Gd ref: 689940); three quarters of a mile north/south by up to 250 yds east/west. This is best approached from the A830 at Beoraidbeg (Gd ref: 677935). Follow the outlet stream from the road up to the loch, a distance of a few hundred yards. In wild weather, particularly when the wind blows hard from the east, you will find shelter in the lee of the hills guarding this loch.

Traditional patterns of fly work best, including Soldier Palmer, Black Pennell, Ke-He, March Brown and Butchers. I also find that sometimes crossing the fingers of the right hand can help as well!

92.
The Ides of March

Unlike poor Julius Caesar, wild trout anglers need not "Beware the Ides of March". For us, it is the beginning of the new season and the most welcome time of the year. There are, however, a few waters that don't open on 15th March, including two of my favourites, Watten and Heilen in Caithness. We have to wait until May 1st to fish them.

Early-season trout fishing can be savage entertainment. Some years ago The Manager, my wife Ann, and I fished Dunalistair Reservoir in Perthshire in late March. We were barely afloat when it began to snow. The friends we were with had more sense. They headed straight for the nearest pub. Ensconced before a roaring fire, they smiled when a local burst in and exclaimed, "You will never guess what I have just seen, two idiots fishing the loch!"

But some lochs and rivers can often provide excellent sport in the early days of the season. The day after our blizzard on Dunalistair we fished the River Tay upstream from Aberfeldy and had great fun. It was warmer, and, happily, there was a good hatch of March Brown which encouraged the local residents to rise eagerly to our flies.

Loch Rannoch, to the west of Dunalistair, can also be kind early in the season. It is particularly famous for large ferox trout and these can sometimes be caught in the early months when bank fishing in the vicinity of feeder streams; along the north shore at Bridge of Ericht, Killchonan, Aulich, and from the south shore at Finnart, Camghouran, Dall and Carie.

As a youth, I always started the season on the River Tweed, upstream from Innerleithen on a stretch of the river known as the Red Yetts. I can't remember ever having a blank opening day. The trout were always accommodating. When we lived in Northumberland, I used to fish the South Tyne near Bardon Mill on opening day. A wonderful pool below Hardriding House invariably supplied trout for breakfast.

In Caithness, one of the most productive early-season waters is little Loch Stemster to the north of Latheron on the A9. It is circular, which means that no matter from which direction the wind is howling, there is always an area of bank that is fishable. And I would advise bank fishing, rather than fishing from a boat. In extreme conditions you can always restore circulation by running on the spot for a few minutes.

My best opening day on Loch Stemster produced two trout each weighing about 1lb, and both taken on the same cast. I have a photograph, admittedly a bit blurred because it was snowing, to prove it. Another excellent early season venue is Loch of Swannay in Orkney. One Easter, at the north end of the loch by Costa Hill, whilst the rest of the family huddled in the car, The Manager strode off into a blizzard and returned half an hour later with a splendid trout that weighed just under 2lb.

The next day, whilst bank fishing Swannay from the west shore near Scruit, I hooked and landed two splendid fish, each of which weighed 1lb 8oz. But the trout that I remember most fondly was the 2lb fish that I caught in Loch Stilligarry on South Uist one April 1st. The rest of Clan Sandison had retired 'hurt'. I persevered. But scant praise did I get for my effort. My big son, Blair, simply snorted and said, "Just goes to show that it is not only anglers that are fools today."

93.
Willie Gunn

Some artificial flies catch as many anglers as they do fish and none more so than the Willie Gunn; to be Willie Gunn-less on a Highland stream is to be improperly dressed. I first met the real Willie Gunn when I was archivist for the Skerray Historical Association in North Sutherland.

Whilst studying the admission records for the village school, I spotted the name and wondered if it could be 'the' Willie Gunn? It was. Willie was born on 14th March, 1909 at Skerray Beg and I made a pilgrimage to the ruins of the croft house where his family lived and his father was a crofter/fisherman. This week sees the 10th anniversary of his death, in Inverness on 6th March 1996.

As a young man, Willie started work with the Forestry Commission, helping to plant the first commercial forest in Sutherland on the banks of the River Borgie in the 1920s. Thereafter, he tried farming, which he didn't like. He discovered his real love when he joined the staff of Sutherland Estates.

I met him after he had retired and living in Golspie. Willie told me about his early days with the estate: "Then I was into keeping and working with dogs and the shooting and it was just marvellous," he said.

I asked Willie about the origins of his famous fly. He told me that he had called at Rob Wilson's tackle shop in Brora one day when Rob had just taken delivery of 25 hair-wing patterns of salmon flies. They had been tied for him by an RAF officer, 'Dusty' Miller, who was based at Kinloss in Morayshire. Rob and Miller had been experimenting with variations of these dressings.

Willie examined the flies and then eventually pointed to one: "By gum", he said, "that looks bonny, if I had my choice that would be the one." To which Rob replied, "Then you must have it and we will name the fly after you."

During the course of a day on the River Brora Willie caught six salmon with the fly, and, the following day, a further four. News of the miracle fly quickly spread throughout the north and within a short space of time it had established itself as a principal weapon in the salmon angler's armoury.

Willie discovered fishing when he was on the Loch Choire Estate, a magical glen guarded by Ben Klibreck and the moorlands and mountains of the Ben Armine Forest. He fished for trout on Loch Choire and the River Mallart, a tributary of the Naver. It was on the Mallart that he landed his first salmon, a fish of 16lb.

Willie explained, "Although I didn't exactly lose all interest in trout, salmon just seemed to take over." His heaviest fish was a salmon of 28lb taken from the Bengie Pool on the Brora. Willie's fishing technique was based upon precision: he never fished out a bad cast. If it was wrong, he immediately corrected it.

Willie Gunn was a kindly man. Rob Wilson told me that he once inadvertently fished down a pool on a beat that Willie had for that day. When he realised his mistake, mortified, he apologised to Willie and asked, "Why didn't you say something, Willie?" Gunn replied, "That would never do, I didn't want to spoil your enjoyment."

The Willie Gunn is normally tied on tubes or as a Waddington: tag, oval gold tinsel; body, black wool or floss; ribbing, oval gold tinsel; wing, yellow, orange and black bucktail. No matter where you are in the world, the Willie Gunn will find you a salmon.

94.

Barra

It's that time of year again, when wild brown trout anglers' fingers begin to 'twitch'. The new season opens on 15th March and fishermen will be planning not only early-season outings, but also thinking ahead for longer, more serious summer holiday expeditions.

If you have to take into account the wishes of non-fishing members of your tribe, then I would like to suggest a location that will keep everybody happy; an adventure to a wonderful island where there is something for everyone, regardless of whether or not they are infected with the pleasurable pain of angling.

Barra is the perfect place to combine a family holiday with man's proper function in life, the removal of brown trout from their natural habitat. There are amazing, yellow-sand, near-deserted beaches, excellent hotels, guest houses and self-catering cottages set amidst a vibrant landscape that has remained largely unchanged for a thousand years.

I first arrived in Barra early one morning on the ferry from neighbouring

South Uist. Through the gathering dawn, Barra hills began to form; the stub of Ben Eoilgarry, Ben Erival, Verrisey and Grianan, sweeping up to Barra's highest peak, shapely Heaval. Then, suddenly, as the vessel turned north past Caragrich Island and Orosay, the stark black outline of Kisimul Castle guarding Castlebay.

A single road (the A888) circles the island and all the trout lochs are accessed from this convenient route. Most of the lochs lie within easy reach of the road. The only distant loch on Cadha Mor, a water reservoir has, I believe, been drained and is no longer fished. Loch Ruleos, Lochan nam Faoileann, Loch nic Ruaidhe, Loch na Catrach Loch an Duin contain modest-sized wild brown trout that weigh in the order of three to the pound, whilst Loch an Duin can sometimes produce the occasional sea-trout.

For serious sport, however, Barra has two other lochs, which, in my view are quite superb: Loch Tangusdale (also known as Loch St Clair) and its tiny neighbour, Loch na Doirlinn. Both of these lochs drain into Halaman Bay, which has what must be one of the most beautiful beaches to be found anywhere in the world.

I bank-fished Loch Tangusdale on a windy afternoon, starting at the south end near the ruins of the tower on the little island at the south-east end; built in the seventeenth century when a Barra Macneill married a Sinclair woman from Caithness, hence the alternative name for the loch.

Wading was not uncomfortable and as I worked down the south-west shore I rose and missed three fine trout that would have been 'worth the haudin'. At the north-east corner of the loch, where a small stream flows in from the shoulder of Ben Tangaval, a trout dashed furiously at my tail fly, a size 14 Silver Invicta. After a considerable struggle I managed to 'beach' it. The trout weighed 2lb 8oz, was well-shaped, gloriously red-spotted and in perfect condition. A wonderful prize.

North from Tangusdale I found Loch na Doirlinn. It is very weedy and there is barely enough room for a decent cast, but I had been told by a local angler that it contained trout of up to and over 5lb in weight. I have no reason to doubt the veracity of my informant, but I saw neither fin nor snout, although I was looking, hard, all the time.

Use OS Map 31, Barra, Scale 1:50,000, to find your way round. In

2005, fishing permits cost £2.00 per rod per day, £10.00 per week, and that covered all the lochs noted above. Contact: Barra Community Co-operative Ltd in Castlebay (tel: 01871 810354). For accommodation, contact the Western Isles Tourist Board office in Castlebay on tel: 01871 810336.

95.
Moray Firth Sea-Trout

Saltwater fly fishing is one of the fastest growing areas of our sport, particularly in exotic locations such as the Caribbean and Indian Ocean islands. However, nearer to home, along the Morayshire coast and down to Aberdeen, anglers will find plenty to keep them busy in the sea in the pursuit of seatrout at the mouths of burns and rivers. It is also a lot less expensive than jetting off to Mauritius or the Seychelles.

On the south shore of the Moary Firth, at Cullen, Deskford Burn, Broxy Burn and Glen Burn join and flow into Cullen Bay close to the famous Three Kings sea-stacks. Sport is very much dependent upon high water levels and your best chance of a fish is in the brackish waters after a spate. Contact Seafield Estates (tel: 01542 840777) for further details.

As a general rule, all along the north and east coast, where rivers and burns enter the sea, there is the possibility of catching sea-trout. It is also true to say that these fish put up some of the strongest fights imaginable. Hooking them can be a problem, however, because at that stage in their migrations their mouths are soft, so you will probably lose more fish than you catch when fly fishing. Check out tide times, two hours either side of low tide is about right, and always seek local advice before launching your attack.

Perhaps the most famous sea-trout fishery here is to be found in the four-mile-long Ythan estuary to the north of the Granite City, easily accessible from the A975 Newburgh to Peterhead road. In days past upwards of 2,500 sea-trout could be accounted for each season and although not so many are caught today, the Ythan is still one of Scotland's most famous seatrout fisheries. July is the prime month.

The Newburgh Fishings is the most productive part of the river. There are five beats, three of which are private, but day lets may be available for the other two. At ebb tide the water can be fished as though you are fishing a medium-sized river. When the tide is full, anglers fish from both boat and bank. For bookings, contact Mrs Audrey Forbes on tel: 01358 789297.

When fishing in the sea, be aware of the dangers involved in doing so. It is essential that you seek local advice. Beware of stumbling/slipping on underwater hazards. Be safe, not sorry. Remember also to thoroughly wash your tackle at the end of the day; sea water is highly corrosive. As to which flies, I suggest that you stick to tried and trusted patterns, our old friends Black Pennell, Teal Blue & Silver, Peter Ross, Silver Invicta and Silver Butcher. They work for me and I hope that they will do the same for you.

96.
Valentine's Day

I hope you all did the 'red rose and breakfast in bed' thing last Tuesday? If not, it could seriously damage your angling prospects. After all, no one likes to be taken for granted; least of all the long-suffering women that cheerfully wave us off on our multifarious fishing expeditions and who listen intently to our spurious tales of woe when we return.

Me, I'm lucky. The girl I married is and always has been an angler. I discovered this fact when we first started going out together and I used to recount to her stories of my derring-do with rod and line. OK, so I might have exaggerated a bit, now and then, but so what – I was deeply smitten and anxious to impress.

This ended one evening when we were sitting in a coffee bar in Auld Reekie. I had just finished describing how I had caught a 2lb brown trout from under the branches of a beech tree overhanging a pool near Peebles, when, without saying a word, she opened her handbag and produced a photograph. It showed a brown trout, with a ruler above it, and the fish looked to be much closer to 3lb than it was to 2lb.

When I asked where it had been caught my discomfiture was complete: it had been taken high in the Cairngorm Mountains in the days when the only way in was by hoof. I know that she still has that photograph, but it has never been mentioned again, at least not by me.

I have no doubt that one female angler will be more successful than any 10 men. Not because they are more proficient than we males, but rather because they are more persistent. When we men are sitting on the bank having a dram and swapping stories of the ones that got away and the few that didn't, they are still out there, catching them.

The most successful woman angler I ever knew was Mrs Tom Kelly. When I was a boy, she and her husband were my fishing mentors. They regularly fished Loch Leven and, to my utter delight, invited me to join them for a day; including providing a train ticket from Edinburgh Waverley and a taxi at the station to collect me and deliver me to The Pier.

Mrs Kelly used to sit in the bow, casting a short line, quickly drawing it back towards the boat, whilst her husband, like most men, cast to the horizon. She invariably caught most fish. On one occasion she took more trout to her rod that the combined catch of the Perth and District Angling Club, who were fishing a competition on the loch on the same day.

Some years ago I fished with Fiona Armstrong, another natural and successful angler; we shared a boat together on Loch Craggie near Lairg in Sutherland. I also had the great pleasure of meeting the late Conrad Voss-Bark, a hero of my angling youth, and found that his wife, Anne, was every bit as proficient with a trout rod as she was at running the Arundell Arms Hotel (tel: 01566 784666) at Lifton in Devon. And Grace Oglesby, the wife of Arthur Oglesby. If there were fish about, then these ladies would catch them.

If you have perchance forgotten St Valentine's Day, there is still time to rectify that mistake. It might cost you substantially more in cash than it would have if you had delivered the goods last Tuesday, but try to think of it as an investment. Well, at least if you want to be cheerfully waved off fishing for the rest of the season.

97.
Lights, Camera, Action!

Making an angling film that will please everybody is like trying to thread a size 28 fly onto your cast whilst standing blindfold in the middle of a thunderstorm. It can be done, but only with great difficulty; as is confirmed by the ever-increasing number of television programmes, videos and DVDs about fishing now flooding our way.

In them, there are anglers trying to be actors and actors trying to be anglers. Some are more hooked on entomology than they are on hooking trout, whilst others are more concerned with promoting and presenting fishing tackle than they are with promoting and presenting the magic of our well-loved art to those not so blessed.

Your correspondent has been involved in this circus on a number of occasions; most famously, I suppose, with Paul Young in *Hooked on Scotland*, when I caught a trout by singing an excerpt from George Frederick Handel's *Messiah* to make it rise. Honest. That is how it happened, nothing was faked or prepared and no one was more surprised or astonished when it worked than I was, other than our sceptical producer, Ricky Walker.

The new DVD about fishing for ferox trout that landed on my desk the other day doesn't claim to be that elusive masterpiece that makes everyone happy, but it is well done and packed with information about this amazing species. It features Aberdeenshire anglers Scott Park and Mike Parker hunting for ferox in the Great Glen. The DVD, *Wild Trout Wild Places*, is available from Somers (01224 210008) and Smiths (01224 625161) and costs £14.99. You should also be able to buy it online on www.amazon.co.uk.

Ferox trout are the descendents of fish that have lived in northern waters since the end of the last Ice Age. Two Swedish lakes, Vattern and Mjøsa, have produced ferox trout that weighed 48.4lb and 50.6lb and some of these huge fish can live for more than 20 years. In Scotland, ferox can be found in most of our deep lochs, such as Lomond, Tay, Rannoch, Awe, Ericht, Loyne, Ness, Morar, Sionascaig, Assynt and Loyal. The heaviest caught in Scotland was taken from Loch Awe on 15th March 2002 by Brian Rutland. The fish weighed 31lb 10oz and Scott and Mike's DVD includes an account of its capture.

I once nearly fished for ferox. A few years ago, Ballantine's whisky decided to try to break the British record for a rod and line caught brown trout and I was invited to join the team. The venue was to be Loch Quoich, where we would fish, continuously, in relays for 48 hours. I opted out. After all, I had never fished for ferox before whilst there were others, much better qualified than I was to do the business. At the time, though, it hurt, thinking about all those drams that I would be missing. The attempt failed, but ferox were caught and the 'water of life' was, I am told, great.

The 'guru' of ferox fishing in Scotland is Ron Greer, an unashamed conservationist and remarkable personality. Ron's background as a freshwater biologist includes 20 years' experience of studies on Arctic charr (the primary prey species of ferox) and brown trout, together with 10 years' specialisation on angling for specimen wild trout. His book, *Ferox Trout and Arctic Charr*, published in 1995 by Swan Hill Press, is essential reading for anyone thinking about fishing for ferox. Get a copy through your library, or do a book search on Amazon or Abebooks. Thus armed, with the DVD and the book, all you ever wanted to know about the aquatic 'wolf' from the Ice Age will be revealed.

98.
An Adventure

I had a call from an angler the other day asking for advice about where to find a fishing 'adventure' for himself and his young son; preferably remote, involving a walk, but not too far for little legs and with the certainty of catching wild brown trout.

Happily, I am experienced in these matters having brought up our four children in the art of angling; or, as the Chinese have it, 'brain-washing'. I make no apology. Giving little ones a love of fishing is more valuable than putting money in the bank for them: money comes and goes but a love of fishing brings with it a lifetime's pleasure.

Scotland is well-blessed with such locations and nowhere more so than to the north of the Great Glen amidst the wilds of Inverness-shire, Wester Ross, Caithness and Sutherland. Further afield, in the Western Isles, Orkney and Shetland, are many more fishing venues where the only disturbance will be the sound of loch water lapping on the shore and the call of curlew as you return from the hill.

The most important aspect of these expeditions is to be well-prepared. You must carry a compass and map and know how to use them. Be properly clothed to cope with whatever the weather brings. Travel light: rod, reel and line and a few flies are all that you really need. Tell someone where you are going and when you expect to return.

One of our regular haunts when we lived in Caithness was Loch Ruard (OS Map 11, Thurso & Dunbeath, Gd ref: 142430). It lies in the Flow Country about two miles west of the Latheron/Thurso road. Park at Gd ref: 178437. At the halfway point, at Acharaskill, make sure that you continue on the right bank of the outlet stream from the loch, not the left, which is a nightmare tramp.

As you approach the loch you may be tempted to angle across the heather to save distance. Don't. It is boggy and difficult. Stay on the track until you reach the shore of the loch then turn left to find the old boathouse. Just to the south of Ruard is dark Loch Dubh. To the best of my knowledge it is fishless; if there are trout there then they keep very quiet about it. Personally, I have never seen so much as a snout above the surface.

Ruard is shallow and approximately one mile north/south by up to a few hundred yards wide. A boat may be available, but bank fishing is just as rewarding. The north and south ends tend to be weedy and the most productive fishing area is the west side, from either boat or bank. Most standard patterns of Scottish loch flies will do the business and the trout average in the order of 8oz, although I have had a few fish of over 1lb in weight.

The principal delight here, however, apart from fishing, is the surrounding wildlife. I remember one afternoon, fishing with my wife, Ann, when the trout suddenly stopped rising. Ann 'nodded' to me, looking ahead. Just off the bow of the boat was an otter. He was lying on his back with his front paws crossed on his chest, examining us critically. He dived, and resurfaced to swim slowly round the boat so close that I could almost have reached out and stroked his head. Which I dearly wanted to do. It was a never-to-be-forgotten moment. This is what true adventures are all about.

99.
Durness and the Parph

One of Scotland's senior anglers, Walter Hepburn from Fochabers, and I recently shared memories of fishing on the Parph Peninsula and the famous Durness Limestone lochs. Walter's best trout was a 5lb 8oz fish from Loch Caladail and one of his most memorable evenings was spent sea-trout fishing on the Kyle of Durness when he and his wife, Olive, caught eight fish weighing between 2lb 8oz and 4lb.

However, the Durness limestone lochs are not for beginners and I have had more blank days there than I care to remember. But they offer such an outstanding angling challenge that they draw me back time and again, and, when conditions are right, there are few finer places to fish in all of Scotland.

My favourite Durness loch is Lanlish, although it often drives me to distraction; seeing huge fish head-and-tailing and being unable to tempt them to take any of my flies. The loch is fished from the bank and the water is crystal clear.

I remember, when fishing there in the simmer-dim of a warm June night, hearing the magical, electrifying sound of seriously large rising trout. The heaviest fish taken from Lanlish weighed over 14lb and this magnificent trout used to be displayed amongst the amazing display of glass-case specimens in the old Cape Wrath Hotel.

Less well known are the trout lochs of the Parph Peninsula, accessed via the ferry across the Kyle of Durness from Keodale to Daill. The Cape Wrath Lighthouse bus passes close by two of them, Lochan nam Breac Buidhe and Loch Inshore. Both are guaranteed to restore your angling confidence if the limestone lochs have been unkind. They contain good stocks of pretty little trout that are not too particular about which flies they take.

For the angler who enjoys an adventure, greater pleasure lies to the south of this road amongst a series of lochs that drain into the Kyle from the east shoulder of Fashven (460m). Approach them by hiking up the Daill River, which, in itself, can offer sport with salmon and sea-trout. The first of these lochs is Loch Bad an Fheur-loch and a mile on is Loch Arigh na Beinne, which is your best chance of encountering salmon.

Half a mile west from Arigh na Beinne is Loch na Gainmhich, the headwater loch of the Kervaig River; mainland Scotland's most northerly salmon stream that flows north for four miles to reach the sea across a splendid beach to the east of Cape Wrath. It is only really fishable after heavy rain, and then only in the section between the road and the sea.

Loch Keisgaig, west again from na Gainmhich, is reputed to hold the largest trout of all the Parph waters. I have had reports of fish of up to 3lb being taken. The only problem is getting there; it is a hard tramp of nearly three miles south from the Cape Wrath road and, unless you propose to camp out, you need to link up again with the bus on one of its return journeys from the lighthouse to Daill.

Also be aware that the Ministry of Defence use the Parph as a live bombing range, so when the boys in blue are flying by much of this area is out of bounds to members of the public, including intrepid piscators. Whatever, if you are looking for something different for the trout season that lies ahead, and for a memorable angling experience, make your way to the Parph and you will not be disappointed.

100.
Garvault and Badanloch

The most tortuous road in the north is the B871 between Syre in Strathnaver and Kinbrace in Strath Helmsdale. I travelled that way last Saturday to the River Helmsdale where the proprietors had opened their stream, free of charge, for the first four days of the season.

It was a good-to-be-alive morning. The sun shone on gold-burnished moorlands. I stopped to photograph a group of stags silhouetted on the crest of a hill. To the south, Loch Rimsdale, Loch nam Clar and Loch Badanloch sparkled silver and blue and I remembered the many happy hours my wife, Ann, and I had spent exploring this area.

There is enough trout fishing here to last a lifetime; easily accessible waters like the three named above, and many more at the end of an invigorating tramp into the wilderness, such as Coire nam Mang and Druim a'Chliabhain that lie in the flows between Ben Griam Beg (580m) and Ben Griam Mor (590m).

One glorious expedition started from the Garvault Hotel (tel: 01431 831224). We followed the Coire Nam Mang track, but, where it turns east, continued north for three miles to reach Caol-loch Beag and Caol-loch Mor. After fishing them we headed south-west for a mile and a half to find Loch Sgeireach. All of these lochs hold wonderful little trout that fight with great dash and spirit.

We returned to the hotel round the south shoulder of Beinn a'Mhadaidh (403m) in the midst of one of the most horrendous downpours that I have ever experienced, much enlivened by an accompanying gale. But that day still remains in the fishing-bank of our minds as being one of our most memorable.

Apart from the lochs, great sport can also be had in the small burns that flow south to feed the Badanloch waters. I first discovered them when I was a boy, fishing with an old greenheart rod. My parents had dropped me off at the bridge over the Allt Lon a'Chuil burn and gone on to fish Loch Rimsdale.

I stalked the burn north to as far as Loch Molach, following its twists and turns with increasing delight and pleasure. There had been heavy rain, so the burn was full. The pools where the flow changed direction produced brown trout of my dreams, wonderfully marked, red-spotted, yellow-bellied fish of up and over 1lb in weight.

Another unforgettable memory of that first visit to Strath Hemsdale and Strathnaver is of Father's car breaking down one night somewhere between Garvault and Syre. We huddled in the back whilst Dad did things under the bonnet, but to no avail. Just as all seemed to be lost, including Father's temper, a man appeared out of the gloom on an old bicycle, followed by an old sheepdog.

He stopped and asked if he could be of assistance. He then disappeared under the bonnet and, eventually, called on Dad to "give it a turn". The engine sprang to life. I still remember Father trying to thank our benefactor, who refused all offers of payment for his help. "You must be a mechanic," Father said. "Oh no," came the reply, "I'm a Mackay from Strathnaver."

101.
Ice Cold in Sutherland and Caithness

Nothing could be less like fishing weather. As I write a huge gale accompanied by horizontal rain howls round our cottage here in North Sutherland. Nevertheless, and regardless of the weather, a battalion of anglers will be braving the elements today as they launch their assault on the famous Helmsdale River.

For the third year in succession the proprietors have opened the whole of their river for the first four days of the season (11th/12th/13th/14th January) free of charge to all-comers. All that is required is to turn up and register to be allocated a beat.

My experience of the early months of the season is dominated by memories of frozen rod rings, frozen fingers and, well, I suppose, just about frozen everything. I'm not sure if this can be described as pleasure. Perhaps the phrase 'savage entertainment' is a more appropriate way in which to describe these occasions.

When I was not as old as I am now, and living in Edinburgh, I could hardly wait for 1st February, the opening day on Tweed. I was always there at first light and although I never connected with a fish, the anticipation of doing so kept me warm all day. But I saw salmon, silver bright, surging upstream, and once helped to land one.

The salmon was far more experienced than the angler and, eventually, above and beyond the call of duty, I waded in waist high and hoicked the fish onto the bank. "My first salmon!" he exclaimed, serving himself with a dram from his hip flask. He shouldered the fish and marched off without as much as a thank you, leaving me still in the river.

It took me years to hook my first spring fish. Apart from Tweed, I did the snowman bit in streams that should have been kinder – the Ayr, Tay, Dee, Spey and Kirkaig – but to no avail. I thereafter determined that it would be wiser, and a lot more comfortable, to wait until the darling buds of May began bursting before taking out my salmon rod.

When we moved to Caithness, however, the reputation of the Thurso as a spring salmon stream persuaded me to try again. Consequently, on a cold, blustery March morning I found myself standing on the bridge at the top of the river where it flows out of Loch More, wondering if this was going to be any different from the other days that I had spent freezing in pursuit of salmon.

A cheery voice called "hello" and I turned to greet Eddie McCarthy, the Thurso River superintendent. "Have a cast in the pool below the fish ladder," he advised. I cast into the flow and immediately hooked a fish. It seemed to me that I played that fish for an eternity, trying to prevent it from running under the arch of the bridge. Eventually, the fly came loose and I felt that special agony that every angler knows at these times.

Nevertheless, I will never forget that moment or the sheer, unbridled power of the salmon on the end of my line. I very much hope that the anglers plying the Helmsdale will experience the same thrill that I did with my Thurso fish, without, of course the pain that accompanied losing it. If you are up for it, there are still two days to go. Why not drag out the thermals and head north now!

102.
Rum Do on Rum

Most of the anglers I know value what is not in the water as much they do what is. They are environmentalists at heart and understand the importance of preserving every aspect of Scotland's wild landscape and its precious flora and fauna. Fishing might be the primary reason for their interest, but they are just as fulfilled by being at one with the other creatures that surround them during their angling adventures.

Few places more completely meet this purpose than the Island of Rum, one of the Small Isles of the Inner Hebrides, owned and managed by Scottish Natural Heritage. The island is an important nature reserve and was the site for the reintroduction of sea eagles to Scotland. It is also a centre for red deer research by Edinburgh and Cambridge Universities; one of the longest-running studies of this kind in the world. Rum hosts a remarkable array of wildlife including otters, feral goats, seals, seabirds, as well as lochs blessed with wild brown trout.

Find Rum on OS Map 39, Rhum & Eigg, Scale 1:50,000. Before anyone comments on the spelling, 'Rum', or 'Rhum', it should be noted that there never has been an 'Rh' prefix in the Gaelic language. The correct spelling is Rum. Victorian and Edwardian lairds tended to introduce a soft 'h' into Gaelic in the mistaken belief that it improved the words they so afflicted; such as in 'ghillie', which should be 'gillie'. Well, that is my understanding of these aberrations.

Rum is a dramatic island, mountainous and wild. The highest peak is Askival (812m) and the sole means of transport for visitors is by Shank's pony. You will need to be reasonably fit to reach the fishing locations and be prepared to encounter all kinds of weather along the way; Rum has one of the highest rainfall levels in Scotland. Accommodation is limited to Kinloch, where the ferry arrives in Loch Scresort on the east coast, and is primarily centred on the magnificent sandstone pile of Kinloch Castle (tel: 01687 462037), although there is also a camp site nearby (tel: 01687 462026).

A number of tracks and nature trails lead west and south from Kinloch and the trout lochs can be accessed from them. To avoid disturbing the nest sites of birds, not all of the lochs are available for fishing. However, there are more than enough to keep you busy and exercised during your visit: a'Ghillie Reamhra (Gd ref: 345997), Long Loch (Gd ref: 364985), an Dornabac (Gd ref: 355975), Coire nan Grunnd (Gd ref: 406958), Fiachanis (Gd ref: 357947).

In all of these waters, expect to catch pretty little trout, but look out for larger fish in Loch Fiachanis, a 12-mile hike there and back, and in Coire nan Grunnd, a vigorous five-mile round trip. Salmon and sea-trout can be found, sometimes, depending on water levels, in the Kinloch River, and in the lower reaches of the Abhainn Rangail in Glen Harris. Adjacent to the mouth of the Raingail is a large mausoleum, built to hold the mortal remains of the Bullough family, previous owners of the island and who built Kinloch Castle.

Bank fishing all the way and remember to avoid wading because it only scares the fish out into the depths. Offer the residents standard pattern Scottish loch flies such as Ke-He, Black Pennell, Solider Palmer, March Brown, Silver Butcher and Silver Invicta. It is important to check access details before setting out to fish. They can change, depending on the varying needs and requirements of managing the island. Do so by contacting the Reserve Office (tel: 01687 462026) and enjoy good sport in the grandest of surroundings.

103.
New Year's Eve

Anglers appreciate New Year's Eve. We have a lifetime's fishing to look back on whilst being comforted by the thought that the next season is just about to begin. The best way to enjoy it is in front of the fire with your fishing partner; in my case, with my wife, Ann, The Manager, my fishing companion for, well, more years that either us would care to confess.

They have been wonderful years, full of happy days on river and loch, mountain and moor, when sometimes we caught a few and more often than not we didn't; tramping to remote lochan with the children line astern across the hill, the youngest, Jean, invariably on her big brother Blair's shoulders. Where have those years gone?

Years were 'proper' when I was a younger. Now they fly by as though on wings. When The Manager and I were hitched we lived in a cottage with no electricity or water. We collected water from our next-door neighbour,

Jeannie Simpson. She was a marvellous old lady who used to say, wistfully, "Things are no' the same the day." And of course she was right.

A little river ran by our cottage and in the evening I would sit on the bridge watching a trout of about 1lb feeding in the shade of an overhanging willow. I coveted that trout. Eventually, I devised a cunning plan. I lowered a size 16 Greenwell's Glory through the branches to its lair on a length of nylon.

The trout took and I hauled him up to my waiting hand and transferred him to a bucket of water that I had brought for that purpose. Triumphant, I carried the bucket and fish back home to show Ann how clever I had been. "Put it back, now!" she said. "You should be ashamed of yourself. Never do that again." Chastened, but wiser, I did as I was told.

Over the years, catching fish becomes less important. Just to be out and about with a fishing rod is sufficient unto itself. Well, that's how it has been for me. If we let it, angling can take us into a complete world of sheer delight; peopled by otter, wild cat and red deer, golden eagle, peregrine and buzzard, bright with wild flowers and the scent of bog myrtle and heather.

I remember the days we spent at Poca Buihde, a bothy at the south end of Loch na h-Oidhche in Wester Ross. We walked south again from the bothy across broken sandstone slabs and rough moorland to fish little Loch nan Caber below the majestic north face of Liathach (1,045m), the 'grey one', and sat outside Poca Buidhe in the evening, listening to the silence.

And I also remember the feeling of despair one September when I lost a salmon fishing on Loch Hope. Entirely my own fault, in spite of what I said to my son and grandson who were with me at the time, allegedly 'managing' the boat as I played the fish. It weighed at least 12lb, or, as my son Blair said, "Yes, Dad, and no doubt at least 20lb by the time we get you home."

I wouldn't change anything about my angling life, not even losing that 7lb wild brown trout on Loch na Moine, or any of the other ones that have got away. Fishing, particularly fishing for wild brown trout, seems to me to encompass all that is finest about my native land. I think that it brings out the best in us. Happy New Year when it comes!

104.
One Hundred Not Out!

The Orkney Trout Fishing Association (OTFA) is celebrating its first century. The Association was founded on November 8th 1905 and this milestone has been marked during 2005 by various events, including a weekend festival of fly fishing on Loch of Harray when 40 anglers caught some 700 trout (most of which were released) and a Centenary Open competition, also held on Loch of Harray.

A short history of the association was planned, but this has grown into a major work, *Soft Winds and Sudden Squalls – Orkney Trout Fishing – the first 100 years*, authored by Ian Hutcheon, Malcolm Russell, Alan Shearer and Stewart Wood. Full details can be found at www.orkneytroutfishing. co.uk and all the proceeds from the sale of the book when purchased through the website will go to association funds.

I found Orkney many years ago on a family holiday when we stayed in a cottage at Backakelday overlooking Scapa Flow. Three brothers and three sisters, the Isbister family, owned the farm and I fondly remember their patience and kindness to two small boys who plagued them with endless questions and wanted to do everything and see everything around their farm.

Since then, my wife, Ann, and I have returned often to Orkney with our own children. Now, as they have grown up and left to form their own angling clubs, we still regularly cross the broken waters of the Pentland Firth to explore the moors and cliff paths, the wondrous monuments, and, of course, to fish for some of the most beautiful brown trout in all of Scotland.

Much of the credit for preserving the quality of Orcadian trout fishing is due to the work of the OTFA over the past 100 years. They have grown into a vibrant, focused, organised and committed association with a membership of some 600 local and visiting anglers. The trials and challenges faced and overcome by the association during that period are well recorded in *Soft Winds and Sudden Squalls* and if you are looking for an angling book for Christmas, then this is the one to buy.

Apart from establishing and maintaining excellent lochside facilities for anglers – boathouses, mooring bays and the like – the association has a hatchery programme that was started in 1929 and thrives mightily today. It is headed up by George Skea and Peter Miller, who have progressed to growing fish on to fingerling size, thus thereby greatly enhancing their chance of survival when they are released into the wild.

Much has been done to introduce trout to waters previously devoid of fish, particularly in the North Isles: Lochs Bea, North and Roos in Sanday, Meikle Water in Stronsay, and Burness Water and Saintear in Westray. The results of this work have been outstanding. The fish have grown mightily and some are caught that weigh over 6lb. They do not give themselves up easily, but if you relish an angling challenge, then this is where to go to try to catch your trout of a lifetime.

Perhaps the most significant aspect of the work of the OTFA is that those involved give of their time and knowledge on an entirely voluntary basis. They seek nothing other than to promote and protect their fishing, for their own benefit and for the benefit of generations to come. We never forget this when we visit Orkney and no matter how long or short our visit is, Ann and I join the association. Do likewise and support the efforts of a most remarkable group of anglers. Happy 100th, OTFA!

105.
A Day on the River Findhorn

Before the Royal Highland Show found a permanent home at Ingliston near Edinburgh, it used to travel to a different location each year. The last time it was in Inverness, I was there and managed a day off to fish the River Findhorn with my father and one of his friends. Whilst Dad and his chum lashed away to no avail in search of salmon, I caught half a dozen excellent brown trout, the largest being just over 2lb in weight and I have held the river in high regard ever since.

The Findhorn rises in the Monadhliath mountains and the principal spawning areas lie in the hills above Tomatin. Downstream from Dulsie the river flows through a long, steep-sided gorge past Randolph's Leap, named after the mighty jump of a clansman fleeing from his pursuers. The character of the river embraces a wide range of habitats from wild moorlands above Tomatin, down to Drynachan and the wonderful natural woodlands surrounding the gorge, then the gentle arable fields of the coastal plain where the river enters Findhorn Bay.

Good sport on the Findhorn depends upon hard winters in the hills. As snow melts, fresh water is released into the river drawing fish in from the Moray Firth. The gorge acts as a temperature pool and holds salmon in the lower river until the water temperature rises above 42°F. Opening day is 11th February and the river closes on 30th September. This is a classic Scottish spate stream, no water, no fish.

Much of the best fishing is mountain goat country and, particularly in the 20-mile long gorge, anglers should beware of sudden floods which can raise water levels to a dangerous height very quickly. Most years produce upwards of 1,000 salmon and grilse with the autumn months being the most productive. The average weight of salmon is in the order of 8lb/9lb, but the heaviest fish taken in 2005 was a splendid salmon of 26lb, caught (and released) on the Forres Angling Association Water by Bill Bartlett.

A total of 1,281 salmon and grilse were accounted for during 2005 and river superintendent Albert Duffas told me that more and more anglers were adopting a policy of catch and release. "This season, 52% of the fish caught were released and we very much hope that this trend continues, and grows," he said.

Access to the river is generally available and is in the ownership of the sixteen estates through which it flows on its 65-mile journey to the sea. The lower part of the river, five miles of double bank fishing, is controlled by the Forres Angling Association. For information and contact details, type Findhorn River into your web browser. Also have a look at www.speycaster. net/river_findhorn.htm for Ian Neal's site which offers tuition and guided angling holidays that include fishing on the Findhorn.

The association water limits non-member rods to 10 per day and 10 per week. From February until May it is £20 per day and £100 per week, May to September is £30 per day and £150 per week. Given the quality of sport, this represents excellent value for money. In low-water conditions, which are not infrequent on the Findhorn, the association water can often produce better sport than some of the upstream beats.

For association water bookings, contact Ken Walker or Sandy McCulloch at the tackle shop in Forres (tel: 01309 672936). Arm yourself with Messrs Willie Gunn, Garry Dog, General Practitioner, Munro Killer and Stoat's Tail – and the usual amount of good luck needed when going salmon fishing – and enjoy your time on one of the north's finest salmon streams.

106.
Give Them a Ring

As sleigh bells start to jingle this Christmas, what do you give the angler who has everything? He probably already has enough tackle to fit out an army with rods, reels and lines, and more flies than there are days in a decade; the latest in thermals, wading jackets, waterproof drawers and hats ridiculous; even a top-of-the-range, heated, float tube with built-in drinks cabinet, laptop connection and GPS system.

Fear not, your correspondent has the answer! Ring tones for his mobile phone. What's smart about ring tones, I hear you ask. Well, these are ring tones with a difference and they are pure music to every angler's ear – the sound of a screaming reel; undoubtedly the must-have piscatorial accessory for 2006.

Angler's champion, Orri Vigfusson, chairman of the North Atlantic Salmon Fund, has teamed up with Salmon Reel Limited, a company headed up by Richard Hewitt, former chairman of the Farlows Group and Sportfish. The most famous reels in the world are made by Hardy Bros of Alnwick in Northumberland and Hewitt was granted access to their museum to record emotive sounds from their collection.

These include the Brass Perfect, the Fortuna and the Zane Grey because of their heritage and because of the outstanding quality of the sound of their check mechanisms. Richard Hewitt said, "Our offering also includes the famous brass-faced Perfect, the Field and the Silex Major, and to balance these we have included the Angel, a current production model with a much softer sound."

All the tones can be downloaded from www.salmonreel.com direct to a mobile phone. A simple, step-by-step guide explains exactly how to download the sound of your choice to all makes and models of mobiles. The Perfect, Fortuna, and Zane Grey tones will cost £5.00 each and every time someone buys the sound these famous reels make, £2.00 will go to the North Atlantic Salmon Fund (NASF). Other tones will cost £3.00 and Salmon Reel Limited will also make contributions to the NASF from these sales as well.

The NASF is at the front line of the fight to protect and preserve Atlantic salmon stocks. It has been the most influential and successful body engaged in this task; driven by the sheer energy, commitment and determination of its founder and chairman, Orri Vigfusson. The NASF has negotiated a succession of restrictions on high-seas netting of salmon, thus creating a vast, 'safe-haven' in the North Atlantic where salmon can feed and grow without human interference.

The NASF has also engineered the buy-out of indiscriminate, interceptory coastal netting stations, to ensure that salmon returning to their natal streams can do so without having to run the gauntlet of these nets. The most famous victory was the recent buy-out of most of the North-East of England drift net fishery; in days past it could take upwards of 100,000 wild salmon, fish attempting to reach east coast streams from the rivers Wear and Tyne in England to Scotland's big four salmon rivers, Tweed, Tay, Dee and Spey.

Orri Vigfusson said, "Salmon Reels are not only donating a large part of the money the tones raise to the NASF, but every time the tones are heard they will increase awareness of our sport and provide an immense platform for our efforts to restore stocks of wild Atlantic salmon." This year, for the angler in your life, give him the sound of a screaming reel – and help to protect and preserve the 'great leaper', *salmo salar*, the King of Fish.

107.
The Children of the Mist

The River Teith, the principal tributary of the River Forth, is one of Scotland's most attractive streams. It flows through the country of Clan Gregor, the outlawed 'Children of the Mist'; such was their notoriety that in 1603 the Privy Council in Edinburgh passed an Act ordering "the extermination of that wicked, unhappy race of lawless lymmaris callit the MacGregour".

My grandmother was a MacGregor, born in Callander, and I feel a special kinship with the broken lands of The Trossachs; its secret places, wild mountains and amazing array of streams, lochs and rivers all offering outstanding sport with salmon, trout and sea-trout.

When the headwater lochs of the Forth were impounded and their waters redirected westwards to slack the thirst of Glasgow, the Teith became the primary sporting river of the system. It rises from the hills surrounding Inverlochlairg, near the home of Rob Roy MacGregor, and the infant stream gains force in lochs Doine and Voil; hurrying by the Braes of Balquhidder as the Balvag River to reach Bonnie Strathyre and Loch Lubnaig.

As the Teith exits from Loch Lubnaig it flows past St Bride's Chapel and bursts over the Falls of Leny, gathering in the slow-flowing waters of Eas Gobhain from Loch Venachar before reaching Callander. The best of the fishing is from here downstream to where the Teith joins the Forth near Stirling, at Drip, watched over by the gaunt tower of the Wallace Monument.

The river is divided into eight beats, including Callander Town Water, Gart Estate, Cambusmore, Lanrick, Denston, Blair Drummond, Ochtertyre and Blue Bank. The season is from 1st February until 31st October with the peak months being in the autumn. Nevertheless, good sport may also be had in the spring, and summer brings with it a substantial run of grilse. There are brown trout and sea-trout, but they are largely left to their own devices.

The Cambusmore Fishings are factored by Jim Henderson of Country Pursuits in Callander (tel: 01786 834495; fax: 01786 834210). You will find more information on Jim's excellent website www.country-pursuits.com. Cambusmore is three miles downstream from Callander and the fishing is divided into four beats, each fishing either two or three rods, over 26 named pools.

This is good value-for-money sport, particularly the Syndicate offer of one day's fishing a week during each week of the season, 39 days in all, for £390 + VAT (2005 prices). Day tickets may also be available at between £25 and £60 + VAT per rod per day depending upon the time of year. One of the largest salmon taken from the Teith came from Cambusmore, a fish of 44lb 8oz landed in 1986. Another specimen salmon of 31lb was caught in 1997.

The four beats produced 186 fish this year with 25 of them weighing over 15lb and the heaviest a salmon of 25lb, caught on the fly by Strathaven angler David Colington. Cambusmore is classic fly water, with deep pools and inviting runs. The beats are well managed and easily accessible. Bankside vegetation is kept under control and there are fishing huts and rod racks on each beat.

Vary the size of your fly to suit water levels and offer them Ally's Shrimp, General Practitioner, Munro Killer, Stoat's Tail and Silver Wilkinson. Catch-and-release is mandatory during the spring months, but Jim tells me that of the 186 fish taken this year, more the 70% were returned to fight another day. Although spinning is allowed most anglers prefer to use the fly. There are few more pleasant places in Scotland to do so.

108.
One for the Pot

Poaching salmon is a Scottish tradition. The writer John Buchan immortalised the habit in his book *John MacNab*, the story of illegally taking a salmon and a stag during the course of one day, and in his fine poem about an angling friend, 'Fisher Jamie'.

My experience of poaching is limited, the first being when I fished the River Ayr near Mauchline on a cold spring day. When it started to snow I retired to Poosie Nancy's Tavern to thaw out over a dram. My companion was made of sterner stuff. He arrived with an 8lb salmon. "There you are, Bruce," he crowed, "that's how it's done."

Ten years after this event I discovered the truth. He had been hurrying pub-wards when he was stopped by a boy and asked if he wanted to buy a salmon. Opening his coat, the boy showed the fish, tied by string in a loop hung from his shoulder. The fish was bought and my decade of discomfiture followed.

The only time I have been offered an illegally caught salmon was at Lyne Footbridge on the Tweed, upstream from Peebles. It was a winter's day during the close season. We had been for a walk. A local asked me if I wanted to buy a salmon and, Mauchline-fashion, opened his coat to show the fish hooped round his shoulder. I declined the offer.

Another incident was when my father and I were fishing downstream from the bridge over the Tweed at Innerleithen. Well, I was. When I looked for him he was on the bridge, seemingly giving directions to a local angler about where the fish were lying in the pool below. On a particularly vigorous back-cast the angler's fly got caught in the branches of a tree and I, a youth then, shinned up to retrieve it.

What I untangled was no fly. It was a heavy, bare hook of about five to six inches in length. Obviously, the man was trying to foul-hook salmon, known as sniggering, and my dad was helping him. "What sort of fly is this?" I asked, handing him the hook. "It's a Scott Jock and none of your business," he replied. "Get away with you!"

Turning poaching into a business is unacceptable. Our east coast and south-west rivers are showing encouraging signs of recovery. More than 60% of rod-and-line caught salmon are now released. Those who engage in illegal fishing and poaching damage all the hard work that is being done to restore our rivers to their former glory. They deserve to feel the full weight of the law when caught doing so.

But I confess to having a secret admiration for the romantic notion of taking one of the Laird's fish without his permission. John Buchan's poem 'Fisher Jamie' exemplifies this notion. Jamie worked as a gillie on Buchan's estate on the Tweed and was known to have a 'poaching whim'. On the outbreak of World War I he went to France with Buchan but didn't survive. Buchan wrote the verses as a memorial to his friend.

> He thinks of Jamie in heaven.
> I picter him at gloamin' tide
> Steekin' the backdoor o' his hame
> And hastin' to the waterside to play again the auld, auld game
> And syne wi' saumon on his back
> Catch't clean against the Heavenly law,
> and Heavenly byliffs on his track
> Gaun linkin' doun some Heavenly shaw.

I don't know if it snows in heaven, but I am quite sure that if there are salmon there, there will also be poachers.

109.
The General's Loch

Two anglers were reading the morning papers in a North of Scotland hotel when news arrived that a deceased landowner was to be buried that afternoon. The front page of a *Times* twitched. After a pause, the one said to the other, "I don't suppose the General will need his loch today?" They folded their newspapers and made for the car park.

The hotel was the Scourie Hotel in North-West Sutherland, which Clan Sandison discovered, well, more years ago than I care to remember. In those days it was in the ownership of Ian and Mary Hay who carefully maintained the traditions that had made the hotel into one of the most famous angling establishments in Scotland.

We also met the late Stanley Tuer, one of the hotel's most respected boardmasters. With almost 300 lochs to choose from, a system was devised to fairly allocate fishing and it was managed by a senior guest, known as the 'boardmaster'. On arrival, the name of each guest is entered on a blackboard.

After dinner, the boardmaster offers the guest at the top of the list first choice of the following day's fishing location, and so on down the list.

In the morning, the name that was top goes to the bottom. If a guest leaves, his name is still kept on the board, as a 'ghost', so that the orderly progression up the board continues undisturbed. This prevents those in perhaps third or second position from being suddenly catapulted to the top, thus missing valuable second or third choices.

In times past, when the hotel had one bathroom, the boardmaster had the right to use it first. He was also known as Chief Fork; when guests sat round one table in the dining room, the Chief Fork was served first. When separate tables were introduced, to avoid the possibility of undue influence being brought to bear on him in regard to the allocation of the following day's fishing, the boardmaster dined alone.

The best of the Scourie fishing, at least it is in my opinion, lies in the hill lochs scattered round Arkle, Foinaven and Ben Stack. They are well provided with wild brown trout that vary in size from a few ounces right up to glass-case specimens; in May, Stuart Crooks had a trout of 8lb 12oz whilst Colin Munro took a fish of 7lb 1oz. A total of 4,631 brown trout were landed during the season.

Stan Tuer new every inch of the area, and, I often thought, every trout by name. Indeed, he had personally named many of them; small fish that he caught and then released into an adjacent lochan, to be left there to prosper. This is why, when fishing at Scourie, you should always have a cast or three in the little waters you meet along the way.

My wife, Ann, and I tramped many miles with Stan, a splendid companion and wonderful angler. The events surrounding our outings remain a treasured memory of fish that got away and a few that didn't, but most of all of Stan's unfailing good humour and courtesy. You will find all of these attributes alive and well at Scourie today.

Oh, and should I complete the story of the senior anglers' visit to the General's Loch? They returned fishless, which is probably exactly what they deserved.

110.
Care, Courtesy and Consideration

Anglers are traditionalists. There are things they always do and things they never do. For example, no member of Clan Sandison would ever go afloat without wetting the landing net first. It would be bad luck not to do so. A fish hooked anywhere other than in the mouth goes back, regardless of size. However, our most important and strictly adhered to family tradition is that Father must always be allowed to catch the first trout.

Many of the things that we call 'tradition' are in fact simply good manners. Like the aforementioned practice of letting me catching the first fish. But, in truth, particularly when boat fishing, they are common sense; habits evolved over the years to ensure fair play and communal respect for our companions. Never fish in your boat partner's water; always reel in when your partner is playing a fish; take your share of duty on the oars.

The late David Street, author of that wonderful book, *Fishing in Wild Places*, was one such individual. The last time I fished with David was on Loch Watten in Caithness, a couple of years before he hurried off to that great trout loch in the sky. It was cold, wet and windy and the fish were most noticeable by their absence. I eventually hooked a good trout and, with freezing hands, reached for the landing net. It had been extended, with the handle immediately adjacent to my left hand.

Professor Norman Simmonds, who wrote *Early Scottish Angling Literature*, was one of the best boat companions that it has ever been my pleasure to fish with. I met him some years ago, almost by accident, when I was bank fishing Loch Croispol near Durness in North-West Sutherland. The shoreline is rocky and wading uncomfortable. Two men were fishing from the only boat at the south end of the loch.

I saw them reel in and begin to row towards me. "Good morning!" called the bow rod. "Would you like to join us? Plenty of room and bank fishing is not very pleasant." That was my introduction to Norman and his fishing companion Angus MacArthur. If they were ever asked by a passing boat how they had got on, Angus would invariably reply, "Just the two, just the two," regardless of the number of fish they had or had not caught.

When a friend of mine was staying at Castle Sandison, I arranged for him to fish the Association Water of the River Naver. He returned home in the evening with a 12lb salmon, well pleased with his day. He told me that an elderly man had spoken to him, showed him the beat, pointed out where the best lies were, how to cover them and which were the most likely patterns of flies to use to persuade the fish to take. This kindly 'mentor' had also asked to be remembered to your correspondent. This was the last message I had from Angus MacArthur before he too left life to fish elsewhere.

If fishing is about anything other than catching fish, then it is about sharing our experience with those we meet along the way; about care, courtesy and consideration for others as well as for our quarry. I have been enormously lucky in my fishing lifetime to have found this in full measure everywhere that I have fished. Perhaps best of all in the many happy hours my wife, Ann, and I have spent on loch and river with our children, when, courteously, they invariably allowed me to catch the first fish.

111.
Foreign Airts

What's a poor angler to do, now that the season is over? Yes, we can mount a grayling fishing expedition, which can be cold hard work, or visit our local stillwater pond and fish for stocked rainbow trout, but if that is not your scene then choices are limited.

Increasingly, many of us take off to foreign airts in search of sport: the Falkland Islands, Tierra Del Fuego, the Argentine, Chile, New Zealand and Australia. All these places offer outstanding fly fishing for sea-trout and brown trout, particularly in South America where our winter is their summer.

A few years ago, I spent two Scottish winters (October through to April) in Chilean Patagonia, fishing on Lago Yelcho, about 1,000 miles south from Chile's capital city, Santiago, hosting fishing at a lodge on an island at the south end of the 26-mile long lake.

I was there as an employee, which was just as well given the cost of getting there as a guest. But it was a great experience and one that I enjoyed enormously. I met some super people and caught some super fish; trout of up to and over 5lb in weight were the rule rather than the exception.

However, anglers are travelling ever further afield in search of sport not just with salmonids, but increasingly for saltwater species, such as marlin, bone fish, trevally, triggerfish, milkfish, tarpon, sailfish, tuna, strippers, wahoo, dorado and the elusive grander and silver king, and others whose names I can barely pronounce.

And the world truly is their oyster: Bahamas, Belize, Ecuador, Tobago, Galapagos Islands, Angola, Papua New Guinea, Christmas Island, Costa Rica, Mexico, Panama, Seychelles, Venezuela, Fremantle, Tahiti, Hawaii and a host of other locations around Africa, Australia and New Zealand.

I have to confess that it is many years since I fished in the sea, and it certainly did not encompass any exotic locations; unless, that is, you consider the pier end at St Abb's in Berwickshire or the harbour at Newhaven in Edinburgh to be exotic? I did, in those days, and spent many happy hours fishing for, well, whatever happened to take my bait.

This is probably how many boys (can't remember girls being there) become hooked on fishing. During school holidays we often stayed at Kinghorn in the Wee Kingdom of Fife where my brother and I fished for flounders from a boat in the bay, and risked our lives in stormy weather hurling weighted lines from the rocks beyond the harbour wall.

The largest limiting factor when it comes to fishing in far-flung places is, of course, cost. A week in the Seychelles does not come cheap, or, for that matter, in any other locations mentioned above. Nevertheless, it is not a crime to window-shop what is on offer and you might perhaps be persuaded to award yourself a treat; or, even better, convince nearest and dearest that you deserve a special holiday.

Do an internet search by typing into your browser the place you fancy visiting linked with saltwater fishing. You could also have a look at some of the companies that offer packaged saltwater fishing holidays. Frontiers

International (www.frontierstravel.com) is a good place to start, as is Fish the World (www.fishtheworld.com).

There is so much information available about everything you ever wanted to know about saltwater fishing – species, tackle and techniques and costs – that by the time you have waded through it winter will have passed and the new season sprung. I can't think of a better way to spend the long, cold fishless months that lie ahead. Can you?

112.
Over the Sea to North Uist

On my first visit to the Uists we sailed from Uig on the Isle of Skye across the turbulent waters of the Minch; behind us, a distant prospect of snow-capped Cuillin, westwards, Lochmadday and the gentle hills of the Hebrides, Beinn Mhor, Corodale, Hecla and Eaval.

Even the most careful examination of the Ordnance Survey map can't really prepare the angler for the shock of joy at the vast number of freshwater lochs. Nearly a third of North Uist is covered by water and around every corner blue lochs beckon.

Almost no matter where you stop, within minutes you can be fishing. Roadside lochs and lochans abound, whilst a walk over the moors tempts you ever onwards, from one gem to another. Many of the lochs are such a wild scatter that on the same loch there seem to be an endless number of different lochs.

For instance, Loch Sadavay meanders in and out round headland and bay for a distance of 50 miles. There are hundreds of little islands, reputed to number one for each day of the year, and many of them are adorned with their own lochans.

One of the most exciting North Uist lochs, and perhaps my favourite, is Loch na Geireann. It is situated in the north of the island, close to the road and, like its near neighbours Scadavy and Fada, the shoreline of Geireann is crooked and wandering.

There are several islands on Geireann and on one of them, Aird Reamhar, Neolithic pottery remains have been found; indeed excavations yielded up so much that it is possible that the kilns on the island once supplied most of North Uist with crockery.

Geireann offers good brown trout fishing and the chance of sport with occasional sea-trout and salmon. Use OS Map 18, Sound of Harris, Scale 1:50,000 to find your way round. The loch can't be seen from the road, but park at Gd ref: 843737 and follow the track past the old hatchery building to find a boat mooring bay after a couple of minutes.

Boat fishing is the best way of exploring the loch which is two miles north/south by up to half a mile east/west. If you are going to encounter sea-trout or salmon, then you will most probably do so on a drift between Aird Reamhar and Eilean Glas, and in the bay to the east where the flow from Loch Ceardaich enters Geireann. Brown trout are everywhere and average 8oz, but there are larger fish as well so treat every rise with due respect.

For a special treat, visit the Geireann sea-pool, a three-quarter-mile walk north from where you parked the car. There are areas of soft sand, so, unless you are accompanied by a local angler, follow round the west shoreline to reach the pool. Find it at Gd ref: 846747 bounded by Rubha Glas to the west and Clett to the east.

Plan to start fishing about two hours before low tide and fish on until about two hours after the tide has turned. The rocks are seaweed-covered and slippery so take care. It is just possible to wade safely at the north-west corner of the pool. Offer them John Kennedy's famous Clan Chief, Loch Ordie, Black Zulu, Black Pennell, Silver Butcher and Teal Blue & Silver.

I have wonderful memories of this magical place; of clear, crystal water, surging through the gap in the rocks, bringing with it salmon and sea-trout that shatter the silence with their mighty leaping. If I were given but one place to fish in North Uist, then it would most probably be the Geireann sea-pool.

113.
Going to the Dogs

Man's best friend ain't necessarily so in a boat. It might ultimately depend upon the size of the dog in relation to the size of the boat, but in my experience the two are not really compatible.

Nightmares I still have about Heathcliff, my wife Ann's first Yorkshire terrier. We were fishing Loch Toftingall in Caithness when she made a particularly vigorous cast at a rising trout and inadvertently knocked the little beast into the loch.

You may not know this, but most Yorkshire terriers can't swim; at least none of the breed that I have had the misfortune to be associated with could. It was a damned close run thing, and I just managed to get the landing net under him as he was going down for the third and the last time – the only time the net was used that day.

Even proper dogs like my golden retriever, Breac, the Gaelic name for trout, could be a problem. I was with Kyle Laidlay, the Tomich Fishery Manager, on Loch na Beinne Moire in Inverness-shire, and had left Breac tethered to a post at the mooring bay. The boat was adequate for two large men, but not for two large men and a large dog.

Kyle was rowing. He was smiling and nodding at me as I sat in the stern. Looking behind, I saw Breac snuffling through the waves, swimming towards us. Hauling him into the boat was challenging and wet work. Breac did the same on Coal Loch, north of Altnabreac in the Caithness flow county and almost overturned the boat in the process.

Breac loved the water. When I was bank fishing he would parallel my progress along the shore. He did so at a distance from the bank that was in my preferred casting area. Eventually, I learned to cast ahead of him, and, honest, I often caught trout within a few feet of his black nose. The trout didn't seem to mind Breac's presence.

I concluded that we anglers were perhaps over-precious when it came to trying not to disturb our quarry. This view was almost confirmed to me when, a few years later, I stood on the bridge across the mouth of the Howmore River in South Uist.

Below me in the pool I saw about half a dozen sea-trout. The largest was in the order of 4lb, the smallest about 2lb. Breac dashed in and swam over to bark at me. The pool was not deep and his feet appeared to be almost touching the backs of the fish. They completely ignored this intrusion and remained resolutely in their selected positions.

I left the bridge and called Breac to 'heel'. Back on the bridge again, when I looked down, the sea-trout were still there. Congratulating myself upon having discovered a great angling 'truth', I turned to share it with Ann, who had arrived with the ever-faithful Heathcliff.

Before I could utter a word, Heathcliff had scampered down to the water's edge where he put barely an offside-front toe into the river. Instantly, the sea-trout fled. "Yes," said Ann, "and exactly what is this great discovery?" Heathcliff, his hairy face twisted into a white-toothed, hideous grin, leered up at me. "Nothing, really, Ann," I replied. "Nothing at all."

Heathcliff and Breac are no longer with us. Heathcliff is buried on the slopes of Ben More Assynt; Breac lies asleep with a view of Ben Loyal. And yes, I miss them both, but not necessarily in a boat.

114.
The Bathymetrical Survey

The end of another fishing season. Perhaps it's just my imagination, but seasons are no' the same as they were when I was a boy. They are not as long as they used to be. Unless you are careful you can miss whole chunks. September was here and gone before I noticed. And why is it that October through to March drags? It doesn't seem right to me.

This winter, I have decided to renew my acquaintance with Sir John Murray (1841–1914). I met him about 30 years ago when I was writing my first book, *The Trout Lochs of Scotland*, and he has been one of my heroes ever since. Murray produced what in my view is one of the greatest books on Scottish lochs ever written, *The Bathymetrical Survey of Fresh-Water Lochs of Scotland*, a monumental achievement that took him nearly 10 years to complete and finally published in 1910.

The survey was made possible by the generosity of Laurence Puller, a businessman from Bridge of Allan and a life-long friend of Murray. In the early years of the survey, Puller's son, Fred, worked with Murray, but drowned in 1901 whilst trying to rescue a young woman in a skating accident. Several hundred people were skating on Airthrey Loch near Bridge of Allan when the ice broke. Although Fred could have saved himself, he refused to abandon the woman and they both drowned.

I don't think Murray was an angler, but we are all in his debt. He surveyed a total of 562 lochs, charting their depth and identifying more than 700 species, including 450 invertebrates and nearly 200 algae. Twenty-nine of these species were described as being new. The deepest loch was found to be Loch Morar (1,017ft). Loch Ness held the greatest volume of water. Loch Awe is the longest loch in Scotland (25.47 miles), followed by Loch Ness (24.24 miles) and Loch Lomond (24.23 miles).

The maps are wonderfully detailed, giving a grid of the depths of the lochs surveyed. Murray chose the lochs on a common sense basis: "The only Scottish lochs left unsounded were those which had no boats on them, or to which boats could not readily be transported," he said. Many smaller lochs and lochans were excluded, but not all of them. For instance, Loch Setter in Shetland, and lochs Heilen and St John's in Caithness.

The Caithness lochs were of particular interest to me, given that I lived in Caithness then in a house overlooking Loch Watten. From the survey maps, I discovered that no area in the loch was deeper than 12ft, and that the average depth was about 8ft. Loch Heilen, one of my favourites, is only 5ft deep, whilst Loch St John's is a maximum of 6ft.

This knowledge is vital when it comes to planning the removal of trout from their natural habitat. On Watten, for example, no matter where you drift, from the middle to the margins, you will always be over fish. Knowing the depth is also useful on vast waters like Loch Morar and Loch Arkaig. If you know where the shallows are, you can adjust your drift accordingly and thus increase your chance of sport.

The Bathymetrical Survey was published in six volumes and is really only available in a reference library. Put aside a whole day to study them. After all, what better way is there to spend your time during the close season, than devising cunning plans for the season to come? For starters, log on to the website of the National Library of Scotland: www.nls.uk and follow the links. A treasure trove awaits.

115.
The Crooked Loch of Assynt

I discovered the Cam Loch and Loch Veyatie more years ago than I care to remember and I have never forgotten them. These wonderful Assynt waters offer just about everything that I hold dear in angling: wild brown trout, magnificent scenery, solitude and perfect peace.

They lie between two of Scotland's most dramatic mountains, Cul Mor (849m) to the south and Suilven (731m) to the north, and are accessed from the A835 Ledmore to Ullapool road near the old schoolhouse in Elphin. They are fed from the east by the Ledmore River from Loch Borralan and the Na Luirgean burn from Loch Urigill.

The collected flow streams from Veyatie into the Fionn Loch and the River Kirkaig, cascading over the 60ft-high falls at the head of the river before hurrying westwards down the steep-sided glen to reach the sea in Kirkaig Bay to the south of Lochinver.

Cam Loch, 'the crooked loch', is almost two and a half miles long by up to three quarters of a mile wide and is best fished from the boat. As the name suggests, there are myriad bays and fishy corners to be explored, particularly round Eilean na Gartaig in the bay where the boats are moored, near the cemetery.

Bank fishing is not really advisable because the water deepens quickly from the shore. Cam is over 100ft deep towards the west end. Remember this if you do go ashore. The bow of the boat may be resting on terra firma, but the stern could be over deep water. Always exit the boat from the bow.

Cam trout average 8oz in weight, but there are much larger fish as well, particularly if you use the old Scottish fishing method of trolling. One of the largest fish caught in recent years was a ferox of 16lb in weight, caught in 1993 by W. R. Clark from Gateshead.

If you do decide to bank fish, concentrate your efforts at the north bank at the head of the loch, where a stream flows in from between Creagan Mor (240m) and Meall na Braclaich (375m). Work eastwards from here, paying particular attention to where small burns tumble in to Cam.

Veyatie, Loch Cam's neighbour, is four miles long by up to 400yds wide and can often be wild and windy. Again, boat fishing brings the best results and is the most convenient way of exploring this superb loch. Pack spare fuel for the outboard, otherwise it's a long row back. Also, as with Cam, take care if you are tempted, or are forced by the wind, to bank fish. The water shelves quickly from the shore. Avoid wading. Be safe, not sorry.

Towards the head of Veyatie, before it narrows into Uidh Fhearna leading to the Fionn Loch, stop and have a cast in Loch a'Mhadail. In high water levels a'Mhadail is sometimes joined to Veyatie and it also holds some excellent trout. A fish of 9lb 8oz was caught here, on a Black Pennell, by an angler fishing from the bank.

Other flies that work well on both Cam and Veyatie include Ke-He, Woodcock & hare-lug, March Brown, Greenwell's Glory, Grouse & Claret, Kingfisher Butcher and Silver Butcher. Veyatie often has a good Mayfly hatch, towards the end of June and in early July, when dry fly fishing can produce excellent results as well as wet flies.

Much has changed in recent years in Assynt, with much of the land, and the fishing, now in community control. For details, contact Cathel Macleod at Polcraig Guest House in Lochinver (tel: 01571 844429). Cathel can arrange and advise on fishing on Cam and Veyatie, as well as on nearly 300 other trout lochs in the area.

116.
There is Always Hope

My wife, Ann, The Manager, and I invariably have a day at the end of September on Loch Hope. This year it looked as though the wind was going to defeat us but after a careful examination of forward weather forecasts we decided to give it a go last Saturday.

My first task on arrival at the mooring bay at South End was to bail the boat. It was full to the brim with storm water. I then returned to the car to pull on my waders, which is when I discovered that I had brought Ann's (size 7) rather than my own (size 12). I heaved them on and minced delicately back to the boat like a Chinese barmaid.

I couldn't really complain. I had organised our fishing gear and loaded the car. Nevertheless, it would have been kinder if my fishing partner had commiserated with me, rather than falling about laughing, her only comment being, "Don't worry, Bruce, you will be up and about again on all fours by tomorrow morning."

Task two was to get the boat to the water. The recent gales had blown it almost into the birch wood that borders the bank. Ann was brilliant. Not so much because she is physically strong, although she is, but because she is determined and a wonderful director of operations which is great news for my newly acquired hernia.

Having got the boat afloat, I set up the electric outboard and staggered down with battery for said motor. It was the first time that I had encountered the brute, and, believe me, it weighed a ton. With everything ship-shape, we eventually we made it across the loch to Beat 2 at the mouth of the Strathmore River and began fishing.

To be precise, I did start fishing, briefly; then spent 'some time' attending to my fishing partner's cast, which the naughty old wind had tangled. We were being driven onshore and I pondered my options: bring in the drogue, raise the outboard motor to avoid damaging the propeller on rocks, abandon Ann's tangled cast – which by this time had also caught me – row like hell to keep the boat offshore, or just pray.

I decided to abandon ship and threw myself over the side, collecting two boot-fulls of icy water in the process. I grabbed the bow of the boat and heaved it safely to terra firma. I was soaking, my own line was snagged somewhere under the boat and my feet were killing me. "Well, done," said The Manager, "a perfect place for lunch."

Did I mention that Ann had brought Hareton, her wretched Yorkshire terrier, with her? No, I didn't, sorry. I managed to free him from the soggy drogue and the landing net and carried him ashore. He recovered his customary ill humour after wolfing down a boiled egg and my finger will soon be better after he bit the hand that fed it to him.

In the afternoon, the wind got really worked up and we decided to head home. If we hadn't had the electric outboard we would never have made it across the storm-tossed loch. Even then, I had to row like a galley slave to help it along whilst Ann steered. With the boat secure, I humped the dread battery back to the car.

But it was a wonderful day and we did manage to catch four sea-trout, all taken on a size 12 Ke-He. Ann caught three and I caught the rest. Mind, if my feet hadn't been clamped in a vice, it might have been an entirely different story.

117.
Monymusk

In 1078 AD, King Malcolm Canmore rested at the Aberdeenshire hamlet of Monymusk whilst on his way north to quell yet another uprising in Moravia. Using his spear, he marked on the ground the outline of the church he would build there if granted victory over the rebels. There is a church on the site to this day.

One of Scotland's most important religious relics is the Monymusk Reliquary. This 7th century casket, said to contain a bone of St Columba, was carried before the Scottish army at the Battle of Bannockburn in 1314 to inspire the troops.

The quality of game fishing at Monymusk is also of outstanding interest and inspires anglers from all over the world to come and fish there. The Monymusk Estate fishings extend for a distance of some 10 miles and are booked through the Grant Arms Hotel (tel: 01467 651226); a comfortable and welcoming establishment built in the eghteenth century as a coaching inn.

There are 13 salmon beats with 24 pools. Beat rods are, generally, for one rod fishing salmon, the other rod for trout. However, beats 4, 5 and 12 are reserved for a single rod. Catch-and-release is encouraged and to preserve stocks all hen salmon taken after 30th June must be returned. The upper beats produce the best early-season sport, the lower beats are best during autumn months.

Monymusk also offers challenging brown trout fishing and has some of the finest dry fly water in Europe. The most successful patterns of fly are March Brown and Greenwell's Glory. These two good friends of fishermen account for most of the large trout caught and the best time to use them is in May and June, early morning and late evening.

Some outstanding baskets have been taken over the years, including trout of up to and over 3lb in weight. One of these was even caught by your correspondent, on a very hot, difficult fishing day. The trout was taken near Pitfichie in the shade of branches which overhung the bank. I got the fly there by sheer luck, having one last, wild cast as I nearly lost my footing on the gravelly bottom.

Today, as a conservation measure, the strict rule is that all trout under 12ins, or over 2lb in weight, must be returned to fight another day, and there is a bag-limit of six trout per day. As a further conservation measure, the salmon fishing season on the Monymusk water finishes at the same time as the trout fishing, 30th September. This prevents late-season salmon anglers from inadvertently hooking and damaging out-of-season trout.

My wife, Ann, and I were less than successful when we spent a happy day fishing Paradise Wood. Monymusk House, built in 1587, became the property of Francis Grant, Lord Cullen, in 1712. His son, Alexander, established a million trees each year over a period of 50 years, including Paradise Wood.

We parked our car near to the old mill and walked through a dappled day of sunlight and shadow amidst ancient oak and beech, loud with bird-song. When we decided to surrender, I took Ann's rod, to carry it home, but in doing so I drove a size 14 hook into her thumb.

Ann retired behind a huge beech tree. When she returned, the hook having been removed, she said, "Give me the rod, please, best if I carry it myself." Thinking back to the days of Malcolm Canmore, I wondered if he would have been quite so understanding?

118.
Magnificent Harray

The Loch of Harray is Orkney's largest and most popular freshwater loch and each season it produces several thousand trout. These fish are of a very high quality, silver and pink fleshed, marvellous to catch and to eat. Their average weight is in the order of 10oz/12oz but larger specimens have been taken over the years: a magnificent trout of 17lb 8oz was landed in 1964 and fish of up to 5lb in weight are taken most seasons.

Harray is six miles long by up to one and a half miles wide and encompasses an area of 2,500 acres. The loch is shallow and consequently warms up quickly so spring fishing can be spectacular. It all depends upon the weather. Trout may be caught throughout the whole loch and most anglers launch their attack from boats. However, bank fishing can be just as productive and, in high winds, one of the most rewarding aspects of fishing Harray is that it is always possible to find a sheltered corner from which to cast.

One of the most productive bank fishing areas is at the south end, close to the Standing Stones and Maeshowe. Fish round to the mouth of the burn that feeds Harray from the moors of Nisthouse and Heddle. In a west wind, make for Mill of Rango, close to the A967 and fish down past Whilliastane to Pontooth on Ness of Tenston. When the storm howls in from the east, head for Bigging and ply the shoreline southwards past Nistaben to Ballarat

House. There are endless bays, headlands and fishy corners all waiting for your well-presented fly and you do not need to cast far to be amongst them.

Afloat is a different matter. The loch is full of skerries, barely submerged rock outcrops. Most fish are caught round them, just as the water begins to deepen. Finding these feeding areas is not easy and my best advice is to seek local knowledge. The way to do so is by joining the Orkney Trout Fishing Association. The high quality of Orkney sport is maintained by the association who expend much time and effort in looking after the island's fisheries. Membership of the association allows visitors access to all the association sites on the major lochs and fellow members are always willing to guide the newcomer to the most productive drifts.

Merkister Bay, at the north-east of the Harray is a popular fishing area, but is shallow and can be downright dangerous in low water conditions if you are unfamiliar with the loch. Buoys mark the safe channel out from the jetty. Stick to it.

A highly productive drift can be arranged halfway down the loch, between Ballarat House on the east shore and Ness of Tenston on the west bank. The shallow bay of Ling Holms on the west shore, down to Bockan, can also often provide breakfast. As a general rule on Harray, if you can't see the bottom then you are probably fishing too far out; keep to the margins and shallows.

When Loch of Harray is good, it is very, very good and you could happily spend all your time on Orkney fishing this wonderful water. In my view, Harray is one of the finest trout lochs in the world, set amidst outstanding scenery and cared for by the most welcoming anglers that I have ever met.

119.
Arthur Wood's Dee Salmon

Ballater is a bustling little town on the River Dee and a favourite angling centre. But the most famous fish I remember seeing there was in the centre of town, rather than in the river: the cast of a salmon in the Country Wear tackle shop in Bridge Street. The fish weighed 42lb and was caught by

Arthur Wood on June 18th, 1926, landed by his gillie, Tom Macphearson of Invercauld Estate.

The town of Ballater was developed in the late eighteenth century when visitors came to sample the waters from the health-giving springs at Pannanich. Such was the popularity of the area that it was planned to extend the railway up the glen to Braemar. Queen Victoria was 'not amused' by the prospect of her royal peace being disturbed so the line was stopped at Ballater.

I had the privilege of meeting Tom Macphearson in the mid 1980s, when he told me that his brother was also a gillie and keeper on an estate by Loch Maree in Wester Ross. "In those days," Tom said, "we would go out on the loch and take 20 to 30 sea-trout regularly, grand fish of up to 14lb. The best fly was always a Red Spider tied on a size 10 hook." Sadly, because of disease and pollution from fish farms in Loch Ewe, those days have long since gone.

Tom fondly remembered Arthur Wood, probably the most successful Dee salmon fisherman. For a number of years Wood leased the Cairnton Fishings, one of the finest of the Dee's 45 salmon beats. From 1913 until 1934 Wood landed a total of 3,490 salmon there but he is best known as the inventor of the then revolutionary greased-line method of salmon fishing.

This technique was employed during low water and involved using a line, greased to make it float, and a small fly; quite the opposite of traditional tactics then used on the Dee. Wood's success with the new method was instantly publicised and brought him great notoriety. For miles around, anglers followed suit, fishing a greased line with a small fly called the Blue Charm.

But not everyone agreed. Jimmy Ross, who worked on the Dee when he was a young man, also met Wood and he told me: "I knew his gillie and used to see him in the pub at nights, so I asked him about all these salmon being killed on a wee Blue Charm. 'Don't you believe it; it was a great big Jock Scott doing all the work, and everyone for miles around lashing away with these little Blue Charms they had been reading about in newspaper articles.'"

The heaviest salmon caught on the Dee was taken by another famous gillie, J. Gordon, on the Ardoe Water in 1886. It weighed 57lb 8oz, although, as with many of these 'ancient' fish, the weight is open to dispute. However, there is no dispute about the salmon caught on Park Water on October 12th, 1918, by M. Ewen; a fish weighing 52lb and the official record for the river.

The average weight of Dee salmon today is in the order of 8lb and in recent years catches have improved dramatically, particularly in connection with the increasing numbers of 20lb+ salmon that are now being caught, including a fish taken in the spring of 2008, which was almost certainly over 44lb in weight. Since 1995, when the Dee Board instituted a catch-and-release policy, more than 26,000 fish have been returned to fight another day. For details of fishing log on to FishDee or telephone 01573 470612.

The Dee is a wonderful river, a river to treasure, bright with memories of the great feats of Arthur Wood and his gentle, courteous gillie, Tom Macphearson of Invercauld.

120.
The Glen of the Wind

During service for Queen and country, more years ago than I care to remember, I led convoys of vehicles through rebel-infested mountains in Southern Arabia. This does not, however, qualify me for map reading in the north of Scotland. Clan Sandison claim that trail blazing, if left to me, would mean spending the day going round and round in ever-decreasing circles and why should they want that?

This is how I found myself pausing one morning in Inverpolly, Wester Ross, whilst my wife, Ann, The Manager, planned the way ahead. Our objective was one of my favourite lochs, Doire na h-Airbhe, which lies between dramatic Loch Sionascaig and the north face of Stac Polly.

Spring sunlight warmed my back as I followed Ann down into Gleann na Gaoithe, The Glen of the Wind, where a small stream tumbles over moss-covered rocks and boulders. This is the outlet burn from the loch and with mounting anticipation and quickening step we followed it up the glen.

Loch na h-Airbhe is one mile long by a quarter mile wide. The name means loch of the oak grove and along the south shore a cluster of trees provide welcome shelter when cold winds blow. However, that morning, the weather was perfect and our first action on arrival was to cool off with a splash in the loch.

The west end, where wading is safe and easy, produces an endless flow of small, well-shaped trout. As you progress eastwards, however, the water deepens and the bank becomes much steeper. Sooner, rather than later, it is 'mountain goat' time and you find yourself casting from high above the loch.

Concentrate, because the fishing is excellent all the way along this steep bank, from the start of the first bay, round to a lone hazel tree. We had constant sport and kept three fish each weighing just less than 1lb. Landing them was difficult. A long-handled net would have been a great asset. Otherwise, get your partner to hold on to your heels whilst you reach down. Important not to have fallen out with partner first, otherwise you could have a closer look at the fish than you expected.

The east end of Doire na h-Airbhe is less taxing to fish and every bit as exciting. You will find a shelf of rock over shallow water where excellent trout lie. Eastwards again, the hillside is tree-clad and idyllic. We had lunch there and lazed and slept in the afternoon sun.

When we wakened, an hour's wasted fishing time later, we headed home. For variety, that day, we walked round the north shore of the loch and stopped for a few casts in an unnamed lochan on the hill. Here again, trout rose readily to the fly, hard-fighting and averaging about three to the pound. The walk back to the Polly Lochs was typically Ross-shire: wet, soggy and tiring.

We arrived at the upper River Polly and followed it downstream to where it flows out into the lower river. It is possible to cross dry-shod here, although it involves some minor mountaineering, over fences and across a narrow 'suspect' bridge. We made it safely and walked through golden evening woods, arriving at the car just before the midges. A monument to excellent planning.

Find your way round using OS Map 15, Loch Assynt, Landranger Series, Scale: 1:50,000. Park at Gd ref: 084138; Glen of the Wind: 090124; Loch Na h-Airbhe: 103127. For permission and further information contact Inverpolly Estate Office, tel: 01854 622452. The estate has a self-catering cottage that is let with fishing on other lochs in the area.

121.
Berneray Beckons

And now for something completely different, a glimpse of one of Scotland's most remote and least known trout lochs, Loch Bhruist on the Island of Berneray in the Outer Hebrides. Find it on OS Map 18, Sound of Harris, Scale 1:50,000 at Gd ref: 918826.

Berneray lies in the Sound of Harris between North Uist and South Harris and until recently reaching the island from Mainland Scotland involved a fair degree of planning.: ferry from Uig on Skye to Lochmadday in North Uist followed by another sea-crossing from Newtownferry to Bays Loch on Berneray.

Today, a fine causeway links Berneray to North Uist making getting to this Hebridean jewel a lot easier. Neither will you be disappointed when you arrive because Berneray is a complete delight with something to keep every member of your tribe happy whilst you do battle with Loch Bhruist trout.

The causeway was opened on 8th April 1999 by Berneray's most celebrated guest, HRH Prince Charles, a regular visitor to the island over the years. One of the island's great characters who has been involved with improving fishing on the island is 'Splash' MacKillop (tel: 01876 540235; email: splashmackillop@burnsidecroft.fsnet.co.uk) who also offers visitors comfortable B&B accommodation.

Splash told me that the trout in Loch Bhruist came from North Uist. Those of you familiar with North Uist will know that the majority of lochs on that island are acid and whilst they hold good stocks of native trout, the average weight of these fish is rarely more than 1lb, and more often than not in the order of 6oz/8oz.

Loch Bhruist, however, is a classic machair loch that benefits from the shell sand blown in by the not infrequent Atlantic winds. As such, the Bhruist is lime rich and the fish there thrive mightily and grow to a considerable size. Splendid trout of up to 10lb have been taken.

To preserve the quality of fishing, and to allow the trout to establish themselves, the rule here is strictly 'catch and release', and all fishing is from the bank. A day permit costs £5.00 and is available from The Lobster Pot shop and café, also known as Ardmaree Store (tel: 01876 540288), on your right about a mile or so after you come off the causeway.

Loch Bhruist is shallow, approximately half a mile north/south and up to 400yds wide. It rests on the machair between Berneray's only two modest hills, Beinn Shleibhe (93m) and Borve Hill (85m). The loch can often be wild, but because of the shape of the loch this doesn't hinder fishing.

Because the Bhruist is so shallow, the water on the west side is coloured that magical Hebridean milky-green, shading into dark blue about 15 yards out as the water deepens. There are inviting points and corners down the east shore and trout may be taken from all round the loch.

The three-mile-long beach to the west of the Bhruist, backed by sand dunes of up to 50ft in height and washed by white-crested Atlantic waves, is considered to be one of the finest in Europe. In June, the machair is carpeted with an astonishing array of wild flowers, peopled by busy red-billed oystercatchers.

For further adventure, look west from Berneray to its near-neighbour, the uninhabited island of Boreray. It has one loch, Loch Mor, about which very little is known. It is undoubtedly a machair loch amd I can think of no reason why it should not contain trout. Splash MacKillop will advise you on getting there. If you go, I would be delighted to receive a report on how you got on.

122.
Loch Assynt and the Broken Lands

The broken lands of Assynt offer anglers exciting wild brown trout fishing, something for everyone, from roadside lochs where supper is assured to challenging hikes in search of 'one for the glass case'. The Inchnadamph

Hotel (tel: 01571 844496) has presided over this treasure for more than a century and you will find a warm welcome there and great sport.

I discovered Assynt more years ago than I care to remember, in the days when the late Willie Morrison ran the hotel. Willie was the epitome of the Highland gentleman; ever courteous, self-effacing and always ready with encouragement and advice about the removal of trout from their natural habitat.

OS Map 15, Loch Assynt is essential reading for those seeking adventure amongst the hills and mountains that surround Loch Assynt. For beginners, there is no better place to start than on little Loch Awe (Gd ref: 247153). This island-clad, roadside loch has trout which invariably oblige and weigh in the order of 6oz/9oz. Nevertheless, a 3lb fish has been taken this season so be prepared for the unexpected as well as for breakfast-size trout.

Boat fishing only on the loch and concentrate your efforts in the vicinity of the islands and where the feeder burn enters from Cnoc an Leathaid Bhuidhe, half-way down the west shore. Awe trout are not particularly particular about what flies they take, but try Ke-He, March Brown and Silver Butcher first.

Loch Awe used to produce salmon each season, as did the River Loanan which drains Awe into its majestic neighbour, windy Loch Assynt; six miles long, three quarters of a mile wide and up to 280ft in depth. Few are caught now as West Highland salmonid stocks continue to decline.

However, Loch Assynt offers sport with brown trout, and, of course, the chance of a ferox, the 'aquatic wolf of the Ice Age'. Willie Morrison once showed me a basket of three such fish, all between 9b and 11lb, taken by trolling near the dramatic ruins of Ardvreck Castle.

One of my favourite Assynt lochs, Mhaolach-coire (Gd ref: 277193), lies on the southern skirts of Conival (987m) at the end of a splendid tramp up the River Traligill; the word Traligill being Norse, meaning 'troll' or 'giant'. Along the way you pass the famous limestone caves at Gd ref: 275208. As you approach the loch listen for the sound of the outlet burn, deep underground, still cutting its passage through the limestone to join Traligill burn.

Mhaolach-coire is better known as the Gillaroo Loch because it used to contain trout that resembled the Irish species of that name, still found in loughs such as Melvin, Mask and Corrib. It is most unlikely that any remain in Mhaolach-coire, but the loch does produce trout of exceptional beauty that average 8oz to 12oz in weight, with occasional specimens of up to 2lb.

Given that the loch lies at about 280m, it doesn't really begin to fish until late May. Even then, Cansip and Ben More Assynt can be snow-capped so be prepared for the odd flurry. Arrange a drift along the west shore, about 10 yards out, and take the boat right down to the south end of the loch where the feeder stream enters from Beinn nan Cnaimhseag (Gd ref: 276193).

Fly patterns that produce results, at least for me they do, include Black Pennell, Greenwell's Glory and Kingfisher Butcher. The Gillaroo Loch will make you work hard for a brace or so of fish and it can be dour at times, but I know of few lochs in Scotland that are more dramatic to fish.

123.
Teach them Fly Fishing
and Stay Sane

I have often been asked to comment on how I introduced my children to fly fishing, or, as has been less than kindly alleged, 'brain-washed' them into the gentle art. Quite simply, it seemed to me to be the natural thing to do and the fact that they all still fish, and have introduced their own children to fly fishing, suggests that it worked pretty well.

My first trout rod was a heavy, 12ft greenheart affair with a spike in the butt so that the rod could be stuck upright in the ground when not in use, thus avoiding the possibility of standing on it by accident. The spike got in the way when I was casting, but I survived without doing too much damage to my personal bits and pieces.

A greenheart gives a smooth, all-through action, the only problem being that it has a tendency to break easily and without warning. Eventually, when the patter of tiny feet grew louder in Castle Sandison, I decided to have the rod whittled down to about six feet six inches in length. This was ideal for little ones, light enough for them to use easily, and clearly a 'proper' rod that they could be proud of.

Rod technology has advanced considerably since the dark ages when I was a boy. Today, because rods are so light, it is possible for children to begin with a nine-foot rod. When our grandchildren came along, that is how I started them. In the garden, not on river or loch. I firmly believe that that is the best way to begin. Introduce the basics: no further back than 2 o'clock, pause on the back-cast to let the line straighten out, no further forward than 10 o'clock.

I tried to make it fun, having them walk round, false-casting as they did so, keeping the line in the air. For me, a key point has always been to encourage beginners to watch what happens to the line above their heads. After dinner, we would have friendly competitions, trying to cast a fly onto a plate, lengthening the distance appropriately as they mastered the technique involved in doing so.

Thus, when I finally took them to a river or loch, they were well prepared and had as good a chance as anyone else of connecting with a fish, which they all did, relatively easily. Over the years I have been constantly amazed by the number of people I meet fishing who seem to spend more time worrying about their casting technique and unfankling tangled casts than they do fishing.

This is very sad, because, often, they are on an annual fishing holiday and they should be enjoying every precious moment of it, rather then lashing the water into a hopeless, fishless foam. Ten minutes of casting practice on a few evenings a week, in the garden or in a park, would make all the difference. I believe that if they did so, they would get even greater pleasure out of the act of fly fishing. Casting comfortably and confidently is an integral part of that process.

The downside of teaching others to fly fish is that you might be transferring your own faults to the pupil. For instance, my casting technique has sometimes been described by so-called nearest and dearest as 'father's afflic-tion'. Maybe, to be safe, you should place your children in the care of a qualified instructor. For details contact the Scottish Anglers' National Association (tel: 01577 861116; email: admin@sana.org.uk) They will put you in touch with an instructor in your area.

124.
Mother Knows Best

For 10 years we lived in a house overlooking Loch Watten in Caithness, but having moved west into the wilds of Sutherland, more than a decade passed before I revisited the loch. It was like coming home and happy memories flooded back as I headed out from Factor's Bay in search of adventure.

One of the last times I had done so was when I took my elderly mother fishing. She could raise my blood pressure with just a look, and we had had a terrible fight before getting afloat because I insisted that she should wear wet-weather gear. She was just as insistent that she was not going to parade about in public looking like a Telly Tubby. I won, but it was exhausting doing so.

I motored over to behind the island and turned the boat into my favourite drift, down Whin Bank. This was when I discovered that I had left both rods at the mooring bay. I restarted the engine and headed back up the loch. I was accused of forgetting my cigarettes and lectured about the evils of the 'weed'. But she roared with laughter when I stepped ashore and came back with the fishing rods.

Mother had noticed a 4lb 8oz trout in our freezer, which I had caught on Loch Heilen, and I knew that she coveted it. I hardened my heart and told her that if she wanted a trout to take home with her, then she would have to catch it herself.

Back at Whin Bank, I handed over her rod. She has never been an elegant caster, probably because I had taught her how to fish, but always seemed to manage to catch her supper. Within half an hour, sure enough, she hooked a splendid trout. I reeled in and watched her playing the fish, obviously enjoying every moment.

As I bent down for the landing, she let out a startled yell. I looked up just in time to see the trout flying through the air and landing in the middle of the boat. It had leapt from the loch, straight into the boat of its own accord. The fish, which weighed about 1lb 8oz, was despatched and subsequently travelled home to Edinburgh with its delighted captor.

On another occasion, waiting one evening for my big son, Blair, to come off the loch, I asked a returning angler how he had got on. "Got on!" he spluttered. "I got not a damn thing. I'm only fishing the loch because I read an article Bruce Sandison wrote about it. If I could lay my hands on him now I'd tell him a thing or six. He lives somewhere nearby, do you know him?" Discretion seemed to me to be the better part of valour. "No, can't say I do," I replied.

It was with these thoughts in my mind that I cast my Ke-He, March Brown and Silver Butcher into the clear waters of the loch; I remembered the beautiful 3lb fish I caught a few yards out from the Oldhall boathouse; an otter and her cubs dancing along the Lynegar bay shore; the huge trout I hooked and lost in Shearer's Pool where the flow enters from Loch Scarmclate.

No angling life is complete until you fish Loch Watten. I can't guarantee that trout will jump into your boat by themselves, or that you will see a family of otters, but I can promise you a magical day out on one of Scotland's finest wild brown trout lochs. Bookings from Hugo Ross in Wick, (tel: 01955 604200) and best of luck when you do.

125.
Pennell Point

Hiking boots this morning, please, for a six-mile round-trip to explore a series of lochs in the shadow of Ben Stack (721m) in North-West Sutherland. You will need OS Map 9, Cape Wrath, Scale 1:50,000 to find your way about and you should pack a compass and whistle as well; it is easy to get lost here, even on a fine day. Tell someone where you are going and when you expect to get back.

Park at Gd ref: 190454 on the A894 Laxford Bridge/Scourie road and head for Loch a'Mhuirt (Gd ref: 202201). Walk the south shore and continue south-east past Gorm Loch (Gd ref: 211441), again on the south bank. After a further mile you will reach the west end of dark Lochain Doimhain and Pennell Point (Gd ref: 224430).

Each season, the first person to stand on the point noted above and cast a Black Pennell an inch or so right of centre, is rewarded with a 1lb trout. I know this is true because I heard the story from the late Stan Tuer, a famous Scourie Hotel 'Boardmaster', and my wife, Ann, and I were with Stan when he demonstrated the fact, catching a 1lb trout with his first cast in the process.

A few years later, Ann and I walked this way with our son, Blair, and his wife, Barbara. Just to show off my superior knowledge concerning all things piscatorial, I told Blair the story and said, condescendingly, "There you are, Blair, give it a throw." "That's very kind, Father," he replied, "but I insist that you begin; after all, you catch so few fish that it would be churlish of me to deprive you of at least one opportunity to do so."

I strode confidently to the point and cast out a size 12 Black Pennell in the approved direction, "an inch or so right of centre". Nothing. Not even an offer. I cast again, further this time. Nothing. I heard sniggering behind my back. "OK, then, if you are so smart, Blair, you have a go." Blair walked up, making line as he went, and cast his Black Pennell in the same direction. The instant it touched the water it was grabbed by a 1lb trout which Blair duly landed.

Loch Doimhain can be unforgiving, but the small waters that surround it offer splendid sport with fish that weigh between a few ounces up to 5lb. It is a Scourie tradition that anglers take small fish from large lochs and place them, secretly, in adjacent lochans. These become that anglers 'private larder', where the fish are allowed to grow undetected and undisturbed, other, that is, than by the fisherman who put them there.

None of these waters are named on the OS Map, but they have local names: Boot Loch, Otter Loch, Pound Loch, Aeroplane Loch and others. I won't give you the exact locations, because it would spoil your pleasure in discovering them for yourself. In normal circumstances you would probably just ignore them and walk by without having a cast. I fished one, not too far distant from Loch Doimhain and about the size of a couple of swimming pools. My reward was a trout of 2lb 12oz.

When so much fishing today is made easily accessible, managed and manicured, angling at Scourie takes us back to basics. Discover this joy for yourself in the wilds of North-West Sutherland. Fishing from the shore costs in the order of £5.00 per rod per day, so it won't break the bank. But, be warned, it might break your heart when that monster you have hooked disappears back into the depths.

Bookings from Reay Forest Estate, tel: 01971 500221; also Scourie Hotel, tel: 01971 502396.

126.
Whisky in the Wind

Get away from the madding crowd this summer to the wonderful island of Islay; a land of near-deserted, gold sand beaches, outstanding wildlife and a different 'water of life' distillery for each day of the week. And, most important of all for those of us afflicted with angling, some of Scotland's most lovely, easily accessible and inviting trout lochs.

The Dunlossit Estate lies between Bridgend and Port Askaig to the south of the A846 road. Find your way round using OS Map 60, Islay, Scale 1:50,000. The estate offers fishing on four principal waters: Ballygrant (Gd ref: 405661), the largest, Loch nan Cadhan (Gd ref: 404669) a step north of Ballygrant, and Lossit (Gd ref: 409653) to the south.

The fourth loch is Loch Allan (Gd ref: 425677), south from Port Askaig and close to the narrow channel that separates Islay from its wild neighbour, Jura, the 'island of deer'. The famous mountains, the Paps of Jura, dominate the view; Beinn a'Chaolais (733m), hill of the narrows, Beinn an Oir (784m), the hill of gold, and Beinn Shiantaidh (755m), the holy hill.

Further south still, along an estate track, there are three more lochs lying on the moor between Beinn Bhreac to the west and Beinn Dubh to the east: Loch Fada (Gd ref: 410637), Loch Leathann (Gd ref: 410632) and Loch Bharradail (Gd ref: 393633). Reaching them requires about 15 to 20 minutes' vigorous leg work, but they are splendidly isolated and just the place for anglers who enjoy a good walk with their fishing.

Ballygrant is best fished from the boat. The water is crystal-clear and trout average about 8oz/10oz in weight, although there are larger specimens. The Ballygrant narrows into a finger-like bay at the east end and this is the place to begin your assault. Boat fishing also brings good results on nan Cadhan, Lossit and Allan.

The largest trout taken so far this season weighed 2lb 8oz and was caught on Allan. The estate, along with members of the Port Ellen Angling Club, is working to increase the average weight of fish by stocking, but doing it in the 'proper' way: transporting fish from lochs which have an abundance of small trout to lochs that can sustain a higher population.

The estate has three new boats on their lochs this season and also a purpose-built boat for the use of disabled anglers. Permission to fish is available from the Dunlossit Estate Office on tel: 01496 840232 or the Port Askaig Shop (tel: 01496 840245). Boat hire costs £20 per day, £10 per half day.

The artificial flies you use to tempt them is a matter of choice, but, as always, you can do little better than stick to well-trusted, traditional patterns: Soldier Palmer, Black Zulu, Blue Zulu, Black Pennell, He-He, March Brown, Silver Butcher and Silver Invicta. Vary the size according to prevailing wind conditions.

During your day you may be visited by one of the 'managers', the rare-breed pigs that roam the estate as an integral part of estate management. They are very friendly and may wander up to share your lunchtime picnic. The Middle White breed, particularly, is inclined to say 'hello'. They are docile and easily managed; a bit like your correspondent providing he has caught a trout or two during the morning.

I am also reliably informed that the hairs from their tails are much-prized by fly-tiers, although I have no information on exactly how the animal reacts should you try to 'acquire' some. I guess that they may be less docile during the process and advise against attempting to do so. Concentrate your efforts on the trout. Much safer.

127.
Ferox Trout

Some years ago, Ballantine's of Scotch whisky fame organised a determined attempt to catch a new British Record brown trout. The chosen venue was Loch Quoich at the head of the Inverness-shire Garry system and I was invited to take part. The plan was for a team of eight expert ferox anglers to share the task of fishing continuously for 48 hours to try to break the record.

Not being an expert ferox angler, I had to decline the invitation and the event went ahead without me. The British record wasn't broken, but several double-figure ferox were caught and I am sure that it is only a matter of time before the loch does produce an award-winning specimen. The heaviest brown trout caught in Britain came from Loch Awe on the opening day of the 2002 trout angling season. It weighed 31lb 12oz and was landed by Brian Rutland.

Personally, I'm not really sure if Mr Rutland's fish should qualify for the 'heaviest' distinction because Loch Awe has been plagued over the years with escapes from fish farms. At one stage several hundred thousand farmed rainbow trout did a runner, much to the advancement and appetite of the local ferox population, not to mention the appetite of the droves of fishermen who descended on the loch to catch their fair share. This gives Awe ferox access to an artificial food supply which is not available in other lochs that host ferox.

Loch Quoich ferox have to make their way in life as their ancestors have been doing since the end of the last Ice Age, by preying mainly on Arctic charr, and, of course, on anything else that happens their way, including their smaller brethren. Quoich also contains pike and a considerable population of traditional wild brown trout that average in the order of 8oz/10oz, as well as good numbers of larger fish.

The loch is distinguished by being set amidst some of Scotland's most majestic scenery. A cluster of Munros (mountains 914.4m in height) surround this nine-mile-long water: Sgurr Mhaoraich, Gleouraich, Creag a'Mhaim, Spidean Mialach, Gairich, Sgurr Mor, Sgurr nan Coireachan, and mighty Sgurr na Ciche. The south shore is trackless, but the north bank is bordered by a minor road for half its length, until it climbs north-east through the hills to reach the eastern end of sea Loch Hourn.

The safest and most useful way to fish Quoich is from the boat. Bank fishing is generally uncomfortable and dangerous, with a great depth of water close to the shore in many areas. There are exceptions, however, such as where the River Quoich flows in at the north end of a finger-like extension to the main body of the loch (Gd ref: 019065 on OS Map 33, Loch Alsh & Glen Shiel, Scale 1:50,000).

For those of you who relish a little pain before pleasure, then there are two remote hill lochs in the vicinity that will more than meet your needs: Loch Fearna at Gd ref: 056032 lies in a hollow at 500m, below the crags of Spidean Mialach, and Loch nam Breac at Gd ref: 905996, clutched between the intimidating heights of Druim Chosaidh to the north and Ben Aden to the south.

If you are ready to face the challenge of Loch Quoich, contact the Tomdoun Hotel (tel: 01809 511218), one of the oldest and most welcoming hostelries in Scotland for permission to do so. The hotel also offers fishing on Loch Garry, Loch Inchlaggan and Loch Poulary and on other surrounding hill lochs.

128.
Climb Canisp First

If golf is a good walk spoiled, then hill loch fishing must surely be a good walk improved. Find the best of both worlds, fishing and walking, during this hike into the glorious wilderness of the Glen Canisp Forest in Assynt, North-West Sutherland.

Park off the A837 Ledmore to Lochinver road at the north end of Loch Awe. Cross the outlet stream and head up the hill to reach Loch na Gruagaich. Tempting though it may be to stop for a cast, keep walking. Gruagaich does contain trout, but because of the poor availability of food in the loch the fish are only a few ounces in weight, in spite of being several years old.

Indeed, before fishing anywhere, climb to the summit of Canisp (846m). It would be churlish not to do so prior to attending to the removal of trout from their natural habitat. It is an easy walk and when you reach the top you will be rewarded with a vista encompassing some of Scotland's most dramatic peaks; Ben More Assynt (998m), Suilven (731m), the Viking's 'Pillar Mountain', the long ridge of Quinag (808m) and the mountains of the Inverpolly National Nature Reserve: Cul Mor (849m), Cul Beag (769m) and little Stac Polly (613m).

From the summit you will also be able to plan future fishing expeditions. To the south-west lies the silver ribbon of Loch Veyatie and Cam Loch, the 'crooked loch'. The small lochans here, on the skirts of Suilven and above Loch Veyatie, rarely see an artificial fly from one season to the next: Lochan Nigheadh, Loch nan Rac, Loch Gleannan a'Madaidh and their satellite waters.

But our primary objective this morning is to examine an unnamed lochan on the grey shoulder of Canisp, two and a half miles distant from the start point. Find it on OS Map 15, Loch Assynt, Second Series, Scale 1:50,000 at Gd ref: 220183. A step to the north of the loch, on the eastern slopes of the hill, lie Loch Dubh Meallan Mhurchaidh, Loch na Faoileige and Loch nam Meallan Liatha, full of small trout that fight hard. Nearby, however, there are other, smaller waters here, some of which contain much larger fish.

All the lochs on Canisp are managed by the Assynt Angling Group. Permission to fish them can be obtained from a number of outlets in Lochinver including the Tourist Office, Inverlodge Hotel, the Post Office, Lochinver Fish Selling Chandlery, Polcraig Guest House, and the Altnacealgach Hotel (tel: 01854 666260), the latter being the most convenient place to buy your permit if you are arriving from the east.

The first time I passed this way, I gave our little unnamed lochan a cursory glance; the day was stormy and the surface angry and white-foamed. Lying on the 450m contour line, surely it would be fishless? Usually, when hill walking I pack a telescopic rod, reel, spool of nylon and half a dozen flies, but not that day. Next time, I promised myself, I would be properly prepared have a cast to "mak sicker".

What happened? Well, you will have to tramp there for yourself to find out. Whilst nothing other than uncertainty is certain in fishing, you should not be disappointed. If the fates are unkind and you tramp home supperless, then it will probably be because you failed to pay your respects to the summit cairn on Canisp prior to fishing. Can't say fairer than that, can I?

129.
The Trout of a Lifetime

I have never caught the fish of a lifetime, a dream-trout to warm the angling memories of my sunset years. But I know someone who has: the inestimable Hugo Ross from Wick in Caithness. Hugo runs a fishing tackle shop in the High Street (tel: 01955 604200) and he is known to fishermen throughout the UK for his kindness and courtesy. Nothing is ever too much trouble for Hugo when it comes to lending a helping hand to both local and visiting anglers alike.

So I was delighted when I heard that Hugo had caught one of the most beautiful wild brown trout that I have seen in years; a specimen fish weighing 6lb 4oz and taken from little Loch Bea on the Island of Sanday in Orkney. The fish was photographed and carefully returned to fight another day. Of course, much heavier fish are caught on a daily basis from stocked fisheries, but to land a wild trout of such perfect beauty is one of angling's supreme joys.

Most anglers visiting Orkney concentrate on the excellent Mainland lochs, Harray, Stenness, Swannay and Hundland, and few ever explore the lochs on the adjacent islands. They are easy to access, but it does involve a fair bit of pouring over ferry timetables to organise a fishing expedition.

Those who do so will be well rewarded for that effort because these lochs are some of the finest and least fished waters in Scotland; undiscovered gems, treasured by the few who know their real worth.

Loch Bea lies adjacent to the B9068 road a mile or so north from Kettletoft Pier where the ferry arrives. Bea is shallow and lime-rich and fish are taken from the shore all round the loch. No one place is substantially better than another. As the season advances, from July onwards, weed can become a problem so it is best to launch your attack in April or May. For permission to do so, contact Mr E. Groundwater, Castlehill, Sanday (tel: 01857 600285). The trout average around 1lb in weight but in recent years fish of up to 8lb have been taken from the loch.

Sanday has two other significant lochs that deserve your attention, Roos Loch and North Loch. Roos Loch lies close to the sea on the west side of the island at the end of a minor road branching off the B9068 to Bellevue and Airon. Cautious bank fishing here, and not for the faint-hearted because Roos is dour, but there are some exceptional fish waiting for your well-judged cast. Sea-trout may also be caught in the sea at Roos Wick, although they are fewer in number now than they were in times past. Seek advice on tide tables before fishing.

North Loch is the largest water on Sanday, three quarters of a mile long by up to half a mile wide. Turn right from the B9068 at Isgarth and follow the minor road out to Galilee. North Loch is exposed and sometimes windy, not unknown in these airts. It is shallow and is easily examined from the shore. The trout, whilst not as large as those in Bea, are very pretty and average about 10oz/12oz in weight. There is also the possibility of sport with sea-trout in the Bay of Sandquoy to the west of North Loch. There is one unnamed loch at the northern tip of the island (OS 5, Orkney – Northern Isles, Scale 1:50,000, Gd ref: 685466) of which I have no knowledge. If you pass that way, let me know how you get on, please?

130.
Down the Tube

I think that fishing from a float tube is an American innovation. Whatever, an American introduced me to float-tubing when he visited a lodge I was looking after on an island in Lago Yelcho in Chilean Patagonia. He wanted to try out his tube on the 1,000ft deep lake and assured me that he was an expert, but for some reason the tube was not properly inflated. When he got into it, from a boat in the middle of the lake, he promptly turned somersault. We had a hard time getting him out alive and I took the blame for this misadventure.

Therefore, when a friend stopped me in the village the other day and mentioned the 'float tube', I greeted the information with a degree of trepidation, if not with down-right dismay. "When you're finished in the post office, come and see it," he said. "John took five lovely trout from that roadside loch you told him about." I was now very interested, because I knew that the said roadside loch held some seriously large wild brown trout, the only problem being getting at them because of reeds. Indeed, I mentioned it in this column last July.

My friend's son, John, is a keen angler. When I arrived, however, I found him complaining about bruised ribs, from playing football. "Never mind," he said, "I will just have to fish through the pain barrier." As I said, John is keen, very keen. The tube was produced in all its green-waterproof glory and I was impressed. It was similar to a huge, comfortable, legless armchair, complete with about everything other than the kitchen sink: pockets, gadgets for hanging things from, landing nets et al. Neither was it heavy; even I could lift it easily.

My first question was, "John, how do you inflate it and make sure that it remains inflated?" John replied that once the float tube was correctly inflated, he just left it that way and carried it on his back to wherever he was going; including up a mountainside to some excellent trout lochs above Loch Eriboll. "It is awkward," he explained, "it clips your ankles on the way up and bangs against the ground on the way down, but it really is worth the trouble because once afloat you can reach places that you could never reach when bank fishing." It is also manoeuvrable, ultra-safe and environmentally friendly, apart, that is, to unsuspecting trout.

So why do I have reservations? It's not easy to explain, and I hasten to add that these are purely personally reservations, but I just have a gut-feeling that, somehow, it's not fair: creeping up on your quarry, catching him un-awares, giving fish little warning of evil intent. Well, I happily fish from a boat, so what's the difference? Thinking about it, were the truth told, I now invariably fish for trout from the shore. I used to put that down to idleness; being too lazy to lug outboards to the water's edge, or to heave on oars in a raging gale all day. But maybe, subconsciously, it is because I think that fishing from the bank gives trout a more sporting chance.

Nevertheless, have a go at float-tubing and make up your own mind. A good place to start is with Mike Barrio (tel: 07810 868897) at the Haddo Trout Fishery between Methlick and Old Meldrum. Be assured, you will be in far safer and more competent hands than those that dangle from the arms of yours truly.

131.
Bearing Up

Black, Grizzly, Polar or otherwise, bears scare the hell out of me. I am reliably informed that the key point to remember, should you be confronted by a bear when fishing, is not to run away. Apparently, this only encourages the beast to chase after you and that could lead to a catastrophic rearrangement of your precious bodily parts.

Two American friends of mine panicked and ran when they came face to face with a bear when salmon fishing in Alaska. The bear followed in hot anticipatory pursuit. After a few hundred breathless yards one of the intrepid duo stopped to retie a shoelace that had come undone.

His companion screamed at him in terror: "Good God, Jim! What do you think you are doing? Run faster!" His friend smiled and replied, "No hurry, Hank. I don't have to run faster than the bear. All I have to do is run faster than you – and I have been able to do that for years."

This story may be apocryphal but it always springs to my mind when talk turns to reintroducing to Scotland species that have become extinct; particularly large, predatory carnivores such as bears and wolves. I agree in principle that they could, and probably should be reintroduced, but I question the practicability of doing so.

It certainly would be one way of reducing Scotland's massive red deer population. A few hundred ravenous wolves and bears roaming our hills would soon rearrange their numbers. The problems would begin when this readily available supply of venison dried up, or, to be more accurate, was eaten up.

Bears and wolves, no doubt by then thriving mightily, would turn to other available sources of food like sheep, cows, hens or anything else that happened along; including, and no one can deny the possibility, the odd unsuspecting hill-walker or angler.

But the presence of these animals would greatly add to the excitement of a day out in the hills and records from countries where these beasts live naturally suggest that they pose minimal risk to human life or to farm stock. In any case, landowners would quickly persuade their friends in government to pay them compensation and grants to reimburse them for any alleged loss of income. Your average Highland laird can spot a grant-aid opportunity quicker than a golden eagle spots a wounded hare in the heather.

There is, however, one animal, the European beaver, native to Scotland 400 years ago, that could be reintroduced without cause for alarm and I fully support Scottish Natural Heritage's (SNH) intention to do so. I believe that beavers will enhance our freshwater habitat. The dams they build store organic matter, which is recycled in rivers, bestowing benefits upon all the creatures that depend upon that habitat for survival, including trout and salmon.

Not all fisherpersons agree with my point of view in regard to the reintroduction of beavers. There are valid and reasonable concerns that beavers might be detrimental to angling, particularly in Argyllshire where the reintroduction is planned to take place. Some may also wonder why SNH is happy to spend hundreds of thousands of pounds on beavers, but seems to have done very little to protect a species that, after nearly 10,000 years in our rivers and lochs, is now facing extinction: West Highland and Islands wild sea-trout.

Whatever your opinion might be, I have just thought of another important attraction of reintroducing beavers to Scotland, rather then wolves and bears. Should the need arise I am pretty certain that I could quite easily outrun even the most fleet-footed of their kind.

132.
Loch Coruisk

The sun was dipping behind Sgurr Alasdair sending shafts of light glancing amidst Cuillin Hills when our boat glided into the sheltered waters of Loch na Cuilce on the Island of Skye. Before supper, we crowded ashore to stretch cramped legs and, unsteadily, climbed the iron ladders on the breakwater to terra firma by the outlet stream from Loch Coruisk. The river, sad in autumn drought, had barely enough force to reach the sea.

We scrambled to the top of Meall na Cuilce and looked down on Coruisk, once one of Scotland's most exciting sea-trout fisheries, guarded by magnificent peaks: Sgurr Alasdair (993m), Sgurr na Banachdich (966m), Sgurr Ghreadaidh (973m), Sgurr nan Gillean (965m) and the long ridge of Druim nan Ramh.

The best account of sea-trout fishing on Loch Coruisk is contained in a marvellous book called *Fishing from Afar* by Stephen Johnson; a game fishing classic now sadly out of print. Johnson wrote it whilst a prisoner of war in Germany during the last war. To while away the long hours of imprisonment, he described pre-war fishing holidays spent at Coruisk and Camasunary.

Johnson's account of his exploits, and the exploits of the other members of his family, makes fascinating reading. His father once took 30 sea-trout from Coruisk, weighing a total of 40lb. Their best sea-trout, caught whilst trailing a salmon fly behind the boat, weighed 13lb 8oz.

Sea-trout are fidgety beasts, particularly when they have just arrived home from the sea. Their mouths are soft, and, consequently, more are hooked and lost than are hooked and caught. Their outstanding quality, however, is the strength with which they fight and many anglers consider sea-trout much more exciting fish to catch than salmon.

Once hooked, sea-trout seem to run forever. A big fish can have your reel down to the backing quicker than you can say Izaak Walton. Nor is there much you can do to stop its mad rush, other than row or run after it. Another notable basket of Coruisk sea-trout, caught at night, contained 15 fish weighing 73lb, including eight fish of over 8lb and one of 9lb.

When you get to Coruisk, try a Camasunary Killer, a fly that evolved from an original dressing by Stephen Johnson that he called his 'Blue Fly'; hook, size 12 wet; thread, black; tail, blue wool; body, half blue and half red; rib, oval silver; wing, soft black hackle. I generally fish it as the tail fly on a cast of three.

Loch Coruisk, like other West Highland waters, does not produce the number or size of fish that it did when Johnson enjoyed its pleasures, and remember that getting there involves considerable effort; not the least of which, if walking out from Camasunary, is negotiating the famous 'Bad Step' when you have to traverse a narrow ledge above a sheer drop of some 30ft/40ft into the sea.

But Coruisk is one of the most dramatic lochs in all of Scotland and a splendid place to spend a day. For permission, contact the John Muir Trust office in Straithaird and expect to pay a fee in the order of £5.00 per rod per day.

On my last visit, as I stood at the mouth of the river, reluctant to return to the boat, in my mind's eye I saw Johnson and his friends stalking their prey through the long summer nights; saw the bend of the rod as a heavy fish took; heard the wild scream of the reel and their cries of excitement. When I turned to go, a sea-trout leapt in the bay, a bar of purest silver, bright against the darkening sky.

133.
Fine Sport on Loch Ericht

Loch Ericht is one of Scotland's great lochs, 15 miles long by up to one mile wide at the south end. The most people ever see of it is a quick glimpse of the north end as they speed by Dalwhinne on the A9 Inverness/Perth road. However, those seeking sport with wild trout should pause awhile: Loch Ericht could provide you with that ever-elusive monster for the glass case of your angling dreams.

Use OS Map 42, Loch Rannoch, Landranger Series, Scale 1:50,000 to find your way round. The east shore is largely trackless, but the opposite bank is accessible for most of its length from the dam at Dalwhinne (Gd ref: 632844) to Benalder Cottage (Gd ref: 499680). The cottage is reputed to be haunted but is much enjoyed by hill walkers on their way to explore the surrounding peaks: Ben Alder (1148m), Beinn Bheoil (1019m) and Beinn a'Chumhainn (902m).

You may also access Loch Ericht from a track on the north shore of Loch Rannoch (Gd ref: 507577). This track ends a mile or so short of Alder Bay. One of Scotland's most famous hill walkers, Bonnie Prince Charlie, hid in a cave above the bay following the disaster of Culloden in 1746. The cave was named after his supporter, Ewen MacPhearson of Cluny, laird of Badenoch.

Whilst Loch Ericht is full of traditional, small wild brown trout, it also contains some monster ferox, the aquatic 'wolf' that has survived in Scottish waters since the end of the last Ice Age. These are most often encountered when using the old Scots fishing method of trolling live or dead bait or artificial lure at a depth of up to 30ft/40ft from behind a slowly moving boat.

The best description of fishing the loch is probably the one recounted by John Inglis Hall in 1960, when he used to stay at the Loch Ericht Hotel when Davy Matheson was proprietor. Sandy Craib was his gillie. The day was wild and wet and the pair trolled a few hundred yards out from the east shore, halfway down the loch.

Their first fish weighted 2lb 8oz, and, as he landed it, Sandy remarked to Hall, "Your net's no' very large. I don't know what we'll do when we get the big one." The next fish weighed 4lb 8oz. "Never two without three, "said Sandy, "they're on the take; we might do it."

The third fish proved to be a monster, estimated to be well over 12lb in weight, and some 18 inches too long for the landing net. They played the fish for more than half an hour, hardly aware of the driving rain and rising gale. But after several failed attempts to land the trout, the cast broke and their prize escaped back into the depths.

Today, bank fishing is the most-used fishing method on the loch, and, as always, avoid wading. Ericht is a part of a hydro-electric generating system and the margins can be soft and dangerous is some places. Stay safe ashore. Also be aware that we are talking serious walking to reach the remoter parts of the loch, particularly the south end where the fishing is generally accepted to be best.

If you have your own boat, it may be possible to obtain permission to use it and, if so, this will greatly help in exploring this vast water, but you will most likely need a 4x4 vehicle to be able to get the boat to the water to launch it. Contact the estate factor on tel: 01528 522253. Otherwise, bank fishing permits are available from Dalwhinne Garage (tel: 01528 522311) at about £9.00 per rod per day. The glass case is extra.

134.
Golden Days

How big is a big salmon today? Anything over 20lb seems to be the answer; exemplified by William Newlands with his 24lb 5oz fish taken from the Tarroul Pool on Wick River last Monday.

But compared to the size of fish caught in times past, the 'big' salmon of today are unremarkable. The most famous is, of course, Georgina Ballantine's 64lb fish, caught on 7th October 1922 on the Boat Pool of the River Tay downstream from Dunkeld. The Duke of Portland commented at the time, and you can almost hear his teeth grinding with envy, "I understand that her father was rowing home in the evening with a large spinning bait trailing behind the boat. The bait was suddenly seized and Ballantine told his daughter to catch hold of the rod. She did and kept the point up."

A rival for the biggest UK rod-and-line caught salmon was a fish of 69lb 12oz taken by Lord Home on Tweed in 1743. There is no doubt that the fish was caught and accurately weighed, but what is not known is exactly how many ounces equalled one pound in those days, so Lord Home's fish can't be accepted as the record rod-and-line caught salmon.

Another famous Tay salmon story is about one that got away; hooked by Bishop Browne and played for ten and a half hours before the cast broke and the fish escaped. Not for long, however, because two days later the fish, which weighed 71lb, was taken in the nets – with Bishop Browne's Phantom lure still in its jaw.

The River Tweed also has its share of 50lb+ salmon to boast about, including 57lb 8oz (Mr Prior, 1886), 55lb (Mr Brereton, 1889), 55lb (Mr W. A. Kidson, 1913) and 50lb 8oz (Mr Rudd, 1925). As for 'lesser' Tweed fish, John Ashley-Cooper comments about Tweed in his book, *The Great Salmon Rivers of Scotland*, "Forty-pounders are far too numerous to list here. The last one of 43lb was caught at Tillmouth three years ago [1977]."

The River Awe was also justly noted for the size of its salmon. Three remarkable fish have come from the river, two of them caught by the same woman, Mrs G. B. Huntington: 55lb, from the Errachd Pool in September 1927, and a fish of 51lb from Stepping Stones in May 1930. The third 'big' Awe salmon was caught by Mr Huntington. It weighed 57lb and came from Cassan Dhu Pool in July 1921.

These were perhaps the golden days of salmon fishing in Scotland. Between 1883 and 1922, 23 salmon of 50lb and over in weight were taken from the Tay. The River Deveron produced two 50lb+ fish: Colonel Scott's 56lb salmon taken in 1920 and Mrs Morrison's 61lb fish in 1924. The glorious Spey, the UK's fastest-flowing stream, can recount similar stories of mighty salmon, not the least of which is Duncan Grant's famous 54lb fish, hooked in Mountebank, and landed 12 hours later at the head of Lord Fife's water below Aberlour.

Whether or not these 'golden days' will ever return is uncertain, but it seems to me that an increasing number of 20lb+ salmon are being caught, at least in Scotland's east and south-west streams. Perhaps better river management and the work of people like Icelander Orri Vigfusson and his North Atlantic Salmon Fund are beginning to take effect. Let's hope so.

135.
Spring in Your Step

Spring sprung last week. Snowed in on Monday, Wednesday onwards bathed in warm sunlight; birds cheepin', buds bustin' and a happy start to the brown trout fishing season. Winter seemed to go on forever and I am delighted that it is over. Time to drag out the rod and head for little Loch Hakel, a few minutes from our front door. Ke-He on the 'bob', March Brown in the middle, Silver Butcher on the 'tail'. Wild brown trout for breakfast. Never fails.

I might even suggest a trip across the Pentland Firth to fish Mainland Orkney. In years past The Manager and I have had excellent early-season sport there, particularly bank fishing on my favourite Orcadian water, Loch of Swannay. I will ask The Manager tonight. We need to go to Orkney. By the way, always have a Black Pennell on your cast when fishing Swannay, no matter what time of year it is.

Further back in my fishing life, when I lived in Auld Reekie, the spring months often found me fishing in The Trossachs; that sparkling, mountain-bedecked wonderland of rivers and lochs where time is endless and a new angling delight beckons around every corner; Lubnaig, Voil, Katrine, Ard and Loch Venachar, and the fast-flowing, foaming River Teith.

Perhaps the most memorable fact of Trossachs fishing is the clarity of the water, crystal clear, and the beauty of the wild brown trout waiting to be caught there, red-speckled and fighting fit. All these memories came to mind when I was talking to Mark Wilkinson about fishing Loch Venachar. Mark has a new venture, The Venachar Club. The club (www.trossachs-leisure.co.uk) and is committed to improving access and fishing on the loch.

The start-point for the exercise was a status survey of the loch, carried out by one of Scotland's leading experts in these matters, Dr Andy Walker from the Freshwater Lab in Pitlochry. A stocking programme is now in place to help the native brown trout population recover, and bag limits have been established for each of the 25 boats available to both Venachar Club members and visitors alike.

Morris Meikle is head gillie for the Venachar Club, which also offers excellent salmon and sea-trout fishing on the rivers Teith, Earn and Tay. Corporate fishing days can be arranged and Angling Clubs are welcome. A new loch-side fishing lodge with café, shop and toilets will be up and running in mid-June. So far this season, Venachar anglers have enjoyed great sport, with trout that average around 1lb 8oz in weight with a few fish of up to 2lb.

Trout have been rising to traditional patterns of loch flies, fished in the traditional fashion, in front of a drifting boat, and boat-fishing definitely brings the best results on this three-and-a-half-mile long loch. The shallow west end of Venachar is the place to begin, in the vicinity of Lendrick on the north shore, and along the south shore past Invertrossachs to where the outflow stream from Loch Drunkie enters.

Anglers will also be pleased to know that Loch Katrine might soon reopen to fishing. The problem has been to do with health and safety regulations and the refusal of permission to use petrol outboard engines. Mark Wilkinson believes that when a new treatment plant has been completed, then permission to use outboard engines could follow. Let's hope so. Few angling locations compare with fishing in the shadow of Ben Ledi on Venachar and Ben Venue on Loch Katrine in the heart of Scotland's 'Bristling Country', the amazing Trossachs.

136.
Fishing the White Loch

Scotland's most famous basket of brown trout was caught on the Fionn Loch in Wester Ross on 12th April 1851 by Sir Alexander Gordon Cumming of Altyre. Osgood Mackenzie, who was nine years old at the time, later described the fish in his book, *A Hundred Years in the Highlands*: "There were four beauties lying side by side on the table of the small drinking room, and they turned the scales at 51lb. The total weight of the 12 fish caught that 12th day of April by trolling was 87lb 12oz."

The 'white loch' is six miles long by up to one and a half miles wide and falls to a depth of 150ft near Carnmore Bothy. Draining westwards down the Little Gruinard river, Fionn reaches the sea in Gruinard Bay; guarded by infamous Gruinard Island, used for anthrax experiments during the last war, now 'decontaminated'. Eastwards, Fionn is dominated by magnificent peaks: Ben Lair (861m), the Mountain of the Mare; A'Mhaighdean (936m), the Maiden; Meall Mheinnidh (731m), the Grassy Hill and Beinn a'Chaisgein Mor (857m), the Forbidding Mountain.

The only forbidding aspect of Fionn, however, is getting there. On foot, it is a walk in of more than six miles. When The Manager and I visited, we got there in a bone-shaking Land Rover. Even then it was is a long journey, but worth every rattle and lurch of the way because Fionn is one of Scotland's special places and offers everything that is best in fishing: solitude, silence, wild empty hills, a circling eagle and the exciting sound of rising trout.

In 1963, one happy angler took 21 fish weighing 63lb, the heaviest being 11lb and even today, with trolling banned, most seasons can produce trout of over 5lb in weight. Salmon and sea-trout also enter Fionn by way of the Little Gruinard River but few anglers fish for them, preferring to concentrate upon their smaller, more accommodating cousins. You would have to be the greatest duffer in the world not to catch trout on the Fionn Loch, regardless of weather conditions.

Use OS Map 19, Gairloch & Ullapool, Second Series, Scale 1:50,000 to find your way round. The bays at the north end, split by the promontory of Aird Dhubh (Gd ref: 937820) offer good sport and another favourite area is in the shelter of Eilean Fraoch (Gd ref: 945804) off the east shore. There used to be an inn here, on the line of an old cattle drove road. But perhaps the most productive drift is down the south-west shore, from New Boathouse Bay. Boat fishing only and hasten slowly. Huge underwater rocks, shallows and sudden, deep pots lie in wait to catch you unawares.

Our day on Fionn proved the truth of the quality of fishing. It was not just a bad day. It was appalling. The wind howled. We sat, rain-soaked and frozen with teeth gritted, determined not to give in. When we were finally forced ashore, to avoid the onset of hypothermia, there were 12 fish in the boat. My wife Ann caught six, our fishing partner caught six and I caught the rest. Well, after all, I suppose even the greatest of duffers can have their off days?

Permission: all enquiries in regard to access and fishing in this area should be addressed to Ms Barbara Grant, Letterewe Estate, Loch Maree, Achnasheen, Ross-shire, 1V22 2HH. tel: 01445 760207; fax: 01445 760284. Permission is entirely at the discretion of the Estate, which also has a number of comfortable, self-catering properties which are let with trout, sea-trout and salmon fishing.

137.
Inver Park and the River Braan

The little River Braan bustles into the mighty Tay just upstream from Dunkeld, near Inver Park in Perthshire. When I was a Boy Scout our troop camped at Inver one long-ago summer and I instinctively knew then that I had discovered something very special. The ever-present smell of wood-smoke and pine essence pervades the senses. The sound of the river lulled us to sleep. It was a good-to-be-alive place, a place for all seasons.

I also found the Braan's wild brown trout when I explored the Hermitage, an ornate folly overlooking the Black Linn Fall and built in 1758 as a 'surprise' for the 2nd Duke of Atholl by one of his nephews. There is a balcony here, high above the foam-fringed pool below the falls from where I watched bright, red-speckled trout rising through the crystal-clear water to take surface flies. The mirrors that once lined the walls of the building have gone, but the view is still spectacular and even more so when the river is in spate.

The poet William Wordsworth with his sister Dorothy visited the Hermitage, as did the composer Felix Mendelssohn. Another famous and entirely Scottish musician knew and loved the Hermitage: Neil Gow (1727–1807), the fiddler who is widely regarded as being the 'father' of Strathspey and Reel music. He was born at Inver and lived there all his life. Robert Burns met Gow in 1787 when Gow played for Scotia's bard. I like to think of Gow, as a boy, perhaps guddling for trout in the Braan.

Fishing the lower river, downstream from Black Linn Fall, is difficult because of bankside undergrowth, but the upper river is easily fished, particularly in the vicinity of Amulree, where my paternal grandmother was born. The stream is narrow here and the fish are not large, but they are challenging to catch. Use light tackle to try to do so, and offer them a delicately presented dry fly: Iron Blue Dun, Greenwell's Glory, March Brown, Partridge & Yellow. Find your way round using OS Map 52, Aberfeldy & Glen Almond, Second Series, Scale 1:50,000.

Loch Freuchie (Gd ref: 865377) lies astride the headwaters of the River Braan in Glen Quoich and also offers the opportunity of good sport with brown trout. Both boat and bank fishing are available and, when bank fishing, begin at the north end of the loch in the shallow bay where the Braan flows in. Fish average approximately 8oz, but there are much larger trout as well, the heaviest taken in recent years weighing 6lb 8oz. Dapping is a popular and productive fishing method from the boat. When wet fly fishing, from bank or boat, try Black Pennell, Grouse & Claret, and Silver Invicta.

Salmon fishing on the lower river is preserved; for trout fishing contact Kettles of Dunkeld (tel: 01350 727556). For fishing the upper river, and for fishing on Loch Freuchie, contact Janis and David Henderson, the new owners of the Amulree Hotel (tel: 01350 725218). The hotel is also an excellent centre from which to explore the surrounding area. There is something here for every-one, angler and non-angler alike; vigorous hill walks through magnificent desolate scenery; gentle forest walks; the delight of Dunkeld's splendid cathedral and the famous 'little houses' round Atholl Street.

But my favourite place is on the bridge across the Braan near the Inver cottage where Neil Gow was born. In the late evening, sitting on the bridge watching moonlight glinting above Craig a Barns from a blue-black, star-speckled sky, I swear that I could sometimes hear the haunting strains of the master's fiddle accompanying the soft music of the stream.

138.
In the Footsteps of BPC

I have never had much time for Bonnie Prince Charlie (BPC) or for the lairds who supported him. They brought ruin to their people and paved the way for the mass-depopulation of the north of Scotland. Only one thing impresses me about BPC: his ability to hike for miles through some of the most inhospitable terrain in the world. Had he confined himself to seeking wild brown trout whilst doing so, rather than a crown, a lot of heads would have remained on their shoulders and a century of Highland misery might have been averted.

'The Road to the Isles' is littered with memorials to BPC's passing. Get a hold of OS Map 40, Loch Shiel, Second Series, Scale 1:50,000 to find some of them: where he hid above the Stage House Inn at Glenfinnan, the cave on the shoulder of Sgurr na Ciche (1040m), The Prince's Cairn at Loch nan Uamh, where he arrived, and, eventually, departed these shores. You will also find here some of the most remote and challenging trout lochs in Scotland; both for the quality of the fish they hold and for the effort required to reach them.

Top of my list is the scatter of lochs that lie between Loch Ailort and Loch Moidart, including Loch nam Paitean (Gd ref: 725740), Loch Dearg (Gd ref: 736742), Lochan na Craoibhe (Gd ref: 727751), Lochan Meal a'Mhadaidh (Gd ref: 718750), Lochan na Caillich (Gd ref: 705746) and Upper Lochan Sligeanach (Gd ref: 715744). This is a paradise for the brown trout angler and for those who love Scotland's wild places and the flora and fauna that call it home. Getting there will stretch limbs and lungs a bit but it is worth it. There are more lochs to the west of Loch nam Paitean that are also recommended. Save them for another day.

Begin your adventure near Brunery (Gd ref: 727720) by the River Moidart. A stalker's path heads north from here, climbing steeply past 'The Three Old Maids' (Gd ref: 721727) to breach the crags between Coire Mor to the west and Leachd Fheadanach to the east. This leads to the south end of Loch Paitean. Although there is a boat house, there is no boat and all the lochs noted above are fished from the bank. Depending upon how fit you are, and how often and how long you stop to admire the view along the way, the journey will take approximately one and three quarter to two hours.

Loch nam Paitean lies like a blue butterfly on the moor and is the most productive water, depending, of course, upon how the fish are feeling when you get there. They average about 10oz/12oz in weight, are very pretty, and fight well. It would really take a whole season to properly explore this wonderful loch. The shoreline meanders in and out through fishy bays, corners and promontories over a distance of some three and a half miles. The island-clad bay on the west bank, to the north of the boathouse, is particularly inviting, as is the south-east wing of the loch.

To enjoy the other waters here will require a few more visits. All of them contain excellent fish and Loch Meal a'Mhadaidh has the reputation of holding the largest. Fish average 1lb and trout of up to 5lb in weight have been caught here, but it has to be said that they do not give themselves up easily. Start with Soldier Palmer, Woodcock & hare-lug, and Silver Butcher. Permission to fish from Mrs N. D. Stewart, Kinlochmoidart House, Loch Ailort, Inverness-shire, tel: 01967 431609. Enjoy.

139.
The King of Fish

Meeting up with Scotland's 'King of Fish', *salmon salar*, is primarily a matter of chance. Or, as others would have it, luck. I'm one of the others. Using a doubled-handed salmon rod effectively, however, is an entirely different matter. Great skill is required and only practice makes perfect. Speaking as someone who has practised for a lot of years, even this is often not enough. The other great 'leveller' that determines success or otherwise in salmon fishing is the weather. Without rain he who casts will cast in vain.

The Wick River in Caithness is an excellent example of this truth. During the 2004 season good water levels produced outstanding sport. The situation was entirely different in 2003, the driest season recorded on the river, when 75 salmon were caught; second only in terms of disaster to the 1984 season which accounted for a mere 56 fish.

But when water levels are right, the Wick can give splendid sport. In 1990, 828 salmon and grilse were caught; 1993 produced nearly 1,000 fish and 2001 more than 800. The river also has a well-deserved reputation for larger than average salmon. The heaviest in recent years weighed 19lb 6oz and was landed in 1992 by Willie Miller. David Mackay had a fish in May 1997 that weighed 18lb 8oz, whilst Ian Swanson took a 17lb 4oz salmon in July 2002. The 10-year average for the river is a highly respectable 400 fish.

The Wick rises to the south of Loch Watten and is formed by the Burn of Acharole and Strath Burn which meet near Watten Village. Thereafter, the river flows east through fertile farmlands to reach the sea in the stormy waters of Wick Bay. From Watten to the sea, a distance of eight miles or so, the river drops in height by barely 10ft, so the Wick is slow-moving and in low water conditions weed can become a problem. A channel has been cut that links the river to Loch Watten and in the winter months, and in times of high water, salmon have access to the loch although few are ever caught there.

There are no beat divisions. The whole river is available to both local and visiting anglers alike. The best sport is upstream from Bilbster Bridge where there are a number of deep holding pools, including The Pot, Cows, Borgie, Tarroul, Quarry Hole, and Wash Pool. Downstream from Bilbster, try Otter Island, Dyke End and Willie's Pool. All legal fishing methods are allowed, depending upon the time of the season, and worming takes most fish. Nevertheless, there is attractive fly-fishing water. The main thing to remember is to keep well back from the banks of this narrow stream, below the horizon. Stalk your fish, no matter what fishing method you use.

Wading is not required and casting is safe, there being few obstructions, trees and the like, along the river banks. Excellent news for the likes of your correspondent. Use a 12ft rod when fly fishing, just in case you encounter one for the glass case, and offer them Garry Dog, Thunder & Lightening, Hugo's GP, and Shrimp Fly. In low water conditions, also try Black Pennell, Ke-He, Invicta.

Further information and permits from: Hugo Ross, Fishing Tackle Shop, 56 High Street, Wick, Caithness, tel: 01955 604200; website: www. hugoross.co.uk and follow the links.

140.
Drumossie Moor

Before the Battle of Culloden in April 1746, Bonnie Prince Charlie's general Lord George Murray devised a cunning plan: the Jacobite army would march to Nairn where the government forces were camped, and attack them as they slept off the after-effects of celebrating the birthday of their commander, the Duke of Cumberland. The plan went horribly wrong when the rebel forces lost contact with each other and the ragged band retreated to Culloden to meet their fate at the points of Cumberland's bayonets the following morning.

I thought of these sad events as I stood by the River Nairn last week at Clava Lodge (tel: 01463 790228), close to the battlefield on Drumossie Moor.

The only fights hereabouts today are between anglers and salmon and Clava Lodge is a good place to begin. Clava has a mile of fishing on the River Nairn and excellent accommodation almost within casting distance of the stream.

Meanwhile, another, happier, army will assemble tomorrow morning at 10.30am at the Jubilee Pool upstream from the Railway Bridge in Nairn when Nairn Angling Association President, Jim Lennon, will make the first cast of the 2005 season. And if the 2005 season is anything like as productive as the 2004 season, then there will be a lot of smiling faces along the river bank during the months ahead. Last year, the club recorded its best ever season with a total of 1,137 fish, the highest number taken since records began in 1922.

The breakdown of the 2004 catch returns detailed 182 salmon, 807 grilse and 148 sea-trout (excluding finnock) caught. Nearly 30% of these fish were returned to fight another day and the club hopes to improve upon this figure during 2005. The heaviest salmon was taken by Elgin-born angler Brian Stewart on an Ally's Shrimp and weighed 4lb 8oz. The best sea-trout was caught by junior member Bill Jeans and it weighed 6lb. Ms Jan Burton took the ladies 'heaviest fish' prize with a salmon of 8lb.

The River Nairn is the 'Wee Gem' of Nairnshire and one of the most attractive salmon rivers in the north. It is not 'intimidating', easy to access and easy to fish. Upstream from Daviot on the A9 Perth/Inverness road, most of the fishing is preserved by the owners, but the Nairn Angling Association has nearly eight miles of river and this is available to both local and visiting anglers alike. Neither does it cost an arm and a leg to obtain sport: day tickets for visitors are £26, and for a week, £100. Junior visitors (up to 17yrs old) are charged £11 per day with a weekly permit at £30.50.

From opening day on 11th February to 28th February, fishing is by fly only on a strictly catch-and-release basis, to preserve spring stocks. Thereafter, to the end of the season on 7th October, all legal methods are allowed with a catch limit of five fish per angler per week. Once this limit is reached, fishing is by fly only using barbless hooks. Be aware, also, that anglers who fail to file completed catch returns will be charged a levy of £10 for adults and £5 for juniors. Catch returns are essential to the proper management of the river.

Permits are available from Pat Fraser's shop, 41 High Street, Nairn, tel: 016667 453038. Devise your own 'cunning plan' and make this the season that you discover the 'Wee Gem'.

141.
Ben More Assynt

Dubh-Loch Mor, the source of the River Oykle, is a small corrie lochan hidden below the towering walls of Conival (987m) and Ben More Assynt (998m), the highest mountains in Sutherland. The river tumbles south between the enfolding arms of Breabag and Sail an Ruthair, gathering in the flow from Dubh Loch Beag and Loch Sail an Ruthair along the way.

A few years ago, The Manager and I fished these last two named lochs in company with Peter Voy, then factor of Assynt Estate. I found the climb from the river to the loch a bit testing, but I suspect that this had more to do with the hospitality I had enjoyed the previous evening than with a general lack of physical fitness. I suffer in pursuit of our well-loved art.

I remember that we had been instructed to return with trout as a starter-course for dinner that evening. We took four small fish home. Peter caught three, Ann caught one and I caught the rest. The largest, a fish of about 14oz that Ann caught, never made it to the table. The moment she had it on the bank, her disgusting thug of a Yorkshire terrier, Heathcliff, grabbed it and dashed off up the hill and buried it, who knows where.

Much more easily accessible, and also great fun to fish, is Loch Ailsh, where the growing Oykle pauses before rushing east to reach the sea in the Kyle of Sutherland. Find Loch Ailsh on OS Map 15, Loch Assynt, Landranger Series, Scale 1:50,000 at Gd ref: 315110. A forest track at Gd ref: 298084 branches north to the loch from the A837 Bonar Bridge to Ledmore Junction road.

Loch Ailsh is shallow, about three quarters of a mile long by up to half a mile wide. A large sand bank has been formed where the river enters the loch, and there is a wonderful, tree- and scrub-covered little island at the south end close to where the loch exits down Glen Oykle. A boat is moored at Gd ref: 323113, near Benmore Lodge and the loch is boat fishing only.

The trout are not large, but they are plentiful and fight well. This makes Loch Ailsh an ideal venue for newcomers to fly fishing. Catching trout is the rule here, rather than the exception. Neither are they particular about which flies the take. Begin with Black Pennell, Grouse & Claret and Peter Ross. There are bigger fish in the loch; a friend of mine, the French writer Marc Sourdot, caught one of the largest taken recently, a trout of just under 3lb in weight.

But what makes Loch Ailsh really special is the fact that it also holds salmon and, particularly, sea-trout. They arrive from mid-July onwards and, in times past, Loch Ailsh had a famous reputation for the quality and number of sea-trout that it produced each season. It still fishes well for these most spectacular of all game fish, although not so many are taken today. This also applies to salmon, but there is generally a better-than-evens chance of encountering them as well.

Although fish rise and are taken all over the loch, from the margins to the middle, the best tactic is to concentrate your efforts about a dozen yards or so out from the shore. This applies especially in regard to connecting with salmon: they lie in very shallow water. Dapping is a classic method of attracting Loch Ailsh salmonids. Something large and bushy will do. Try a Loch Ordie or a Ke-He. Crossing the fingers also helps. Well, it does for me.